CULTURES IN CONFLICT: Perspectives on the Snow-Leavis Controversy

CULTURES IN CONFLICT:
Perspectives on the Snow-Leavis Controversy

David K. Cornelius
Edwin St. Vincent
Randolph-Macon Woman's College

Scott, Foresman and Company
Chicago   Atlanta   Dallas   Palo Alto   Fair Lawn, N.J.

The authors gratefully acknowledge the cooperation of the following publishers for permission to reprint the selections in this book:

George Allan & Unwin Ltd. for excerpt from *Science and the Planned State* by John R. Baker.

The Atlantic Monthly: for "Why Do We Teach Poetry?" by Archibald MacLeish.

Messrs. Ernest Benn: for excerpt from *The Way the World Is Going* by H. G. Wells, pp. 205, 208. Reprinted with permission of Messrs. Ernest Benn, Executors of H. G. Wells.

Cambridge University Press: for excerpt from *The Two Cultures and the Scientific Revolution* by C. P. Snow.

Chatto and Windus Ltd.: for excerpt from *Two Cultures? The Significance of C. P. Snow* by F. R. Leavis and Michael Yudkin.

The Clarendon Press: for excerpt from Preface to *Lyrical Ballads* by William Wordsworth.

Commentary: for "Science, Literature & Culture: A Comment on the Leavis-Snow Controversy" by Lionel Trilling, from *Commentary*, 1962, 33:461–477. Copyright by the American Jewish Committee.

Harcourt, Brace & World, Inc.: for "The Machine Stops" from *The Eternal Moment and Other Stories* by E. M. Forster, copyright, 1928, by Harcourt, Brace & World, Inc., copyright, 1956, by E. M. Forster. Reprinted by permission of Harcourt, Brace & World, Inc.; and for excerpt by James T. Shotwell from *Science and Man* edited by Ruth Nanda Anshen, copyright, 1942, by Harcourt, Brace & World, Inc. and reprinted with their permission.

Harper & Row, Publishers, Incorporated: for excerpt from *The Proper Study of Mankind*, Revised Edition, by Stuart Chase, pp. 3–9. Copyright 1948, 1956 by Stuart Chase. Reprinted with permission of Harper & Row, Publishers, Incorporated.

Holt, Rinehart and Winston, Inc.: for excerpt from *The Sane Society* by Erich Fromm. Copyright © 1955 by Erich Fromm. Reprinted by permission of Holt, Rinehart and Winston, Inc.

Houghton Mifflin Company: for excerpt from *How Does a Poem Mean?* by John Ciardi.

The Hudson Review: for excerpt from "London Letter" by John Wain. Reprinted by permission from *The Hudson Review*, Vol. XV, No. 2, Summer 1962. Copyright 1962 by The Hudson Review, Inc.

The Kenyon Review: for "A Literary Defense of 'The Two Cultures'" by Martin Green.

National Review: for "The Voice of Sir Charles" by William F. Buckley, Jr.

The New Republic: for excerpt from "The Dog That Didn't Bark" by Hilary Corke.

The New Statesman: for articles by Bertrand Russell.

The New York Times: for "'1984' Can Be a Good Year" by J. Bronowski. Copyright by The New York Times. Reprinted by permission.

Pantheon Books: for excerpt from *Two Cultures? The Significance of C. P. Snow* by F. R. Leavis and Michael Yudkin. © Copyright, 1963, by Random House, Inc. © 1962, by Chatto and Windus Ltd. Reprinted by permission of Pantheon Books, a division of Random House, Inc.

Show: for "From the Top Drawer and the Bottom" by Anthony West.

Sidgwick & Jackson Ltd. and the Author's Representatives: for "The Machine Stops" from *The Eternal Moment and Other Stories* by E. M. Forster.

William Sloane Associates: for excerpt from *Off Broadway* by Maxwell Anderson.

The Spectator: for "Grounds for Approval" by Richard Wollheim; and for "The Two Cultures," an editorial.

The Viking Press, Inc.: for excerpt from *Women in Love* by D. H. Lawrence. Copyright 1920, 1922 by D. H. Lawrence; 1948, 1950 by Frieda Lawrence. Reprinted by permission of The Viking Press, Inc.

Contents

Preface

The readings collected in this book deal with a subject of permanent interest. Its implications range from the problem of what subjects students should be required to study in school to ultimate questions concerning the modes of life appropriate to human beings. The issues dealt with here have been debated, in one form or another, for thousands of years, but never more keenly than at present.

No writer in our time has spoken more influentially on the subject of the relative significance of science and the humanities than the author of the first selection, Sir Charles Snow; and no article has provoked more animated intellectual controversy than F. R. Leavis' rejoinder to Snow, from which the second selection is taken.

C. P. Snow's *The Two Cultures and the Scientific Revolution* derives its authority in part from the peculiar qualifications of the author. Snow is, on the one hand, a scientist who has played a prominent role in directing scientific projects as an official of the British government and, on the other hand, a serious, prolific, and successful novelist. He may thus be regarded as a successful practitioner in the areas of both of the "two cultures" which he attempts to define—the "scientific" and the "literary" or "traditional." It should be noted, however, that many of Snow's critics, some of whom are represented in Part One, have seriously questioned his basic assumptions in both of these areas.

The readings in Part One have been chosen in an attempt to represent the main outlines of what has come to be known as "The Snow-Leavis Controversy" and to communicate the spirit of living debate and intense personal engagement on the part of the participants. Part Two undertakes to place the current controversy in a certain historical perspective by presenting a number of comments from previous centuries that bear, directly or by implication, upon the contemporary debate. The readings in the first section of Part Three explore, from varying points of view, opposing methods by which man seeks to understand himself and grasp the world around him. The readings in the second section seek to evaluate the consequences, actual or anticipated, of the increasing dominance of science and technology. The final pages of the book contain study questions and suggested topics for student papers.

We should like to express our gratitude for the advice and assistance rendered by Miss Margaret Thomas, Librarian of the Lipscomb Library, Randolph-Macon Woman's College, and our appreciation of the help regularly and cheerfully extended by the staff of the libraries of the University of Virginia.

A Note on Documentation

Students writing documented papers based on this collection are advised to make their references to the original sources of the readings. To this end, original page numbers have been interpolated throughout. Deleted from this text are (1) all footnotes from the printed version of Snow's lecture, (2) editors' notes on Latin translation from the Bacon and Ruskin selections, and (3) bibliographical references from the Baker excerpt.

PART I

The Current
Debate

The Issue Stated

C. P. Snow

THE TWO CULTURES

Sir Charles Snow (1905 –   ) is an English novelist and scientist. Snow's family was poor, and he early decided that a scientific career offered him the most practicable means of advancement. His studies in physics led to a Ph.D. at Cambridge (1930) and an appointment as a Fellow of Corpus Christi College. Through the thirties he was engaged in scientific work and college administration at Cambridge. During World War II Snow served as the Chief of scientific personnel for the Ministry of Labour and in 1943 was awarded the C. B. E. (Commander of the British Empire). In 1945 he was appointed Civil Service Commissioner.

During much of this period Snow was contemplating, and laying the groundwork for, another career — that of novelist. As early as 1935 he had conceived the idea for a series of novels picturing English life over a long period of modern history. This project, begun after the end of World War II, has born fruit in nine separate but interrelated novels of a projected eleven-volume series. Snow has given this series the general title "Strangers and Brothers." Snow's novels have been praised for solid intellectual content and realistic portrayal of ambition and intrigue among men in positions of power and authority. One novel in the series, The Affair, *has been adapted for the theater by Ronald Miller and was presented with great success in London during 1961 – 1962.*

The following excerpt from Snow's The Two Cultures and the Scientific Revolution *presents about half of the text of that work. The student is encouraged to consult the full text.*

THE TWO CULTURES

It is about three years since I made a sketch in print of a problem which had been on my mind for some time. It was a problem I could not avoid just because of the circumstances of my life. The only credentials I had to ruminate on the subject at all came through those circumstances, through nothing more than a set of chances. Anyone with similar experience would have seen much the same things and I think made very much the same comments about them. It just happened to be an unusual experience. By training I was a scientist: by vocation I was a writer. That was all. It was a piece of luck, if you like, that arose through coming from a poor home.

But my personal history isn't the point now. All that I need say is that I came

From *The Two Cultures and the Scientific Revolution* (New York: Cambridge University Press, 1959).

to Cambridge and did a bit of research here at a time of major scien- /1/ tific activity. I was privileged to have a ringside view of one of the most wonderful creative periods in all physics. And it happened through the flukes of war — including meeting W. L. Bragg in the buffet on Kettering station on a very cold morning in 1939, which had a determining influence on my practical life — that I was able, and indeed morally forced, to keep that ringside view ever since. So for thirty years I have had to be in touch with scientists not only out of curiosity, but as part of a working existence. During the same thirty years I was trying to shape the books I wanted to write, which in due course took me among writers.

There have been plenty of days when I have spent the working hours with scientists and then gone off at night with some literary colleagues. I mean that literally. I have had, of course, intimate friends among both scientists and writers. It was through living among these groups and much more, I think, through moving regularly from one to the other and back again that I got occupied with the problem of what, long before I put it on paper, I christened to myself as the 'two cultures'. For constantly I felt I was moving among two groups — comparable in intelligence, identical in race, not grossly different in social origin, earning about the same incomes, who had almost ceased to communicate at all, who in intellectual, moral and psychological climate had so little in common that instead of going from Burlington House or South /2/ Kensington to Chelsea, one might have crossed an ocean.

In fact, one had travelled much further than across an ocean — because after a few thousand Atlantic miles, one found Greenwich Village talking precisely the same language as Chelsea, and both having about as much communication with M.I.T. as though the scientists spoke nothing but Tibetan. For this is not just our problem; owing to some of our educational and social idiosyncrasies, it is slightly exaggerated here, owing to another English social peculiarity it is slightly minimised; by and large this is a problem of the entire West.

By this I intend something serious. I am not thinking of the pleasant story of how one of the more convivial Oxford greats dons — I have heard the story attributed to A. L. Smith — came over to Cambridge to dine. The date is perhaps the 1890's. I think it must have been at St John's, or possibly Trinity. Anyway, Smith was sitting at the right hand of the President — or Vice-Master — and he was a man who liked to include all round him in the conversation, although he was not immediately encouraged by the expressions of his neighbours. He addressed some cheerful Oxonian chit-chat at the one opposite to him, and got a grunt. He then tried the man on his own right hand and got another grunt. Then, rather to his surprise, one looked at the other and said, 'Do you know what he's talking about?' 'I haven't the least idea.' At /3/ this, even Smith was getting out of his depth. But the President, acting as a social emollient, put him at his ease, by saying, 'Oh, those are mathematicians! We never talk to *them*'.

No, I intend something serious. I believe the intellectual life of the whole of western society is increasingly being split into two polar groups. When I say the intellectual life, I mean to include also a large part of our practical life, because I should be the last person to suggest the two can at the deepest level be distinguished. I shall come back to the practical life a little later. Two polar groups: at one pole we have the literary intellectuals, who incidentally while no one was looking took to referring to themselves as 'intellectuals' as though there were no others. I remember G. H. Hardy once remarking to me in mild puzzlement, some time in the 1930's: 'Have you noticed how the word "intellectual" is used nowadays? There seems to be a new definition which certainly doesn't include Rutherford or Eddington or Dirac or Adrian or me. It does seem rather odd, don't y' know.'

Literary intellectuals at one pole—at the other scientists, and as the most representative, the physical scientists. Between the two a gulf of mutual incomprehension—sometimes (particularly among the young) hostility and dislike, but most of all lack of understanding. They have a curious distorted image of each other. Their attitudes are so /4/ different that, even on the level of emotion, they can't find much common ground. Non-scientists tend to think of scientists as brash and boastful. They hear Mr T. S. Eliot, who just for these illustrations we can take as an archetypal figure, saying about his attempts to revive verse-drama, that we can hope for very little, but that he would feel content if he and his co-workers could prepare the ground for a new Kyd or a new Greene. That is the tone, restricted and constrained, with which literary intellectuals are at home: it is the subdued voice of their culture. Then they hear a much louder voice, that of another archetypal figure, Rutherford, trumpeting: 'This is the heroic age of science! This is the Elizabethan age!' Many of us heard that, and a good many other statements beside which that was mild; and we weren't left in any doubt whom Rutherford was casting for the role of Shakespeare. What is hard for the literary intellectuals to understand, imaginatively or intellectually, is that he was absolutely right.

And compare 'this is the way the world ends, not with a bang but a whimper' —incidentally, one of the least likely scientific prophecies ever made—compare that with Rutherford's famous repartee, 'Lucky fellow, Rutherford, always on the crest of the wave.' 'Well, I made the wave, didn't I?'

The non-scientists have a rooted impression that the scientists are shallowly optimistic, unaware of man's condition. On the other hand, the scientists /5/ believe that the literary intellectuals are totally lacking in foresight, peculiarly unconcerned with their brother men, in a deep sense anti-intellectual, anxious to restrict both art and thought to the existential moment. And so on. Anyone with a mild talent for invective could produce plenty of this kind of subterranean back-chat. On each side there is some of it which is not entirely baseless. It is all destructive. Much of it rests on misinterpretations which are dangerous. I should like to deal with two of the most profound of these now, one on each side.

First, about the scientists' optimism. This is an accusation which has been made so often that it has become a platitude. It has been made by some of the acutest non-scientific minds of the day. But it depends upon a confusion between the individual experience and the social experience, between the individual condition of man and his social condition. Most of the scientists I have known well have felt—just as deeply as the non-scientists I have known well—that the individual condition of each of us is tragic. Each of us is alone: sometimes we escape from solitariness, through love or affection or perhaps creative moments, but those triumphs of life are pools of light we make for ourselves while the edge of the road is black: each of us dies alone. Some scientists I have known have had faith in revealed religion. Perhaps with them the sense of the tragic condition is not so strong. I don't /6/ know. With most people of deep feeling, however high-spirited and happy they are, sometimes most with those who are happiest and most high-spirited, it seems to be right in the fibres, part of the weight of life. That is as true of the scientists I have known best as of anyone at all.

But nearly all of them—and this is where the colour of hope genuinely comes in—would see no reason why, just because the individual condition is tragic, so must the social condition be. Each of us is solitary: each of us dies alone: all right, that's a fate against which we can't struggle—but there is plenty in our condition which is not fate, and against which we are less than human unless we do struggle.

Most of our fellow human beings, for instance, are underfed and die before their time. In the crudest terms, *that* is the social condition. There is a moral trap which comes through the insight into man's loneliness: it tempts one to sit back, complacent in one's unique tragedy, and let the others go without a meal.

As a group, the scientists fall into that trap less than others. They are inclined to be impatient to see if something can be done: and inclined to think that it can be done, until it's proved otherwise. That is their real optimism, and it's an optimism that the rest of us badly need.

In reverse, the same spirit, tough and good and determined to fight it out at the side of their /7/ brother men, has made scientists regard the other culture's social attitudes as contemptible. That is too facile: some of them are, but they are a temporary phase and not to be taken as representative.

I remember being cross-examined by a scientist of distinction. 'Why do most writers take on social opinions which would have been thought distinctly uncivilised and démodé at the time of the Plantagenets? Wasn't that true of most of the famous twentieth-century writers? Yeats, Pound, Wyndham Lewis, nine out of ten of those who have dominated literary sensibility in our time—weren't they not only politically silly, but politically wicked? Didn't the influence of all they represent bring Auschwitz that much nearer?'

I thought at the time, and I still think, that the correct answer was not to defend the indefensible. It was no use saying that Yeats, according to friends whose judgment I trust, was a man of singular magnanimity of character, as well as a great poet. It was no use denying the facts, which are broadly true. The honest answer was that there is, in fact, a connection, which literary persons were culpably slow to see, between some kinds of early twentieth-century art and the most imbecile expressions of anti-social feeling. That was one reason, among many, why some of us turned our backs on the art and tried to hack out a new or different way for ourselves.

But though many of those writers dominated /8/ literary sensibility for a generation, that is no longer so, or at least to nothing like the same extent. Literature changes more slowly than science. It hasn't the same automatic corrective, and so its misguided periods are longer. But it is ill-considered of scientists to judge writers on the evidence of the period 1914–50.

Those are two of the misunderstandings between the two cultures. I should say, since I began to talk about them—the two cultures, that is—I have had some criticism. Most of my scientific acquaintances think that there is something in it, and so do most of the practising artists I know. But I have been argued with by non-scientists of strong down-to-earth interests. Their view is that it is an over-simplification, and that if one is going to talk in these terms there ought to be at least three cultures. They argue that, though they are not scientists themselves, they would share a good deal of the scientific feeling. They would have as little use—perhaps, since they knew more about it, even less use—for the recent literary culture as the scientists themselves. J. H. Plumb, Alan Bullock and some of my American sociological friends have said that they vigorously refuse to be corralled in a cultural box with people they wouldn't be seen dead with, or to be regarded as helping to produce a climate which would not permit of social hope.

I respect those arguments. The number 2 is a very dangerous number: that is why the dialectic /9/ is a dangerous process. Attempts to divide anything into two ought to be regarded with much suspicion. I have thought a long time about going in for further refinements: but in the end I have decided against. I was searching for something a little more than a dashing metaphor, a good deal less than a cultural map: and for those purposes the two cultures is about right, and subtilising any more would bring more disadvantages than it's worth.

At one pole, the scientific culture really is a culture, not only in an intellectual but also in an anthropological sense. That is, its members need not, and of course often do not, always completely understand each other; biologists more often than not will have a pretty hazy idea of contemporary physics; but there are common attitudes, common standards and patterns of behaviour, common approaches and assumptions. This goes surprisingly wide and deep. It cuts across other mental patterns, such as those of religion or politics or class.

Statistically, I suppose slightly more scientists are in religious terms unbelievers, compared with the rest of the intellectual world — though there are plenty who are religious, and that seems to be increasingly so among the young. Statistically also, slightly more scientists are on the Left in open politics — though again, plenty always have called themselves conservatives, and that also seems to be more common among the young. Compared with /10/ the rest of the intellectual world, considerably more scientists in this country and probably in the U.S. come from poor families. Yet, over a whole range of thought and behaviour, none of that matters very much. In their working, and in much of their emotional life, their attitudes are closer to other scientists than to non-scientists who in religion or politics or class have the same labels as themselves. If I were to risk a piece of shorthand, I should say that naturally they had the future in their bones.

They may or may not like it, but they have it. That was as true of the conservatives J. J. Thomson and Lindemann as of the radicals Einstein or Blackett: as true of the Christian A. H. Compton as of the materialist Bernal: of the aristocrats Broglie or Russell as of the proletarian Faraday: of those born rich, like Thomas Merton or Victor Rothschild, as of Rutherford, who was the son of an odd-job handyman. Without thinking about it, they respond alike. That is what a culture means.

At the other pole, the spread of attitudes is wider. It is obvious that between the two, as one moves through intellectual society from the physicists to the literary intellectuals, there are all kinds of tones of feeling on the way. But I believe the pole of total incomprehension of science radiates its influence on all the rest. That total incomprehension gives, much more pervasively than we realise, living in it, an unscientific flavour to the whole /11/ 'traditional' culture, and that unscientific flavour is often, much more than we admit, on the point of turning anti-scientific. The feelings of one pole become the anti-feelings of the other. If the scientists have the future in their bones, then the traditional culture responds by wishing the future did not exist. It is the traditional culture, to an extent remarkably little diminished by the emergence of the scientific one, which manages the western world.

This polarisation is sheer loss to us all. To us as people, and to our society. It is at the same time practical and intellectual and creative loss, and I repeat that it is false to imagine that those three considerations are clearly separable. But for a moment I want to concentrate on the intellectual loss.

The degree of incomprehension on both sides is the kind of joke which has gone sour. There are about fifty thousand working scientists in the country and about eighty thousand professional engineers or applied scientists. During the war and in the years since, my colleagues and I have had to interview some-where between thirty to forty thousand of these — that is, about 25 per cent. The number is large enough to give us a fair sample, though of the men we talked to most would still be under forty. We were able to find out a certain amount of what they read and thought about. I confess that even I, who am fond of them and respect them, was a bit shaken. We hadn't quite expected that /12/ the links with the traditional culture should be so tenuous, nothing more than a formal touch of the cap.

As one would expect, some of the very best scientists had and have plenty of energy and interest to spare, and we came across several who had read everything that literary people talk about. But that's very rare. Most of the rest, when one tried to probe for what books they had read, would modestly confess, 'Well, I've *tried* a bit of Dickens', rather as though Dickens were an extraor-dinarily esoteric, tangled and dubiously rewarding writer, something like Rainer Maria Rilke. In fact that is exactly how they do regard him: we thought that discovery, that Dickens had been transformed into the type-specimen of literary incomprehensibility, was one of the oddest results of the whole exercise.

But of course, in reading him, in reading almost any writer whom we should value, they are just touching their caps to the traditional culture. They have their own culture, intensive, rigorous, and constantly in action. This culture contains a great deal of argument, usually much more rigorous, and almost always at a higher conceptual level, than literary persons' arguments — even though the scientists do cheerfully use words in senses which literary persons don't recognise, the senses are exact ones, and when they talk about 'subjective', 'objective', 'philosophy' or 'progres- /13/ sive', they know what they mean, even though it isn't what one is accustomed to expect.

Remember, these are very intelligent men. Their culture is in many ways an exacting and admirable one. It doesn't contain much art, with the exception, an important exception, of music. Verbal exchange, insistent argument. Long-playing records. Colour-photography. The ear, to some extent the eye. Books, very little, though perhaps not many would go so far as one hero, who perhaps I should admit was further down the scientific ladder than the people I've been talking about — who, when asked what books he read, replied firmly and confidently: 'Books? I prefer to use my books as tools.' It was very hard not to let the mind wander — what sort of tool would a book make? Perhaps a hammer? A primitive digging instrument?

Of books, though, very little. And of the books which to most literary persons are bread and butter, novels, history, poetry, plays, almost nothing at all. It isn't that they're not interested in the psychological or moral or social life. In the social life, they certainly are, more than most of us. In the moral, they are by and large the soundest group of intellectuals we have; there is a moral component right in the grain of science itself, and almost all scientists form their own judgments of the moral life. In the psychological they have as much interest as most of us, though I fancy they come to it rather late. It isn't that they lack the in- /14/ terests. It is much more that the whole literature of the traditional culture doesn't seem to them relevant to those interests. They are, of course, dead wrong. As a result, their imaginative understanding is less than it could be. They are self-impoverished.

But what about the other side? They are impoverished too — perhaps more seriously, because they are vainer about it. They still like to pretend that the traditional culture is the whole of 'culture', as though the natural order didn't exist. As though the exploration of the natural order was of no interest either in its own value or its consequences. As though the scientific edifice of the physical world was not, in its intellectual depth, complexity·and articulation, the most beautiful and wonderful collective work of the mind of man. Yet most non-scientists have no conception of that edifice at all. Even if they want to have it, they can't. It is rather as though, over an immense range of intellectual experience, a whole group was tone-deaf. Except that this tone-deafness doesn't come by nature, but by training, or rather the absence of training.

As with the tone-deaf, they don't know what they miss. They give a pitying chuckle at the news of scientists who have never read a major work of English literature. They dismiss them as ignorant specialists. Yet their own ignorance and their own specialisation is just as startling. A good many /15/ times I have been present at gatherings of people who, by the standards of the traditional culture, are thought highly educated and who have with considerable gusto been expressing their incredulity at the illiteracy of scientists. Once or twice I have been provoked and have asked the company how many of them could describe the Second Law of Thermodynamics. The response was cold: it was also negative. Yet I was asking something which is about the scientific equivalent of: *Have you read a work of Shakespeare's?*

I now believe that if I had asked an even simpler question — such as, What do you mean by mass, or acceleration, which is the scientific equivalent of saying, *Can you read?* — not more than one in ten of the highly educated would have felt that I was speaking the same language. So the great edifice of modern physics goes up, and the majority of the cleverest people in the western world have about as much insight into it as their neolithic ancestors would have had.

Just one more of those questions, that my non-scientific friends regard as being in the worst of taste. Cambridge is a university where scientists and non-scientists meet every night at dinner. About two years ago, one of the most astonishing experiments in the whole history of science was brought off. I don't mean the sputnik — that was admirable for quite different reasons, as a feat of organisation and a triumphant use of existing /16/ knowledge. No, I mean the experiment at Columbia by Yang and Lee. It is an experiment of the greatest beauty and originality, but the result is so startling that one forgets how beautiful the experiment is. It makes us think again about some of the fundamentals of the physical world. Intuition, common sense — they are neatly stood on their heads. The result is usually known as the contradiction of parity. If there were any serious communication between the two cultures, this experiment would have been talked about at every High Table in Cambridge. Was it? I wasn't here: but I should like to ask the question.

There seems then to be no place where the cultures meet. I am not going to waste time saying that this is a pity. It is much worse than that. Soon I shall come to some practical consequences. But at the heart of thought and creation we are letting some of our best chances go by default. The clashing point of two subjects, two disciplines, two cultures — of two galaxies, so far as that goes — ought to produce creative chances. In the history of mental activity that has been where some of the breakthroughs came. The chances are there now. But they are there, as it were, in a vacuum, because those in the two cultures can't talk to each other. It is bizarre how very little of twentieth-century science has been assimilated into twentieth-century art. Now and then one used to find poets conscientiously using scientific expressions, and getting /17/ them wrong—there was a time when 'refraction' kept cropping up in verse in a mystifying fashion, and when 'polarised light' was used as though writers were under the illusion that it was a specially admirable kind of light.

Of course, that isn't the way that science could be any good to art. It has got to be assimilated along with, and as part and parcel of, the whole of our mental experience, and used as naturally as the rest.

I said earlier that this cultural divide is not just an English phenomenon: it exists all over the western world. But it probably seems at its sharpest in England, for two reasons. One is our fanatical belief in educational specialisation, which is much more deeply ingrained in us than in any country in the world, west or east. The other is our tendency to let our social forms crystallise. This tendency appears to get stronger, not weaker, the more we iron out economic inequalities: and this is specially true in education. It means that once anything like a cultural divide gets established, all the social forces operate to make it not less rigid, but more so.

The two cultures were already dangerously separate sixty years ago; but a prime minister like Lord Salisbury could have his own laboratory at Hatfield, and Arthur Balfour had a somewhat more than amateur interest in natural science. John Anderson did some research in organic chemistry /18/ in Würzburg before passing first into the Civil Service, and incidentally took a spread of subjects which is now impossible. None of that degree of interchange at the top of the Establishment is likely, or indeed thinkable, now.

In fact, the separation between the scientists and non-scientists is much less bridgeable among the young than it was even thirty years ago. Thirty years ago the cultures had long ceased to speak to each other: but at least they managed a kind of frozen smile across the gulf. Now the politeness has gone, and they just make faces. It is not only that the young scientists now feel that they are part of a culture on the rise while the other is in retreat. It is also, to be brutal, that the young scientists know that with an indifferent degree they'll get a comfortable job, while their contemporaries and counterparts in English or History will be lucky to earn 60 per cent as much. No young scientist of any talent would feel that he isn't wanted or that his work is ridiculous, as did the hero of *Lucky Jim,* and in fact, some of the disgruntlement of Amis and his associates is the disgruntlement of the under-employed arts graduate.

There is only one way out of all this: it is, of course, by rethinking our education. In this country, for the two reasons I have given, that is more difficult than in any other. Nearly everyone will agree that our school education is too specialised. But nearly everyone feels that it is outside the will /19/ of man to alter it. Other countries are as dissatisfied with their education as we are, but are not so resigned.

The U.S. teach out of proportion more children up to eighteen than we do: they teach them far more wisely, but nothing like so rigorously. They know that: they are hoping to take the problem in hand within ten years, though they may not have all that time to spare. The U.S.S.R. also teach out of proportion more children than we do: they also teach far more widely than we do (it is an absurd western myth that their school education is specialised) but much too rigorously. They know that—and they are beating about to get it right. The Scandinavians, in particular the Swedes, who would make a more sensible job of it than any of us, are handicapped by their practical need to devote an inordinate amount of time to foreign languages. But they too are seized of the problem.

Are we? Have we crystallised so far that we are no longer flexible at all?
. . . /20/

INTELLECTUALS AS NATURAL LUDDITES*

The reasons for the existence of the two cultures are many, deep, and complex, some rooted in social histories, some in personal histories, and some in the inner dynamic of the different kinds of mental activity themselves. But I want to isolate one which is not so much a reason as a correlative, something which winds in and out of any of these discussions. It can be said simply, and it is this. If we forget the scientific culture, then the rest of western intellectuals have never tried, wanted, or been able to understand the industrial revolution, much less accept it. Intellectuals, in particular literary intellectuals, are natural Luddites.

That is specially true of this country, where the industrial revolution happened to us earlier than /23/ elsewhere, during a long spell of absentmindedness. Perhaps that helps explain our present degree of crystallisation. But, with a little qualification, it is also true, and surprisingly true, of the United States.

In both countries, and indeed all over the West, the first wave of the industrial revolution crept on, without anyone noticing what was happening. It was, of course—or at least it was destined to become, under our own eyes, and in our time—by far the biggest transformation in society since the discovery of agriculture. In fact, those two revolutions, the agricultural and the industrial-scientific, are the only qualitative changes in social living that men have ever known. But the traditional culture didn't notice: or when it did notice, didn't like what it saw. Not that the traditional culture wasn't doing extremely well out of the revolution; the English educational institutions took their slice of the English nineteenth-century wealth, and perversely, it helped crystallise them in the forms we know.

Almost none of the talent, almost none of the imaginative energy, went back into the revolution which was producing the wealth. The traditional culture became more abstracted from it as it became more wealthy, trained its young men for administration, for the Indian Empire, for the purpose of perpetuating the culture itself, but never in any circumstances to equip them to un- /24/ derstand the revolution or take part in it. Far-sighted men were beginning to see, before the middle of the nineteenth century, that in order to go on producing wealth, the country needed to train some of its bright minds in science, particularly in applied science. No one listened. The traditional culture didn't listen at all: and the pure scientists, such as there were, didn't listen very eagerly. You will find the story, which in spirit continues down to the present day, in Eric Ashby's *Technology and the Academics*.

The academics had nothing to do with the industrial revolution; as Corrie, the old Master of Jesus, said about trains running into Cambridge on Sunday, 'It is equally displeasing to God and to myself'. So far as there was any thinking in nineteenth-century industry, it was left to cranks and clever workmen. American social historians have told me that much the same was true of the U.S. The industrial revolution, which began developing in New England fifty

---

*Luddites were English workmen of the early nineteenth century who, fearful of unemployment, set out to destroy labor-saving machinery in the Midlands and North of England. Their name is said to derive from a certain Ned Ludd, a villager of low mentality in Leicestershire, who in 1779 went into a rage and broke two frames in a stockingmaker's house—*Editors' note*.

years or so later than ours, apparently received very little educated talent, either then or later in the nineteenth century. It had to make do with the guidance handymen could give it—sometimes, of course, handymen like Henry Ford, with a dash of genius.

The curious thing was that in Germany, in the 1830's and 1840's, long before serious industrialisation had started there, it was possible to get a good university education in applied science, bet- /25/ ter than anything England or the U.S. could offer for a couple of generations. I don't begin to understand this: it doesn't make social sense: but it was so. With the result that Ludwig Mond, the son of a court purveyor, went to Heidelberg and learnt some sound applied chemistry. Siemens, a Prussian signals officer, at military academy and university went through what for their time were excellent courses in electrical engineering. Then they came to England, met no competition at all, brought in other educated Germans, and made fortunes exactly as though they were dealing with a rich, illiterate colonial territory. Similar fortunes were made by German technologists in the United States.

Almost everywhere, though, intellectual persons didn't comprehend what was happening. Certainly the writers didn't. Plenty of them shuddered away, as though the right course for a man of feeling was to contract out; some, like Ruskin and William Morris and Thoreau and Emerson and Lawrence, tried various kinds of fancies which were not in effect more than screams of horror. It is hard to think of a writer of high class who really stretched his imaginative sympathy, who could see at once the hideous back-streets, the smoking chimneys, the internal price — and also the prospects of life that were opening out for the poor, the intimations, up to now unknown except to the lucky, which were just coming within reach of the remaining 99 per /26/ cent of his brother men. Some of the nineteenth-century Russian novelists might have done; their natures were broad enough; but they were living in a pre-industrial society and didn't have the opportunity. The only writer of world class who seems to have had an understanding of the industrial revolution was Ibsen in his old age: and there wasn't much that old man didn't understand.

For, of course, one truth is straightforward. Industrialisation is the only hope of the poor. I use the word 'hope' in a crude and prosaic sense. I have not much use for the moral sensibility of anyone who is too refined to use it so. It is all very well for us, sitting pretty, to think that material standards of living don't matter all that much. It is all very well for one, as a personal choice, to reject industrialisation — do a modern Walden, if you like, and if you go without much food, see most of your children die in infancy, despise the comforts of literacy, accept twenty years off your own life, then I respect you for the strength of your aesthetic revulsion. But I don't respect you in the slightest if, even passively, you try to impose the same choice on others who are not free to choose. In fact, we know what their choice would be. For, with singular unanimity, in any country where they have had the chance, the poor have walked off the land into the factories as fast as the factories could take them.

I remember talking to my grandfather when I /27/ was a child. He was a good specimen of a nineteenth-century artisan. He was highly intelligent, and he had a great deal of character. He had left school at the age of ten, and had educated himself intensely until he was an old man. He had all his class's passionate faith in education. Yet, he had never had the luck — or, as I now suspect, the worldly force and dexterity — to go very far. In fact, he never went further than maintenance foreman in a tramway depot. His life would seem to his grandchildren laborious and unrewarding almost beyond belief. But it didn't seem to him quite like that. He was much too sensible a man not to know that he hadn't been adequately used: he had too much pride not to feel a proper rancour: he was disappointed that he had not done more – and yet, compared with *his* grandfather, he felt he had done a lot. His grandfather must have been an agricultural labourer. I don't so much as know his Christian name. He was one of the 'dark people', as the old Russian liberals used to call them, completely lost in the great anonymous sludge of history. So far as my grandfather knew, he could not read or write. He was a man of ability, my grandfather thought; my grandfather was pretty unforgiving about what society had done, or not done, to his ancestors, and did not romanticise their state. It was no fun being an agricultural labourer in the mid- to late eighteenth century, in the time that we, snobs that we /28/ are, think of only as the time of the Enlightenment and Jane Austen.

The industrial revolution looked very different according to whether one saw it from above or below. It looks very different today according to whether one sees it from Chelsea or from a village in Asia. To people like my grandfather, there was no question that the industrial revolution was less bad than what had gone before. The only question was, how to make it better.

In a more sophisticated sense, that is still the question. In the advanced countries, we have realised in a rough and ready way what the old industrial revolution brought with it. A great increase of population, because applied science went hand in hand with medical science and medical care. Enough to eat, for a similar reason. Everyone able to read and write, because an industrial society can't work without. Health, food, education; nothing but the industrial revolution could have spread them right down to the very poor. Those are primary gains – there are losses too, of course, one of which is that organising a society for industry makes it easy to organise it for all-out war. But the gains remain. They are the base of our social hope.

And yet: do we understand how they have happened? Have we begun to comprehend even the old industrial revolution? Much less the new scientific revolution in which we stand? There never was anything more necessary to comprehend. /29/

A Group of Reactions

C. P. Snow's The Two Cultures *was widely and favorably reviewed in both British and American periodicals. In the general chorus of approval that greeted Snow's essay, the few dissenting voices attracted little attention. Late in February 1962, however, nearly three years after the publication of* The Two Cultures, *F. R. Leavis, in his Richmond Lecture at Downing College, Cambridge, launched a violent attack upon Snow. Leavis' address, which both repudiated Snow's views on the subject of science and culture and also undertook to demolish his reputation as a novelist, was subsequently published in the English magazine* The Spectator *(March 9, 1962) and immediately provoked what Lionel Trilling has called "a miasma of personality-mongering."*

The intense interest generated by this first phase of the debate derived in part from the character of Snow's antagonist. F. R. Leavis is one of the most influential and controversial literary critics of our time. Influenced by Matthew Arnold, he has based his criticism on the conviction that literature is central to a civilization and that the function of the critic is to determine "the best that is known and thought in the world." This conviction has led Leavis to single out from the mass of traditional literature authors and works which he sees as elect, or deserving of classical status. Among those components which make for such status is a preoccupation with mature interests. In The Great Tradition, *for example, he singles out for study those novelists "who are significant in terms of the human awareness they promote; awareness of the possibilities of life."* Life, *for Leavis, means the individual life, not collective life. Here is one of the issues of his conflict with Snow, for his main objection to Snow's essay is that it gives over hope for individual life in the present to focus on collective life in the future.*

The letters, articles, and reviews that appeared in the months following the publication of Leavis' Spectator *article—some supporting Leavis, others Snow—reflect a great variety in point of view and a wide range of attitude. In this section an excerpt from Leavis' essay is followed by a group of selections which represent a cross section of these responses. (A comment upon Snow's work that preceded the Leavis essay—the review-article by Richard Wollheim—has also been included in this section.) Several selections (e.g., the articles by Wain, West, and Corke) which comment interestingly upon personal factors involved in the dispute. Certain articles—especially that of William Buckley, Jr.—touch on the relation of the controversy to the ideological conflict between East and West. Other essays in the group deal with the issues of the debate at varying levels of abstraction.*

F. R. Leavis

TWO CULTURES? THE SIGNIFICANCE OF C. P. SNOW

*Frank Raymond Leavis (1895 –   ) was born in Cambridge, England, where he
has spent his life writing, editing, and teaching. Leavis' work has centered principally
in* Scrutiny, *a critical quarterly that was founded in 1932 by a group, mostly young
research students, who focused about Leavis' home.* Scrutiny *ran for more than twenty
years with Leavis as its main driving force. Out of it grew many of his most important
works –* Revaluation *(1936),* The Great Tradition *(1948),* The Common Pursuit
(1952), and D. H. Lawrence, Novelist *(1956).*

It might seem an odd position for one who proudly thinks of himself as
a major novelist. But I now come to the point when I have again to say, with a
more sharply focused intention this time, that Snow not only hasn't in him the
beginnings of a novelist; he is utterly without a glimmer of what creative literature is, or why it matters. That significant truth comes home to us, amusingly
but finally, when, near his opening, he makes a point of impressing on us that,
as himself a creative writer, he is humanly (shall I say?) supremely well qualified
– that he emphatically *has* a soul. 'The individual condition of each of us,' he
tells us, 'is tragic,' and, by way of explaining that statement, he adds, 'we die
alone.' Once he /38/ says 'we live alone,' but in general – for he makes his point
redundantly – he prefers to stress dying; it's more solemn. He is enforcing a
superiority to be recognised in the scientists: they, he says, 'see no reason why,
just because the individual condition is tragic, so must the social condition be.'
For himself, with tragic stoicism, he says, 'we die alone: all right,' but – which
is his message, the sum of his wisdom – 'there is social hope.'

He is repetitious, but he develops no explanation further than this. It doesn't
occur to him that there is any need, stultifying as anyone capable of thought
can see the antithesis to be. What *is* the 'social condition' that has nothing to do
with the 'individual condition'? What is the 'social hope' that transcends, cancels
or makes indifferent the inescapable tragic condition of each individual?
Where, if not in individuals, is what is hoped for – a *non*-tragic condition, one
supposes – to be located? Or are we to find the reality of life in hoping for other
people a kind of felicity about which as proposed for ourselves ('jam,' Snow
calls it later – we die alone, but there's jam to be had first) we have no illusions?
Snow's pompous phrases give us the central and supreme instance of what I
have called 'basic cliché.' He takes over inertly – takes over as a self-evident
simple clarity – the characteristic and disastrous confusion of the civilisation
he is offering to instruct.

It is a confusion to which all creative writers are tacit enemies. The greatest
English writer of our century dealth with it explicitly – dealt with it again and
again, in many ways, and left to our hand what should be the classical exposure.
But Snow, exhibiting his inwardness with modern literature by enumerating
the writers who above all matter, leaves Lawrence out (though he offers us
Wyndham Lewis – the brutal and boring Wyndham /39/ Lewis). Lawrence,
intent with all his being on the nature and movement of the civilisation of the
West, turned the intelligence of genius on what I have called the characteristic
confusion. He diagnoses it in his supreme novel, *Women in Love*, both discur-
sively and by the poetic means of a great novelist. Concerned with enforcing

From *Two Cultures? The Significance of C. P. Snow* published with *An Essay on Sir Charles Snow's Rede
Lecture* by Michael Yudkin (New York: Pantheon Books, 1963).

in relation to what may be called a quintessential presentment of the modern world the Laurentian maxim that 'nothing matters but life,' he insists on the truth that only in living individuals is life there, and individual lives cannot be aggregated or equated or dealt with quantitatively in any way. . . . /40/

. . . [Snow] dismisses [as "natural Luddites"]—sees no further significance in—Dickens and Ruskin, and all the writers leading down to Lawrence. Yet—to confine myself to the non-creative writer, about whom the challenged comment is most easily made—it was Ruskin who put into currency the distinction between wealth and well-being, which runs down through Morris and the British Socialist movement to the Welfare State.

But for Ruskin 'well-being' or 'welfare' could not conceivably be matters of merely material standard of living, with the advantages of technology and scientific hygiene. And there we have the gap—the gap that is the emptiness beneath Snow's ignorance—between Snow and not only Ruskin, but the great creative writers of the century before Snow: they don't exist for him; nor does civilisation. Pressing on this ancient university his sense of the urgency of the effort to which we must give ourselves, he says: 'Yet'—in spite, that is, of the 'horror' which, he says, is 'hard to look at straight'—'yet they've proved that common men can show astonishing fortitude in chasing jam tomorrow. Jam today, and men aren't at their most exciting: jam tomorrow, and one often sees them at their noblest. The transformations have also proved something which only the scientific culture can take in its stride. Yet, when we don't take it in our stride, it makes us look silly.'

The callously ugly insensitiveness of the mode of expression is wholly significant. It gives us Snow, who is wholly representative of the world, or culture, to which it belongs. It is the world in which Mr. Macmillan said—or might, taking a tip from Snow, have varied his /44/ phrase by saying—'You never had so much jam'; and in which, if you are enlightened, you see that the sum of wisdom lies in expediting the processes which will ensure the Congolese, the Indonesians, and Bushmen (no, not the Bushmen—there aren't enough of them), the Chinese, the Indians, *their* increasing supplies of jam. It is the world in which the vital inspiration, the creative drive, is 'Jam tomorrow' (if you haven't any today) or (if you have it today) '*More* jam tomorrow.' It is the world in which, even at the level of the intellectual weeklies, 'standard of living' is an ultimate criterion, its raising an ultimate aim, a matter of wages and salaries and what you can buy with them, reduced hours of work, and the technological resources that make your increasing leisure worth having, so that productivity —the supremely important thing—must be kept on the rise, at whatever cost to protesting conservative habit.

Don't mistake me. I am not preaching that we should defy, or try to reverse, the accelerating movement of external civilisation (the phrase sufficiently explains itself, I hope) that is determined by advancing technology. Nor am I suggesting that Snow, in so far as he is advocating improvements in scientific education, is wrong (I suspect he isn't very original). What I *am* saying is that such a concern is not enough—disastrously not enough. Snow himself is proof of that, product as he is of the initial cultural consequences of the kind of rapid change he wants to see accelerated to the utmost and assimilating all the world, bringing (he is convinced), provided we are foresighted enough to perceive that no one now will long consent to be without abundant jam, salvation and lasting felicity to all mankind.

It must be recognised, though, that he doesn't *say* 'salvation' or 'felicity,' but 'jam.' And if 'jam' means /45/ (as it does) the prosperity and leisure enjoyed by our well-to-do working class, then the significant fact not noticed by Snow is that the felicity it represents cannot be regarded by a fully human mind as a matter for happy contemplation. Nor is it felt by the beneficiaries to be satisfying. I haven't time to enlarge on this last point. I will only remark that the observation is not confined to 'natural Luddites': I recently read in the *Economist* a disturbed review of a book by a French sociologist of which the theme is (not a new idea to us) the incapacity of the industrial worker, who—inevitably —looks on real living as reserved for his leisure, to use his leisure in any but essentially passive ways. And this, for me, evokes that total vision which makes Snow's 'social hope' unintoxicating to many of us—the vision of our imminent tomorrow in today's America: the energy, the triumphant technology, the productivity, the high standard of living and the life-impoverishment—the human emptiness; emptiness and boredom craving alcohol—of one kind or another. Who will assert that the average member of a modern society is more fully human, or more alive, than a Bushman, an Indian peasant, or a member of one of those poignantly surviving primitive peoples, with their marvellous art and skills and vital intelligence?

But I will come to the explicit positive note that has all along been my goal (for I am not a Luddite) in this way: the advance of science and technology means a human future of change so rapid and of such kinds, of tests and challenges so unprecedented, of decisions and possible non-decisions so momentous and insidious in their consequences, that mankind—this is surely clear— will need to be in full intelligent possession of its full humanity (and 'possession' here means, not confident ownership of that which belongs to *us*—our property, /46/ but a basic living deference towards that to which, opening as it does into the unknown and itself unmeasurable, we know we belong). I haven't chosen to say that mankind will need all its traditional wisdom; that might suggest a kind of conservatism that, so far as I am concerned, is the enemy. What we need, and shall continue to need not less, is something with the livingness of the deepest vital instinct; as intelligence, a power—rooted, strong in experience, and supremely human—of creative response to the new challenges of time; something that is alien to either of Snow's cultures. /47/

John Wain

A CERTAIN JUDO DEMONSTRATION

John Wain (1925–   ) is an English novelist, poet, and literary critic who was described during the fifties as one of the most promising of Britain's "Angry Young Men." His works of fiction include Hurry on Down *(1953),* The Contender *(1958), and* Strike the Father Dead *(1962).*

[O]ur private worries, like yours, are to do with our personal lives, whether we are getting lung cancer from cigarettes, and in general how to get more love and money. At such a time, people welcome diversions, and there have been several on the literary-intellectual scene lately. Much the biggest was a certain judo demonstration given at Cambridge on February 28th, under the title of the Richmond Lecture, when F. R. Leavis, as if to prove that on the eve of retirement he has lost none of his skill, threw Sir Charles Snow over his

From "London Letter," *The Hudson Review* (Summer 1962), pp. 253–260.

shoulder several times and then jumped on him. The lecture was closed to reporters, but garbled reports filtered into some of the /254/ daily papers, and finally Dr. Leavis allowed the full text to appear in the *Spectator*. The whole thing made more of a stir than one would have thought; in central London, where surely a quarrel between two literary men cannot bulk very large, the paper was sold out and unobtainable within a few hours.

Many people, particularly if they hadn't been readers of *Scrutiny* in the old days and therefore familiar with the tradition of all-out personal destruction that magazine so signally failed to make respectable, were genuinely shocked at the brutality of the attack; while such echoes as reached the man in the street appear to have confirmed him in his belief that "intellectuals" are people who spend all their time indulging in passionate feuds of obscure motivation.

Actually, of course, the motivation wasn't at all obscure. For some time, Sir Charles has been blandly offering an account of "the Two Cultures," literary and scientific, which has been — to say the least of it — grossly inadequate in its account of the literary mind and curiously uncompelling in its account of the scientific. This wouldn't have mattered if Sir Charles had not been accepted by the public mind as a Sage, the true voice of mature wisdom in our time, and if he hadn't in turn accepted this as his natural role. Sir Charles is a decent and fair-minded man, genuinely doing his best to grapple with important problems, and one's uneasiness was caused less by what he himself said and did than by the sense that he was being carried upwards on a thrust of half-articulate public opinion, and that sooner or later this thrust would spend itself and leave him very high up with nothing to hold on to. That the *débâcle* would be precipitated by Leavis was something I must say I hadn't anticipated, yet once done it seemed natural enough: two Cambridge men, both widely accepted as Sages but not in the same kinds of circles, and with diametrically opposed temperaments and beliefs.

Leavis, of course, overdid the demolition; Sir Charles's admirers may have claimed for him a distinction that isn't really there, but it is absurd to say "he is intellectually as undistinguished as it is possible to be," as if he were the village idiot. Again, there is point in making a fairly drastic adverse criticism of Snow as a novelist, if your concern is to point out that his acceptance by a large public depends on a special kind of *réclame* that makes him both a distinguished scientist and a considerable novelist. Snow's idea of the novel is exactly Trollope's; his performance may be better than Trollope's or worse — I can't say, because I have never managed to read Trollope in bulk, any more than I have read Galsworthy or Snow in bulk. So I would go along with a reasonably cool appraisal of Sir Charles as a novelist: but I see no reason for Leavis'

> As a novelist he doesn't exist; he doesn't begin to exist. He can't be said to know what a novel is. The nonentity is apparent on every page of his fictions — consistently manifested, whatever aspect of a novel one looks for. /255/

The whole thing left one with a sense of comradely sympathy for Sir Charles, as it might be for a man who had been involved in a serious motor accident. This feeling, however, vanished abruptly one week later. In its issue of March 16th, the *Spectator* published several pages of fiery letters, most of them pro-Snow. It is these pages that deserve serious attention as a barometer of the present state of intellectual England. I have no space to quote: the entire document will be consulted, not once but repeatedly, by anyone (now or in the future) who wants the flavour of 1962 in England. In a word, the quality of the support offered by the Snow faction was such as to prove beyond doubt one of Leavis' main points: that the elevation of Sir Charles to his present position of Tribal Sage is the work of forces which exist independently of him and of which he has become the focus; that he has been "created" by "the cultural conditions manifested in his acceptance." Most of the correspondents who rushed to pull out Leavis' darts, and apply balm of one kind and another, offered such perfect illustrations of the *naiveté* and emptiness that Leavis was attacking that they left nothing for a pro-Leavis party to do. William Gerhardi, for instance, boiled over for several columns with a personal abuse of Leavis that went just as far in the direction of personality as anything Leavis had said about Snow, and seemed the more offensive in being used in the service, not of anything that could be called an idea, but merely a series of reflexive twitches. Mr. Gerhardi was typical of most of the defenders in his anxiety to build up Sir Charles into a figure worthy of the highest allegiance; one of his points, for instance, was that Leavis, who doesn't know Russian, ought not to challenge any of Sir Charles's judgments on Russian literature, for Sir Charles knows the language and reads the literature with the insight of passion. Is this true? I saw something of Sir Charles in Moscow during his first visit, when the foundations of his uncritically admiring attitude were being laid firmly into place, and he certainly didn't know much Russian then; he was content to echo the opinions handed to him by members of the literary bureaucracy, with whom his solidity seemed to me even at that time to be remarkable. That was in 1960; has Sir Charles, in the intervals of his busy life, really had time and energy in the last eighteen months to acquire that inwardness with the Russian language that would justify Mr. Gerhardi's deferring to him as an expert whose judgment cannot be questioned?

Another correspondent, Mr. G. S. Fraser, declared that "men like Snow, at home both in Russia and America, and in a blunt simple way trying to teach these two blunt simple giants to understand each other, may in the end prove greater benefactors of the world than Dr. Leavis." Again, one notices the assumption that Snow is "at home" in Russia: the phrase carries, surely, an implication that he understands the workings of the place, knows how to assess it and deal with it. And again this is what I question. I was, as I say, in the Soviet Union at the same /256/ time as Sir Charles on his first visit, and had the opportunity of seeing just how the all-important first steps in his approach were made, and what kind of people guided them: and my impression, gained at the time and reinforced by all his public utterances since, is that it is Sir Charles, and not the Soviet authorities, who is being "blunt and simple"; that he believes what they tell him and hands it out to a credulous audience at home who mistake him, as Mr. Gerhardi does, for a sensitive exponent of Russian literature, or, as Mr. Fraser does, for a "benefactor of the world." Personally I don't believe that anyone who spreads confusion and misunderstanding, in however well-meaning a way, is a benefactor of anybody. Sir Charles feels "at home," in Mr. Fraser's sense, among bureaucrats; he reveals, in his novels, both knowledge of and sympathy with the workings of the bureaucratic mind; he knows how battles are won and lost on committees. And of course, when he goes to a country like the Soviet Union where an all-powerful bureaucracy rules everything, he feels that this is the place for him. This fact was amusingly illustrated in a recent television interview between Sir Charles and Malcolm Muggeridge (transcript published in *Encounter*, February 1962). Asked about Russian literary taste, Sir Charles explained:

They are, they are making a very serious attempt, now, to translate most people whom they think reach a high standard, a highish standard, who are not actually, in their sense, really hostile. That is they wouldn't publish people whom they would call Fascist.

Muggeridge.   Mm.

Snow.   That would certainly be true. But that said, I think they're in many ways more open-minded than we are.

Muggeridge.   Could you imagine yourself living happily in a Communist society?

Snow.   I think so, It would depend a bit on what I, on my particular profession. You mean me as. . . .

Muggeridge.   Yes, you as you.

Snow.   You mean me as me.

Muggeridge.   You, writer-scientist.

Snow.   Yes, I think so. . . .

The slight difficulty over identification here ("You mean me as *me*?") reflects the bureaucratic habit of mind very accurately. It seems almost as if, in Sir Charles's eyes, nothing as statistically insignificant as an individual person could be quite real. His happiness in a Communist country would depend ("a bit") on what he was doing; that is, whether he was on top, handing it out, or down below, taking it. And when he says "they," of the Russians, he means "the Soviet bureaucracy," obviously, since it is this bureaucracy, not the Russian people, who are /257/ making "a serious attempt" to translate foreign writers of "a highish standard" who "are not actually, in their sense, really hostile." It is they, not the people, who dub all criticism, all scepticism about the perfect wisdom of their own decisions, "Fascist." What the common humanity of the Soviet Union feels about it all, we have to try to feel intuitively, since they have no voice.

But enough of this. Mr. Ronald Hingley, of the *Sunday Times,* has been going through the files of Soviet newspapers and reading their reports of some of the things Sir Charles and Lady Snow have been saying at literary dinners and the like. He promises to publish his findings very soon; and it may be that the kind of comfortable literary Englishman represented by Mr. Gerhardi (who is currently at work on a life of Lord Beaverbrook) will decide, on reading some of these pronouncements, that ultimate wisdom and justice does not, after all, reside in this kind of blunt simplicity. And if so, I predict we shall find ourselves forgetting the whole episode quite speedily. /258/

Hilary Corke

SNOW VS. LEAVIS

Hilary Corke (19   –   ) is a British poet and critic. His collected poems, The Early Drowned and Other Poems, *were published in 1962. The following selection is taken from a review of F. R. Leavis'* Two Cultures? The significance of C. P. Snow.

From "The Dog That Didn't Bark," *The New Republic* (April 13, 1963), pp. 27–30.

I suppose everyone has been more or less forcibly acquainted with the facts. In 1959 Sir Charles Snow, a well-known British novelist and spokesman for the sciences, delivered a Rede lecture at Cambridge, which he named *The Two Cultures*. His theme was, briefly, that the split, the gap in communication, between the "two cultures," of the sciences and the humanities, was already wide and would, unless steps were taken, continue to widen; that this was an unhappy, indeed, a potentially perilous thing; and that it was everyone's concern to try and do something about it. The theme, if neither very original, nor very deeply thought out, nor very memorably expressed, seemed at least meritorious. Coming from someone in the public position that Sir Charles enjoys, its tenets (one felt), though no doubt on the woolly side to begin with, and destined to be filtered through many many tons more of Establishment wool before they penetrated to any vital spot, would culminate in effects that would be, if marginally, more useful than not. But in 1962, in another endowed lecture of the usually cozy Cambridge sort (the Richmond), the critic F. R. Leavis, attacked both Sir Charles and his lecture with an uncontrolled virulence of fury that had hardly been seen in England since the days of *The Edinburgh Review* nearly a century and a half earlier. How had Sir Charles called down upon his head this almost frenetic savaging?

The present volume reprints Dr. Leavis' lecture, together with two prefatory notes to it by himself, plus a long biographical note on him (evidently also either written, or else inspired, by himself), and finally an essay by the Cambridge biochemist Michael Yudkin, written quite independently of Leavis, but equally, though from a different angle and in a very very different tone, attacking the Snow thesis.

What, first, of Snow? Sir Charles is very much what it is fashionable to call a figure of the Establishment. Quite typically, too, he was not born to it but "came up from the ranks" by way of a state school in Leicester. At Cambridge he was a molecular physicist and elected a Fellow of his college in that subject at the age of twenty-five. The war took him, ten years later, out of the university into the Civil Service. At the same time he turned seriously to the novel, and has more or less divided his time between these two latter callings since. His novels are highly thought of by the British Council and similar powers that be. The reasons are not far to seek. The books, which are concerned with men in their public capacities—the inwardnesses of an administrative scandal or of a college election—are written with integrity: their emphasis is on plot rather than character—on the sort of plot, moreover, that is a large part of Establishment experience, but normally left untackled in literature. They can safely be recommended to foreign students as examples both of sound, if unadverturous English style, and of the supposedly solid merits of the British way of life.

More serious students of literature no doubt think of Snow as respectable rather than brilliant, a conscientious writer of the second rank who has astutely made an unfamiliar but important piece of territory his own. They certainly do not in general regard him as anything remotely in the nature of a menacing portent or bogey. His is in fact the type of mind, wide but comparatively shallow, that is usually underestimated, rather than the reverse, by the professional critic—whose own mind will tend to cut pretty deep but, in his case, on a front that is comparatively narrow. A paragraph of a Snow novel yields nothing whatever to deep analysis; his merits lie in the structure and ordering of the whole. His is a typical administrator's mind, not very perceptive over the details, but capable of forming and retaining a well-balanced picture of the entire field. . . . /27/

But Leavis—what of Leavis? Let me say at once, that one's instincts and sympathies are basically with him; or at any rate basically against the sort of blandness and gross oversimplifications that the well-meaning Sir Charles represents. But the tone! Here is pure hysteria. After all, there is really not the slightest reason why the thought of the good Snow should bring blood-flecked froth to the mouth. Indeed, Leavis' fury takes our minds quite off the subject of Snow and turns them instead to himself. Where there is this much disparity between cause and effect, between stimulus and reaction, we look at once for a disorder in the person of the reactor.

As to its nature, this little work provides us every kind of evidence. Wild adulations of Leavis are plastered all over the jacket—"England's foremost literary critic" and the rest. The biographical note is a joy to collectors of the documentation of gloomy self-satisfaction: I don't suppose that ever before, even in the long history of academic folly, has any one thought fit to virtuously and solemnly assure his readers that he has never taken sabbatical leave from his duties. And when we look at the twin prefaces, the note of painfully outraged innocence takes us at once into realms of unconscious comedy of a very high order. "The angry, abusive and strikingly confident utterances of Snow's supporters" he complains fretfully, without for a moment beginning to understand to what infinitely greater extent the epithets must be applied to the raging diatribe that called those supporters forth.

To Lionel Trilling and others, who condemned the pointless virulence, Leavis replies in a very pained way. I was merely destroying a portent, he says, "and the portent as person may very well feel wounded, leaving his friends to accuse one of cruelty." But (he goes on), he was not "cruel," he was merely "unanswerable": 'The unanswerable is the cruelty. . . . It would have been less cruel had it been accompanied, as it was not, by the animus that impels the intention to hurt." Fine words, indeed: but alas! when we examine the lecture itself we find, beyond any shadow of a doubt, that he *was* cruel, and that he was *not* unanswerable. Is not this cruel?—

"As a novelist he doesn't exist; he doesn't begin to exist. He can't be said to know what a novel is. The nonentity is apparent on every page of his fictions. . . . I am trying to remember where I heard (can I have dreamed it?) that they are composed for him by an electronic brain called Charlie, into which the instructions are fed in the form of the chapter headings." . . . /28/

As for his "unanswerableness," the sum effect of Leavis' lecture is that of an attack that seems marvelously incisive and drastic so long as it keeps within general items, but fades and shies curiously whenever it descends to particulars.

"It is characteristic of Snow that 'believe' for him should be a very simple word. 'Statistically,' he says, 'I suppose slightly more scientists are in religious terms unbelievers, compared with the rest of the intellectual world.' There are believers and unbelievers; we all know that 'religious terms' are; or everything relevant in relation to the adjective has been said. Snow goes on at once: 'Statistically, I suppose, slightly more scientists are on the Left in open politics.' The naïveté is complete."

This doesn't begin to touch its target. Snow is exactly aware, as Leavis is exactly not, of the crude sociological context in which he is using the term "believer," and is careful to indicate his own reservations by the words *statistically, religious terms, open politics*. To such indicators Leavis is quite deaf – as indeed he appears to be to almost every aspect of style. This is one of the really disconcerting things about him as a pretender to critical overlordship. It is difficult not to debar (not wholly, but say 90 percent) anyone who is capable of perpetrating the kind of sentences that Leavis endlessly sees fit to pen:

> "Though I spoke of the 'literary world' as 'metropolitan', I wasn't forgetting that, most significantly, an essential element in it (and I don't mean my 'literary' to be taken in a narrow sense – I am thinking of what, borrowing a license from Snow, I will call the whole publicity – created culture) belongs to the universities."

It is not easy, after that sentence and dozens like it, to feel that Leavis can have anything to say about literature at all.

Finally, one is reluctantly forced into Dame Edith Sitwell's conclusion, "Dr. Leavis only attacked Charles because he is famous and writes good English." This dismal conclusion certainly ought not to be true, but I am afraid it probably is. The angry doctor is, in fact, a limpidly evident case of literary per- /29/ secution mania; and one can say this with the better conscience because one is, is one not, merely attacking the portent and only inadvertently wounding the man? And if one wants to play the amateur diagnostician, that is all too easy too. His whole life has been a passionate wooing of Cambridge – he was even born there – but his ardor has only been grudgingly returned, and returned late. He was 45 before he achieved a Fellowship. He was never a Professor. Who then kept him out? Why, They did. And who's They? The Establishment, of course – and that is precisely the bogey that the unlucky Sir Charles has been picked, almost fortuitously, in his single person to represent. (Even specifically: "It wouldn't be at all ridiculous to conjecture that Snow might have decisive influence in academic appointments – and on the side of the humanities.")

But, did They? Undoubtedly They did not. There is not the least question that Dr. Leavis' undeniably exceptional gifts have never come to proper public fruition. But whose fault is that? One does not endear oneself to one's fellows by habits of angry self-aggrandizement and rasping contempt. One must not at the same time call all one's neighbors fools and complain that they will not elect one to their club. And so one comes to the fretful pomposity of "We who ran *Scrutiny* for twenty years . . . were, and knew we were, Cambridge – the essential Cambridge in spite of Cambridge" (this sentence, incidentally, from a man who sneers at Snow for failing to properly define his terms!). And one could drop an ironic tear for the tragi-comedy of Leavis, in his draughty lodgings, busily being the essential Cambridge while all the dons sat happily sipping their sherry in their warm combination-rooms – if one did not bring oneself up short by recalling that this is precisely the basic social situation of every really unpleasant and *unnecessary* revolution of the past century. /30/

The Spectator

THE TWO CULTURES: AN EDITORIAL

Controversy on matters of intellectual principle frequently has the disadvantage of obscuring those issues which it is intended to lay bare. The contribu-

From *The Spectator* (March 30, 1962), pp. 387–388.

tions to the debate started by Dr. F. R. Leavis's criticism of Sir Charles Snow's Rede Lecture, *The Two Cultures,* have not always gone beyond the polemic principle.

On one level Sir Charles Snow's lecture was a plea for more knowledge of science among literary intellectuals and more knowledge of literature among scientists. His title *The Two Cultures* is intended to refer to an increasing separation of interests, which he believes to be dividing intellectual life in Western society and, above all, in Britain. With this thesis it is difficult to quarrel, inasmuch as it is simply a demand for more scientific education and a rather more general curriculum in the schools; nor did Dr. Leavis do so. Certainly, a more general awareness of scientific method and achievements in the average educated man would be an excellent thing. What is not altogether clear is how it can be furthered. It is no use saying that a layman can familiarise himself with that reduction of natural phenomena to mathematical symbols which is so formative an element of scientific thought, and Sir Charles's own instance of ignorance of the second law of thermodynamics seems to require historical rather than strictly scientific instruction to remedy it.

In all of this there is nothing especially controversial. But the Rede Lecture also contains a view of the nature of culture which is deeply controversial. 'Without thinking about it, they respond alike,' writes Sir Charles of scientists. 'That is what a culture means.' But is this so? The history of civilisation is surely one of increasing consciousness and increasing variety of cultural reaction. Certain values can be held in common, but within these there is an almost infinite range of response. It is hard not to agree with Dr. Leavis when he criticises Sir Charles's view of culture. Such an instinctive unity might possibly be called 'a culture' if it occurred in a primitive tribe (and even a primitive culture is done an injustice by this description), but among more civilised peoples it is crippling—and potentially tyrannical.

Sir Charles seems also to be of the opinion that the two cultures are by no means equal. Scientists have 'the future in their bones.' They are impatient to better man's 'social condition.' Only the scientific culture can take the transformations of the modern world in its stride. Literary intellectuals, on the other hand, are 'natural Luddites.' Some of them hold 'contemptible' social attitudes. They are all smothered in 'the traditional culture.' To this Dr. Leavis replies that a Dickens or a Ruskin or a Lawrence has in fact been responsible for some of the profoundest utterances on the transformations of the modern world and its social consequences. 'But for Ruskin "well-being" or "welfare" could not conceivably be matters of merely material "standard of living," with the advantages of technology and scientific hygiene.' Here we come to the heart of his differences with Sir Charles Snow.

For there is one word lacking in the Rede Lectures, the only word which can give significance to an attempt to bring science and literature together, or to unite the efforts of politician and technocrat. The word is 'philosophy,' and in its secular significance it takes the form of that effort to impart moral direction, which is to be found in the best nineteenth-century English writers. After being told that scientists have the future in their bones it is salutary to read the opinion of William James: 'Of all the insufficient authorities as to the total nature of reality, give me the "scientists". . . . Their interests are most incomplete and their professional conceit and bigotry immense. I know of no narrower sect or club, in spite of their excellent authority in the lines of fact they have explored, and their splendid achievements there.' And, it must also be said, that the claim of scientists to play a part in government cannot easily be reconciled with the facility which they have shown in shrugging off the consequences of their work. If a writer had worked for the Nazis as the scientists who developed the V2 worked for them, he would have been condemned by an allied tribunal or, at least, suffered grave inconvenience. He would not have been transported to a position of affluence and authority in the US or USSR. Scientists cannot have it both ways.

In fact, the cult of science and technology /387/ without an adequate sense of moral direction is simply the 'scientism' of the nineteenth century dressed up in the fashionably emotive garments of aid to underdeveloped countries, higher standards of living, and space exploration. Knowledge is power, but it is not the knowledge of how that power should be used. That is the affair of conscience and consciousness. To admire a tyrannical political regime for its technological achievements is on the same level of appreciation as to admire it for having a large army. We can wonder at some colossal feat of engineering as we wonder at the Pyramids, but only an effort of imagination and a sense of human values can enable us to count the cost or to pity the slaves who built them. It is the business of writers, philosophers and moralists to represent those values which can alone give life to culture or direction to the vast human achievements of science. They can and should learn from science and scientists, but the essential role they themselves have to play is not to be thrust aside with talk of 'natural Luddites.' If we think to some purpose, then we shall be able to make the future instead of being carried along by it like children in the arms of an automaton.

The questions which are begged by *The Two Cultures* are precisely those we must answer. /388/

Anthony West

FROM THE TOP DRAWER AND THE BOTTOM

Anthony West (1914–   ), critic and novelist, was born in England, the son of H. G. Wells and Rebecca West. In 1950 he settled in the United States, where he has continued writing essays and novels. His reviews and essays frequently appear in the New Yorker. *Among his novels are* The Vintage *(1950),* Another Kind *(1952), and* The Trend Is Up *(1960).*

Ronald Millar's play made out of C. P. Snow's novel "The Affair" is one of those theater pieces which have a resemblance to an iceberg; two-thirds of its mass are away out of sight under the wine-dark sea and what is visible is only a part of the show. C. P. Snow is a kindly looking, avuncular figure, who beams at the world out of a round face through round glasses in a way which inspires a belief in man's better nature and the benevolence of the universe. He is, too, on the side of the angels in many things, and the basis of "The Affair" is his wholesome sense of outrage at what seemed to him a very crooked and nasty conception of justice. This was a formulation of D. H. Lawrence's which is to be found lurking hideously in his superficially attractive book, "Sea and Sardinia," a book which many sensitive and intelligent literary persons have found possible to admire. Lawrence wrote:

It is a great mistake to abolish the death penalty. If I were dictator, I should order the old one to be hanged at once. I should have judges with sensitive, living hearts: not

"From the Top Drawer and the Bottom," *Show* (December 1962), pp. 34–35.

abstract intellects. And because the instinctive heart recognized a man as evil, I would have that man destroyed. Quickly. Because good warm life is now in danger.

This shocked Snow very deeply, and with cause, since it would be hard to frame a more repulsive foundation for a judicial system. He sat down to write a morality in which the issue could be displayed within the framework of a row about a fellowship in a Cambridge college. A very unpleasant character called Donald Howard is accused of scientific fraud, and because he is a self-assertive, ill-tempered and generally cross-grained man with a gift for putting people's backs up, substantial and cruel injustice is done to him. The charges are not properly investigated, he is found guilty of them, and he is deprived of his fellowship in a way which ends his career as a scientist. This occurs because his judges, the members of the college's court of seniors, consult their feelings and not their intellects. They know that Howard is a nasty fellow, and, as he is also a Communist, they are sure that he is capable of any wickedness. In fact, he has had some faked evidence planted on him by an older man who, inspired by vanity, wanted to manufacture corroboration for an erroneous hypothesis to which he had committed himself. Sir Lewis Eliot, C. P. Snow's highly ideal-ized version of himself, becomes aware that injustice has been done, and "The Affair" describes the complex intramural politics of the struggle to put things right in which he finds himself engaged as soon as his conscience is aroused.

So far all is plain sailing. But it has to be said that there is a trace of the old Adam even in C. P. Snow. He included among the characters in "The Affair" a certain Lester Ince, a lecturer in music, who was quite clearly a thinly dis-guised portrait of the leading exponent of Lawrence's ideas at Cambridge University. The disguise, though thin, is neatly applied. Lester Ince, taken feature by feature, cannot possibly be the redoubtable Doctor Leavis lately of Downing College at Cambridge University, and yet the totality of all the features Snow has given him builds up an unmistakable resemblance. Doctor Leavis is in many ways admirable; he is also quarrelsome to a degree, ill-mannered and intolerant. He is an easy man to dislike and it was very clear from Snow's portrait of Ince that dislike was involved. This was particularly evident when, at a critical point in the maneuvers designed to bring about a reopening of Howard's case, Ince gives vent to a Lawrencian tirade against the arrogance of scientists, and in a despicable manner washes his hands of the whole affair. He is interested in the good warm life, not in abstract intellectual questions of ethics and justice, and he wants no part of them or their diffi-culties. He retires from the field in pursuit of private satisfactions which C. P. Snow is careful to show as trivial and anti-intellectual.

The incident is striking in the book (it was striking enough to produce the violent attack on Snow by Leavis in a private lecture which became public last year and was the cause of a famous row). It is doubly so on the stage. The enlarging and focusing effect which is the theatrical essence makes Ince seem to be a truly disgusting figure. Whatever Doctor Leavis may be he is not dis-gusting, and he is not dishonorable. So that Ince's speech, in which he shows himself to be without honor and without integrity, is truly shocking. It is one of those classic moments in which injustice is done, and in which it can be seen to be done. The moment is, moreover, one in which C. P. Snow stands himself, happily and without knowing it, on his head. His treatment of Ince-Leavis is precisely the treatment accorded to Donald Howard by his college; Snow takes it for granted that because his man holds the Lawrencian ideas which are detestable to him, he will be capable of any infamy.

The third act of the play, like the final section of the original novel, is con-cerned with the rehabilitation of the wronged man and the discovery of a real villain, the college bursar who has suppressed the vital evidence which would have shown who was in fact guilty of fraud. Sir Lewis Eliot-Snow does the unmasking in cross-examination and when the noble work is done, delivers himself of some fine words on the subject of tolerance and generosity. The bursar was intolerant, and intolerance led him into wickedness; because he didn't like Howard's political ideas, he felt justified in resorting to any means, however unethical, to fix his feet. Sir Lewis is deeply shocked by this, as indeed he should be, and plummily rebukes the audience for inclining to think, in the depth of their hearts, that the bursar's Machiavellian ongoings may have had some practical justification.

I enjoyed his lecture, delivered with a sort of juicy insincerity by Brewster Mason in the direction of Miss Brenda Vaccaro who had given a splendidly bitchy performance as the unlovable Howard's unlovable wife, more in love with Communism than with any man. She radiated a sincere indignation right back at Mr. Mason. Perhaps she was thinking of C. P. Snow's other great controversy fought without dignity and without violence over the dead body of one Professor Lindemann a little while ago. This sprang out of an earlier controversy which took place while the Professor was still alive.

He was then the scientific adviser most influential with the British Cabinet and he was fighting for what was to become an independent Atomic Energy Authority which would not be under the control of the civil service. He took the view that the free spirit of scientific enquiry would be stifled if the AEA became an ordinary department of either the Ministry of Supply or the Ministry of Defense. Snow was on the other side of the fence, and in a powerful position as the director of scientific personnel in the civil service. Had the Atomic Energy Authority remained under civil service control, he would have shaped it and in effect determined its policies by exercising his function of selecting its directors and its research workers. He lost his battle with Lindemann and emerged from it as a figure of greatly reduced importance who no longer had a place at the very center of things.

All this took place in the years immediately following World War II, and by now might well have been forgotten by all but the few insiders who were parties to the hard-fought dispute. But after Lindemann's death in 1957, Snow, who had been, apparently contentedly, occupying the first years of his retirement by making a new career and a new position for himself as a novelist, decided to clear his mind of his thoughts about his old adversary. The ultimate form they took were the Godkin lectures which Snow delivered at Harvard in 1960 and which were later published as a small book by Harvard University Press. These lectures are, in form at least, devoted to a high-toned plea for fuller cooperation and understanding between politicians and the scientific community. They contain as vicious an attack on the reputation and achievement of a public figure as has been written in England for American comsumption. Snow knew that his foreign audience would not be up on the details of his controversy with Lindemann, and knew, too, that it would not be familiar with his behind-the-scenes operations which /34/ were doubly cloaked by wartime security, and by the fact that they were in the realm of cabinet secrets. He had a free hand. He could rely, too, on the difficulties which any defenders of Lindemann would encounter, since the record could be cleared only by disclosing who said what, and when, at official meetings and conferences which were, and still are, covered closely by Britain's Official Secrets Act.

Lindemann was, in many ways, a most unpleasant man, rude, arrogant and selfish. With a great deal of skill, Snow made him out to be even nastier than he was; he then proceeded to denigrate his reputation as a scientist, and to saddle him with a number of gross errors of judgment which had a crucial effect on the British conduct of the war. Lindemann did not make these errors, and Snow had to make supple manipulations of some recalcitrant facts to make it appear that he had done so . . . and so there is good reason for the very attractive Miss Vaccaro to fix Mr. Mason with a beady and sarcastic eye when he tells her how important decency is if we are all to live together in this dangerous and precariously balanced world. /35/

Richard Wollheim

GROUNDS FOR APPROVAL

Richard Wollheim (1922–   ) teaches philosophy at London University. His writings include F. H. Bradley *(1959) and* Socialism and Culture *(1961).*

The Two Cultures and the Scientific Revolution is written in a style that is at once personal and modest. But it would be a mistake to take this too seriously. Sir Charles Snow is a former of opinion, and he speaks for an increasingly large body of people who think that there is something very wrong with contemporary British culture, and that what is wrong with it has to do with the place and prestige it allows to science.

In a narrow compass, fifty small pages, Sir Charles deals with an amazing range of topics. He deals with science in its relation to poverty, to education, and to culture, and in each case his plea is the same: that more space be allowed to science. We should make greater use of it, we should absorb it deeper into our minds. Put like this, casually, generally, imprecisely, the thesis cannot fail to make its appeal. When we think of the appalling squalor and disease and overpopulation in Africa and Asia and South America, it is evident that the spread of technology into these countries should be an overwhelming concern for mankind; when we think how much of the future happiness and prosperity of this country depends on the successful maintenance of economic growth, we cannot but be terribly uneasy over the backwardness of our scientific education; and the extent to which total ignorance of scientific learning all but invariably goes hand in hand with the highest pretensions to culture is alarming. But these are no more than the platitudes of the subject. And if Sir Charles were saying no more than this his lecture would be acceptable in the sense of being true, but unacceptable in the sense of being boring. Happily Sir Charles does say more than this. Exactly how much more he says is not always clear, but enough emerges to attribute to his lecture a stronger thesis and a weaker one. The weaker thesis is that our culture in the widest sense pays inadequate attention to science. The stronger thesis is that our culture in the narrowest sense should assimilate the results of science. And by culture in the narrowest sense what he means is higher education and the arts.

On the face of it there are certain obvious objections to this point of view. Curiosity in a modern man would naturally lead him to find out more about the discoveries of modern science, since they are among the most striking achievements of our age; and curiosity is an attribute of mind naturally associated with

"Grounds for Approval," *The Spectator* (August 7, 1959), pp. 168–169.

the man of high education and the artist. But there is another attribute that we associate even more intimately with culture in the narrowest sense, and that is freedom, or choice. Higher education is regarded, at any rate in the tradition of the West, as a means whereby man liberates himself and becomes or endeavours to become what he wants to be: indeed in the last hundred years the liberating role of education has increased, in that through it not merely do individual men free themselves of natural fears and inherited beliefs but whole classes and groups of men manage to break down the social barriers that would otherwise have confined them to an imposed routine. Equally it is part of the whole concept of art as we possess it that it is produced in freedom. A system of education in which people can't learn what they want to learn, a style of art in which people can't say what they want to say, would scarcely count for us as either education or art, and this is none the less true even if we can't imagine— as Sir Charles perhaps can't—how any educated person might not want to know about, and any artist might not want to talk about, modern science. The brutal fact is that certain things bore certain people. Why must they swallow their boredom, or else be deprived of education and denied creativity?

I think that there are certain further doctrines that would lead to an attitude much like that exemplified in this lecture, and it would be interesting to know if Sir Charles embraces them. The first doctrine concerns equality and education. We are entering, it is claimed, an egalitarian society: in other words a society where such social differences as exist will depend upon merit. In such a society wealth, birth, privilege will be dispensed with as ordering principles, and their place will in large part be taken by education, for there can be no better method of discriminating merit than the educational process. Accordingly what is wanted is a system of education in which differences of merit stand out most clearly. A scientific education provides just this, therefore the educational system should be predominantly scientific in character. Sometimes this egalitarian argument is extended so as to relate also to art. The art of the future must make a universal appeal, the only way it can do so is by adopting a content of universal appeal, and this it can only find in science and its many applications.

The second doctrine that might lie behind Sir Charles's plea is doctrine about the nature of culture, a doctrine that has a fairly wide following and from which an argument can be developed that relates specifically, to art and its proper occupation. According to this doctrine a culture is an organic unity; it is a whole that owes its unity to a common bloodstream that runs through and purifies all its parts. In any modern culture the prevailing spirit must be that of science, for it is here that the mind and creativity of man has over the last hundred years most strikingly manifested itself. Accordingly any form of poetry or painting that does not share in this overruling concern of the age is an anachronism, capable perhaps of producing an occasional work of curious beauty, but ultimately sterile, morbid and uninteresting—as Sir Charles says of the poetry of Rilke (surely a case in point for anyone who holds such a doctrine of culture), 'esoteric, tangled and dubiously rewarding'.

These two doctrines—indeed either by itself—lend authority to the appeal for a scientific culture. It is no part of my case to argue their merits, though in passing I could remark that the first I find not without attractions and the second repulsive. My only concern is to indicate how they might have strengthened Sir Charles's position. Since he nowhere subscribes to either of them, his argument must be found the less persuasive.

Sir Charles rightly sees that it is only part of the story to say that modern literary culture is ignorant of the fruits of scientific progress. The truth is that many of its great heroes have been uncompromisingly hostile to the whole forward movement of scientific thought. In a way this might be thought to strengthen the case against literary culture: it might be thought to show it as standing in even greater need of reform. And so, perhaps, it does. But perhaps it also shows something else: and that is the difficulties in the way of such reform. Hostility is a more significant relation than indifference—it shows, that is, more about the terms it relates. May it not be that the bitter hostility shown by nearly all the greatest artists of the modern age to the methods and theories of human improvement reveals some connection which is rather more than coincidental between art and the destructive impulses? In one sense, art is the greatest human victory over the powers of destruction. But its victory lies supremely in its formal aspect, in the management and control of content. And it may be, it often enough seems to be, that the promethean effort demanded of the artist if he is to subdue and mould his content in this fashion, is unlikely to be made unless the content he subdues is in the first place sufficiently unruly.

All this is speculative. We know little /168/ about the sources of art. But if we are to pronounce, however colloquially, on the proper character of human culture, these are matters that should detain us. Sir Charles at one moment makes a distinction between the 'individual condition' and 'the social condition'. The distinction may be facile, but it might have made him wonder whether he had not been led on from a doctrine of social hope to one of individual conformity.

The trouble with the lecture is that it is written absolutely outside any theory of man or culture, and it is this philosophical deficiency that gives it a kind of biscuit-like dryness and places it quite at the opposite end of the scale from discussions of the same matter by, say, Mill or Newman. I have tried at various points to suggest theories that might support or controvert the main thesis. I have done so in the hope that those who agree with Sir Charles's conclusions might be encouraged to work out a richer setting for them. For in the absence of any general conception of man and culture optimistic radicalism can be as depressing and soul-destroying a doctrine as pessimistic conservatism. /169/

William F. Buckley, Jr.

THE VOICE OF SIR CHARLES

William F. Buckley, Jr., (1925–   ) is editor of the **National Review,** *a weekly journal which he founded in 1955 and which expresses a politically conservative viewpoint. Buckley, who describes himself as "a radical conservative," first gained prominence when he published* **God and Man at Yale; the Superstition of Academic Freedom** *(1951), a work in which he accuses his alma mater of pro-collectivism and of anti-religious leanings. Among other works which have aroused controversy is his* **McCarthy and His Enemies** *(1954), a justification of Senator Joseph R. McCarthy.*

Q. *Could you imagine yourself living happily in a Communist society?*
A. *I think so.*

"The Voice of Sir Charles," *National Review* (May 22, 1962), p. 358.

Q. *If you had to, if somebody said you've got to live in America or live in Russia for the rest of your days, I mean supposing it so happened, which would you choose?*
    A. *Well, that is very difficult. . . . I think, to be honest, I could be happy in either of them.*

The voice you have just heard is not that of an IBM machine, which might be equally happy living in Russia or the United States, but C. P. Snow's, transcribed and published in the February *Encounter,* an English-American monthly. (Sir Charles was recently accused by an Oxford professor of writing novels which read as though they had been written by an electronic brain.)

During the last couple of years, C. P. Snow got himself an enormous reputation in England, which means, derivatively, a sizable reputation with the American intelligentsia, primarily as the result of having elaborated the thesis that what's wrong with the world is mainly due to the hostile symbiosis of our "two cultures," the humanistic and the scientific. This is the scientific age, and science should be crowned.

Sir Charles' complaint became the talk-talk of the highbrow set, and Snow, who was originally trained as a scientist, was paid a dizzying amount of attention, which spilled over on his novels, making them best-sellers. In very short order he was certified, on both sides of the Atlantic, and as a matter of fact on both sides of the Iron Curtain, as a seer. He came over to New York a year or so ago and pronounced at a banquet that it is a scientific *certitude* that before ten years have gone by an international accident will set off a nuclear war, unless we have disarmament. His words, which of course were the words of a fetishist, not a scientist, were received with much awe, and Sir Charles' reputation rose even higher.

Now, finally, it has been challenged on one flank, by a crusty Cambridge don, F. R. Leavis, who has moved in on Snow the novelist ("as a novelist, C. P. Snow doesn't begin to exist"), and Leavis has a reputation in the literary world for always getting his man. I don't know what Lloyds of London is quoting on the survival of Sir Charles' literary reputation, but the odds are very different from what they were.

But Sir Charles, as we can see, needs more than a literary going over. What he has been preaching is that final effrontery of relativism: that in the last analysis, there simply aren't any essential differences between the two contending parties in our great war with Communism.

"Mind you," says Snow, "I'm not really a political man, except in a sort of world context. That is, I am strongly for the poor."

Mr. Snow is asked if he thinks something can be done about the world's poverty. "It's perfectly within man's power to correct it, if only Russia and America would stop quarreling," is Mr. Snow's reply.

Would he agree, the interviewer goes on, "that these two regimes, which are normally accepted as representing two opposites, on examination, have enormous points in common"? Snow: "Oh, anyone who has lived in these two countries knows that."

England is the land of eccentrics, but C. P. Snow is not considered one of them, to be laughed at amiably every Sunday afternoon at Hyde Park, as he shakes his little fist at the massive walls of England's Establishment. Snow's views on the nature of our "quarrel" with Communism are held widely, by intellectuals all over the world; and Snow was telling the interviewer what many English intellectuals truly believe. Snow's disease, which so far relieves one of one's vision as to blur into insignificance the differences between life in America and in Russia, seems to strike only at people who are commonly considered to be very cosmopolitan in their outlook; but even so, the disease rages and in America it is the conservative community that seems to be especially afraid of its ravages.

Here is C. P. Snow, world oracle, the beautiful son of the marriage of science and the humanities, preaching this kind of thing, and moving easily in the circles of the English and American elite, where a McCarthyite would be treated as a leper. When indignation meetings storm the country in protest against the sending of jet fighters to Yugoslavia, we hear more than the voice of tactical dissent, we hear the tones of moral outrage, to which, increasingly, the world is growing deaf.

What many Americans who have been denounced as extremists are feeling is a sense that our leaders and our intellectuals are draining the moral content out of our struggle against Communism, that the visits to Geneva, the cultural exchanges, the Spirits of Camp David, the vodka parties, the standing ovations for Khrushchev in Chicago, White House invitations to Linus Pauling, that all these are steps on the road to C. P. Snow.

These Americans have a feeling that they are slowly being swindled out of their moral birthrights. They are less afraid of an increase in genetic mutations caused by radioactivity in the atmosphere than they are of an increase in moral idiocy caused by the predominance of a point of view. The symbol of that point of view is the voice of C. P. Snow, secure in a BBC studio, informing a subject people whose martyrs are slaughtered every day on their stomachs, stopped by machine gun bullets from crawling on their hands and knees to the West — the voice of Sir Charles telling them that they should not have troubled themselves, since the West is no different from what they are fleeing from, dying of. The voice of the machine, in the age of Science. /358/

Martin Green

A LITERARY DEFENSE OF "THE TWO CULTURES"

Martin Green (1927 –   ) was born in London. After graduating from Cambridge University in 1948 he continued his studies at London University, the Sorbonne, and the University of Michigan. He has taught at both the University of Michigan and Wellesley College. In 1961 he published A Mirror for Anglo-Saxons, *a collection of essays discussing his views of life and literature in England and America.*

It is now nearly three years since C. P. Snow delivered the Rede Lecture that was afterward published under the title of *The Two Cultures*. F. R. Leavis' recent attack on it, and on Snow himself, owes some of its popular success to that lapse of time; during those three years a fierce irritation has gathered among "intellectuals" (people who teach, or would in America teach, at a university, let's say) at the publicity given to Snow's thesis. This irritation is to be found among scientists as well as among humanists: there is no name to equal Snow's as a signal, at an intellectual party, for every guest to sharpen his malice and begin a co-operative denigration. And yet — quite apart from the nastiness of this behavior — there has been no answering of his thesis. Dr. Leavis' Richmond Lecture offers the best chance so far to continue (or rather to begin) the debate.

"A Literary Defense of 'The Two Cultures,'" *The Kenyon Review* (Autumn 1962), pp. 731–739.

Dr. Leavis' attack is concentrated on the author's personality, manner, and tone. He claims that these form a context for Snow's propositions that fills out the meaning of his abstract nouns, his compressed judgments, his sweeping metaphors, and his passing allusions, and he asserts that this context defines those meanings as confused, empty, and vulgar. He describes Snow's tone as one that "only genius could justify," he accuses him of a "genially 'placing' wisdom" that condescends to the rest of the world, of seeing himself as a seer and a sage. But supporting these pretensions, Leavis finds only a "crass Wellsianism," a "swell of cliché," an "embarrassing vulgarity," and an "intellectual nullity." Snow is, in fact, the type-product as well as spokesman for a civilization which has lost all cultural standards. He literally does not know what words like culture and civilization mean, and his discussion of them is empty gesturing. "The Two Cultures" therefore means nothing more than an ambitious man's attempt to claim an /731/ advantage for himself. This is the diagnosis, moreover, of other of Snow's literary enemies, though most do not carry it so far or, of course, so publicly.

The first thing to realize is that this is an isolated and belated skirmish in a larger battle. Leavis gives us the clue in his phrase "crass Wellsianism," and later "neo-Wellsian"; he describes H. G. Wells as Snow's spiritual father and Bertrand Russell as his paradigmatic hero. He accuses Snow of misunderstanding, dismissing, disliking all the great creative artists of twentieth-century literature; of not knowing what literature today is. In other words, he sees Snow as the last representative of that encyclopedist movement of the '20s and '30s which was one of his own great enemies: a movement dominated by Wells, Russell, Shaw, etc., the spirit of which was summed up in Wells's three compilations, *An Outline of History, The Science of Life,* and *The Work, Wealth, and Happiness of Mankind:* a spirit of broad general knowledge, national and international planning, optimism about (or at least cheerful businesslike engagement with) the powers of contemporary science and technology, and a philistinism about the more esoteric manifestations of art and religion. For Leavis, this spirit contradicted his own preoccupations so completely that it amounted to a betrayal of every cultural responsibility, announced an ignorance of what culture is, and literature, and history. But it is possible for us now to be glad Leavis felt in this way, and defeated "Wellsianism" for us, without ourselves believing that the latter was "intellectually null."

Indeed, now that Wellsianism is so completely in the past, we can respond with free appreciation to its zest and scope of interest, its fund of common sense, its all-round responsibility. It is hard in fact to remember how powerful it was, and how great a threat to literary standards, so complete has been the success of the minority faction of the time. We can now think of the '30s as the time of the publication of *Scrutiny.* For the last ten or fifteen years the study of literature, and to some extent the general intellectual climate, has been increasingly dominated by a movement very largely antithetical in tendency—a movement which insists on narrow intense knowledge (insights), on the need for personal freedom within the best-planned society, on the dangers of modern science and technology, on the irreducibility of artistic and religious modes. This movement also has its limitations and dangers; and it is now so generally triumphant that these become important. Leavis has a point in calling Snow's style "neo-Wellsian"; this helps us to understand and estimate his ideas; but by the same warrant his own style can be called "neo-Jamesian," and he must submit to an equal, though opposite, pictorialization, as "aesthetic" in his atti- /732/ tude to culture. The quarrel between Wells and James becomes an apt paradigm of some aspects of the present confrontation.

This paradigm, this general setting, does not in itself determine, of course, the validity of Leavis' criticism. But it makes more plausible, perhaps, the contention that he has reacted to Snow's tone as a bull to a red flag. He has not discriminated: he has not registered exactly. Snow's manner, for instance, does not claim for the speaker that he is a genius. Quite insistently it claims that he is a plain man with, by chance, a breadth of plain experience. He does not claim depth or intensity of knowledge; he claims breadth and simplicity. Common sense, not inspiration, is his keynote.

Nor is he pontifical. There is no priesthood of which Snow is the master, no esoteric training one needs to understand him, no dogma without which one is lost. He offers to make his ideas, his reasoning, completely available to his readers, and submissive to their judgments. He is no more a sage than a seer. There will be no disciples. It is precisely not among specialists and enthusiasts that he has any following.

A "genially 'placing' wisdom" certainly describes part of Snow's manner; he obviously does enjoy his position of knowing more than either brand of specialist about the other specialty. But it would be a very ungenerous nature that could not allow him that enjoyment; and participate in it. Because his is essentially a social and co-operative performance. He invites the reader to allow him this indulgence (as, after all, Lawrence invites our indulgence for the liberties *he* takes) and to enjoy his freedom with him. Snow's tone is "Let's agree to abandon between ourselves (between you and me, perhaps) the safeguards of technicalities and indirection. Let's agree to simplify, to colloquialize, to run all the risks of short cuts. We're all shrewd, successful, simple men; since that is what we have in common, let's use that vocabulary—of worldliness, competitiveness, gamesmanship. And let's frankly enjoy the pomp and ceremony our civilization imposes on successful men; it happens to be me that is getting the prizes today, but it might have been you." There is surely no reason to find that tone, as such, offensive; in the present climate of opinion it is remarkably fresh, and, in dealing with such subjects, remarkably interesting; and Snow manages it to lively and subtle effect. It is a humility as well as a sanity in him that he accepts so fully his very difficult position: of representing the intellectuals to the outside world without being accredited as the supreme representative of either science or literature from within. His tone expresses that humility among other things. His position is moreover unique and /733/ self-created; he is not usurping anyone else's place; he is not speaking for literature to any audience Leavis addresses. He has created a new sort of social rostrum, and he is using it to give some large general truths the kind of hearing they otherwise never get. He can make educational and cultural affairs matters of national, even international, concern. Some of those who attack him prefer those affairs to remain private, obscure, neglected, musty, because of their own fear of any brisker climate.

The vulgarity, the nullity, the abundance of cliché which Leavis finds in the style aren't there for anyone who begins without the anti-Wellsian prejudice. He cites "History is merciless to failure" as (typically) meaningless as soon as you reflect on it. But it is a perfectly acceptable way of saying that at a given point in time some particular action may be so necessary that a failure in that will bring about total ruin. He says that Snow's contrast between social hope and individual tragedy is stultifying, invalid, meaningless. "Where, if not in individuals, is what is to be hoped for—a *non*-tragic condition, one supposes—to be located?" But, again, it means that what distresses us in social conditions can be put right by an exercise of collective willpower and intelligence, while what distresses us in our individual condition cannot. The contrast is only invalid if nothing in social conditions does deeply distress us. He says of the phrase "they [scientists] have the future in their bones" both that it "cannot be explained as a meaningful proposition" and that it dismisses the issue, tacitly eliminates the problem, by implying—we presume this is Leavis' interpretation of it—that the future will be something to exult in. But surely the phrase means that scientists habitually deal in kinds of knowledge and power that become socially significant some twenty or fifty years later; so that what is the future for us is contemporary and familiar for them: and that this experience is fundamental in their intellectual life? It does not mean that they rejoice simple-mindedly in the approach of that future. Snow's own warnings about the probability of thermonuclear war surely demonstrate his own sense of that future.

Snow's style, manner, tone are indeed "Wellsian." As such of course they offend against the contemporary intellectual mood. But they are not "crass," and nothing Leavis has said shows that. We must examine his propositions with an open mind, not with a predisposition to find them invalid.

II

When we come to consider those propositions, the ideas of "The Two Cultures," we must grant Leavis one important point. Snow dismisses the /734/ historical record of "the literary culture" far too cavalierly. This lends substance to Leavis' claim that Snow "knows nothing of history" or of the meaning of civilization. When Snow says that the traditional literary culture did not notice the Industrial Revolution, or, when it did notice, didn't like what it saw, then he does expose himself to the sort of scornful reprimand which Leavis is administering. The tradition of culture-criticism, explored by Raymond Williams in *Culture and Society*, is one of the two or three great achievements of modern English thought, and it is predominantly the work of the literary culture. However, Leavis' correctness seems to me in this case a debating triumph; because, if you are deeply aware of that tradition, you are all the more interested in what Snow has to say. It is precisely in the context of those marvellous social insights of Ruskin and Lawrence that the thesis of "The Two Cultures" becomes more than a Sunday-newspaper platitude. The literary culture of the nineteenth and twentieth centuries thought harder and to more purpose than any other group about the human problems created by the Industrial Revolution; and Dr. Leavis is the great inheritor of that great tradition; but they have not, no more than he has, been able to "solve" (analyze satisfyingly) some of those problems, and Snow helps us to understand why. "The Two Cultures" brings new life to that tradition of thought.

Dr. Leavis' other critical points are less convincing. He accuses Snow of slipping from one meaning of "culture" to another unconsciously, of ignoring crucial distinctions. But the cases he cites are all ones where he is imposing his own sense of what the critical distinctions are on the argument. He does not respect Snow's line of thought enough to accord it patient attention. Thus at one point Snow identifies the traditional culture in the nineteenth century with the literary culture. They were certainly different enough, and, from Leavis' point of view, essentially so; but, if there is anything in Snow's argument at all, there is a sense in which the intellectual content of that traditional culture became more and more literary in its bias as it became more and more alienated from science and technology.

Leavis does not bring up the two objections to Snow's use of the word which most literary people raise. Some say that the word can only be used of a society as a whole; others that the intellectual and imaginative habits shared by scientists are not general enough in their implications to deserve the name. But this is, as Leavis implicitly admits, pedantry. There are fifty meanings for the word "culture." Snow uses it to mean fragments of a whole-society culture. We have two cultures in the sense that our two /735/ main sets of intellectual habits and efforts have so little contact and interaction. This is perfectly clear and straightforward.

Then Leavis dismisses as invalid Snow's parallels between people and achievements in the arts and other people and achievements in the sciences. For instance, Snow compared Rutherford's position in the '30s with T. S. Eliot's, and some knowledge of the Second Law of Thermodynamics with having read one of Shakespeare's plays. Leavis says flatly that such things are incommensurable, but here again one feels that he has been too impatient with the argument as a whole to adopt the point of view from which such propositions are meaningful. For a great many research students and teachers of the '30s Rutherford and Eliot must have had parallel positions—and opposite influences; representing to students of English (and all literatures to some extent) and of physics (and all sciences to some extent) not only great intellectual achievement but the specifically modern forms of intellectual life; representing it, moreover, by their personalities, their general attitudes, their lives as well as by their work. The Second Law of Thermodynamics is a key piece in the jigsaw of modern science, connecting with a dozen branches of knowledge, and in itself a most vivid, even melodramatic, concept. To know of it, once to have undergone its imaginative excitement, is very similar to having once read *Macbeth;* not to know it is as clear a signal as not having read *Macbeth* that enormous areas of thought and imagination are cut off from one.

Finally, he accuses Snow of being simple-minded in his use of words like "belief," but here his argument recoils on itself. Snow said that statistically speaking more scientists are unbelievers than believers, in religious terms, and more are on the Left than on the Right, politically. Leavis pours scorn on such simplifications as blurring all the important distinctions, but it is his own recourse to complexities that strikes the reader as the more naïve of the two. Snow's statements are adequate to his argument at that point. To reject them means that you dismiss that kind of statement as such. Leavis, one is bound to suspect, is never interested in whether a man votes Labour or Conservative, whether or not he subscribes to a creed. In a novel, it is true, such categories are so loose they do not tell you much that is interesting about a character; but in effective social thinking they remain indispensable.

Social thinking, however, Leavis treats as something outside culture itself, and to which culture owes a quite single duty of restraint. Great literature, he tells us, asks deeply important questions about the civilization around it, but "Of course, to such questions there can't be, in any ordinary /736/ sense of the word, answers." The questions, moreover, will all be of the sort to make society hesitate, slow down, lose confidence in the future, distrust both social planning and technological advance. Any vigorous hope, any excitement in the new powers, will have to come from outside "culture." Asking such questions, and allowing no answers, literature's contribution to social thought is going to be very lopsided. But with this we begin to enumerate the ways the Richmond Lecture offers evidence for Snow's thesis.

III

The remarkable unanimity of the literary world against Snow simply expresses, of course, a vested-interest anger. Its members have felt themselves criticized. The scientific world has not rallied to his defense because of a more complicated snobbery. Snow's admirers have been among editors, administrators, chancellors; and the intellectual front-line naturally resented the large-toned comments of people from outside and (in terms of power) above. This initial resentment found an intellectual framework in the contemporary taste for pure knowledge, the distrust of popularization, the general reaction against encyclopedism. But there is no more reason to respect these unanimities than those of any other private group when it is criticized from outside. The fundamental issue is something much more serious than that.

The fundamental issue is the meaning of the word "culture." This word, this enormously ramified and tentacular concept, developed, worked on, contributed to by all the greatest writers from Coleridge and Burke to Lawrence and Eliot, commands great intellectual and practical loyalties today. It is a powerful ideal; and among the sets of dedicated people serving and directing it, Dr. Leavis and his various disciples are pre-eminent. Culture, according to their understanding, is a set of standards, both intellectually and morally rigorous, and socially very conscientious; but socially it is also completely on the defensive; against the influences of mechanization, mass-production, mass media, but also, implicitly, against modern science and technology themselves.

There is plenty of evidence of that defensiveness in the Richmond Lecture. Dr. Leavis assures us that he is not a Luddite, but his tone in asserting this is so mild as to be vacuous beside his tone when he attacks those who are any way excited about science or the future. His not being a Luddite is a negation; at best a refusal to join his friends who are actively fighting machines; at worst, one suspects, a refusal to accept the theoretical implications of his practical preferences. The only time he confronts Snow's /737/ claims for the imaginative and intellectual excitement of science — "the intellectual depth, complexity, and articulation" — he swerves away into personal satire. He offers no answer to the challenge, and the irrelevance of the sneer at Snow at that point indicates some embarrassment before it. He goes on to insist that there is a "prior" human achievement to consider, the creation of "the human world," in language and literature. This priority, we gather, is not so much in time as in value, and is so overwhelming as quite to dispose of the claims of other cultural patterns to consideration. He talks at length of a "third realm" to which all that makes us human belongs. This third realm is midway between the merely subjective and fanciful, and the purely objective and materialistic. Literature obviously belongs to this realm, but what about science? Note that the purely objective category includes all "that can be brought into the laboratory and pointed to." There is every evidence that for Dr. Leavis mathematics and physics are matters of counting, measuring, weighing. He makes no mention of those aspects that make them just as finely, poignantly typical of that third realm as literature. His lecture offers no evidence that he "knows what science is," much less that he has any imaginative experience of it to qualify, enrich, mature, validate his sharp distrust. He speaks of "that collaborative human creativity of which literature is the type." But what about science? If literature is *the type* of collaborative human creativity, science — being by any definition very opposite in its structure — must be a very inferior, ineffective, unstimulating version. If science is to have any dignity, any value beyond the materialistic, instrumental, at best simply logical, then the idea of culture, of the third realm of human creativity, must be developed into something of which science also can be a type.

And the consequence of that implicit rejection of science in Leavis is just what Snow remarked in general: an alienation from the essential conditions of modern society. How could it be otherwise, when what is modern and challenging and painful about the present and future is so intimately associated with science, while the humanities deal so much with the past? We have already seen evidence of this alienation in Leavis' account of the duty of culture to modern social thought. And compare his tone about modern America with his tone about the Bushmen: "the energy, the triumphant technology, the productivity, the high standard of living, and the life-impoverishment—the human emptiness; emptiness and boredom craving alcohol—of one kind or another"; with "those poignantly surviving, primitive peoples, with their marvellous arts and skills and vital intelligence." The same thing is implicit in his tone wherever he discusses /738/ politics or the use of power in society. He uses "corridors of power," and for that matter membership of the Athenaeum, quite simply as a condemnation. He identifies Snow with Macmillan, in a moral world beneath polite discussion, and for good measure throws in the intellectual weeklies. They all belong to a world "in which standard of living is the ultimate criterion." He thinks Snow dismissed as Luddites everyone who talks in *any* other terms than "productivity" and "technological progress." All this reveals an extraordinarily fierce distrust of material and social power. He quotes as typical of the truly literary and cultural attitude to social problems Birkin's speech from *Women in Love*, "I want every man to have his share of the world's goods, so that I am rid of his importunity, so that I can tell him: 'Now you've got what you want—you've got your fair share of the world's gear. Now, you one-mouthed fool, mind yourself and don't obstruct me.'" There is plenty of reason to agree that this is typically literary—just as we agree it is quite magnificent in its place in the novel—but we cannot accept it as adequately representing culture, when it so denudes of all dignity those processes of social life which we cannot conduct successfully without feeling them to be important as well as necessary. We shall need our full humanity, we agree, to meet the sharp challenges of the future. But full humanity cannot be guaranteed by a literary sensibility so sharply distrustful of other kinds of intellectual and practical experience.

What Snow has to offer the idea of culture is a hint toward a redefinition. That idea has reached a crucial point in its career, at which its critical powers are very sharp, and its self-confidence perfect, but its posture is completely backward-looking. It is not developing generously. If it can be redefined to include scientific virtues and scientific experience, without losing the sharpness of vision and muscularity of grasp which it has had under Dr. Leavis' direction, then it will also be able to address itself to contemporary social facts with new energy, and its future career can be as successful as its past. /739/

Lionel Trilling

SCIENCE, LITERATURE & CULTURE: A COMMENT ON THE LEAVIS-SNOW CONTROVERSY

Lionel Trilling (1905–   ), a professor of English at Columbia University, is one of America's foremost literary critics. His works include two critical studies, Matthew

"Science, Literature & Culture: A Comment on the Leavis-Snow Controversy," *Commentary* (June 1962), pp. 461–477.

Arnold *(1939) and* E. M. Forster *(1943), and three collections of essays,* The Liberal
Imagination *(1950),* The Opposing Self *(1955), and* A Gathering of Fugitives
(1956). He has also written short stories and a novel, The Middle of the Journey
(1947).

It is now nearly eighty years since Matthew Arnold came to this country on
his famous lecture tour. Of his repertory of three lectures, none was calculated
to give unqualified pleasure to his audience. The lecture on Emerson praised
that most eminent of American writers only after it had denied that he was a
literary figure of the first order. The lecture called "Numbers" raised disturbing questions about the relation of democracy to excellence and distinction.
"Literature and Science" was the least likely to give offense, yet even this most
memorable of the three *Discourses in America* was not without its touch of
uncomfortableness. In 1883 America was by no means committed—and,
indeed, never was to be committed—to the belief that the right education for
the modern age must be predominantly scientific and technical, and Arnold,
when he cited the proponents of this idea, which of course he opposed, mentioned only those who were English. Yet his audiences surely knew that Arnold
was warning them against what would seem to be the natural tendency of an
industrial democracy to devalue the old "aristocratic" education in favor of
studies that are merely practical.

Arnold wrote "Emerson" and "Numbers" especially for his American tour,
but he had first composed "Literature and Science" as the Rede Lecture at
Cambridge in 1882. Its original occasion cannot fail to have a peculiar interest
at this moment, for C. P. Snow's *The Two Cultures and the Scientific Revolution,*
around which so curious a storm rages in England, was the Rede Lecture of
1959.

Sir Charles did not mention his great predecessor in the lectureship, although his own discourse was exactly on Arnold's subject and took a line
exactly the opposite of Arnold's. And F. R. Leavis, whose admiration of Arnold
is well known and whose position in respect to the relative importance of literature and of science in /461/ education is much the same as Arnold's, did not
mention Arnold either, when, in his recent Richmond Lecture at Downing
College, he launched an attack of unexampled ferocity upon the doctrine and
the author of *The Two Cultures.*

In its essential terms, the issue in debate has not changed since Arnold
spoke. Arnold's chief antagonist was T. H. Huxley—it was he who, in his
lecture on "Culture and Education," had said that literature should, and
inevitably would, step down from its preeminent place in education, that
science and not "culture" must supply the knowledge which is necessary for an
age committed to rational truth and material practicality. What is more, Huxley
said, science will supply the very basis of the assumptions of modern ethics.
In effect Snow says nothing different.

The word "culture" had been Arnold's personal insigne ever since the publication of *Culture and Anarchy* in 1867 and Huxley made particular reference to
the views on the value of humanistic study which Arnold had expressed in that
book.* Arnold's reply in "Literature and Science" could not have been simpler,

---

*Arnold, of course, did not use the word in the modern sense in which it is used by anthropologists,
sociologists, and historians of thought and art; this is, more or less, the sense in which it is used by
Snow. For Arnold, "culture" was "the best that has been thought and said in the world" and also an
individual person's relation to this body of thought and expression. My own use of the word in this
essay is not Arnold's. /462/

just as it could not have been more temperate, although it surely did not sur-
pass in temperateness Huxley's statement of his disagreement with Arnold's
ideas; the two men held each other in high admiration and were warm friends.
Arnold said that he had not the least disposition to propose that science be
slighted in education. Quite apart from its practical value, scientific knowledge
is naturally a delight to the mind, no doubt engaging certain mental temperaments more than others but holding out the promise of intellectual pleasure
to all. Yet of itself science does not, as Arnold put it, "serve" the instinct for
conduct and the instinct for beauty, or at least it does not serve these instincts
as they exist in most men. This service, which includes the relating of scientific
knowledge to the whole life of man, is rendered by culture, which is not to be
thought of as confined to literature — to *belles lettres* — but as comprising all the
humane intellectual disciplines. When Dr. Leavis asserts the primacy of the
humanities in education, he refers more exclusively to literature than Arnold
did, but in general effect his position is the same.

It may seem strange, and a little tiresome, that the debate of eighty years ago
should be instituted again today. Yet it is perhaps understandable in view of
the "scientific revolution" about which Sir Charles tells us. This revolution
would seem to be one of the instances in which a change of quantity becomes
a change in kind — science can now do so much more and do it so much more
quickly than it could a generation ago, let alone in the last century, that it
has been transmuted from what the world has hitherto known. One of the
consequences of this change — to Sir Charles it is the most salient of all possible
consequences — is the new social hope that is now held out to us, of life made
better in material respects, not merely in certain highly developed countries
but all over the world and among peoples that at the moment are, by Western
standards, scarcely developed at all.

The new power of science perhaps justifies a contemporary revival of the
Victorian question. But if we consent to involve ourselves in the new dialectic
of the old controversy, we must be aware that we are not addressing ourselves
to a question of educational theory, or to an abstract contention as to what kind
of knowledge has the truest affinity with the human soul. We approach these
matters only to pass through them. What we address ourselves to is politics,
and politics of a quite ultimate kind, and to the disposition of the modern
mind. /462/

II

The Two Cultures has had a very considerable currency in England and
America ever since its publication in 1959, and in England it was for a time the
subject of lively discussion. Indeed, the general agreement in England that it
was a statement of great importance, to the point of its being used as an
assigned text in secondary schools, was what aroused Dr. Leavis to make his
assault on the lecture this long after the first interest in it had subsided. The
early discussions of *The Two Cultures* were of a substantive kind, but the
concerns which now agitate the English in response to Dr. Leavis's attack have
scarcely anything to do with literature and science, or with education, or with
social hope. These matters have now been made a mere subordinate element in
what amounts to a scandal over a breach of manners. The published comments
on Dr. Leavis's attack on *The Two Cultures* were, with few exceptions, directed
to such considerations as the exact degree of monstrousness which Dr. Leavis
achieved in speaking of Sir Charles as he did; whether or not he spoke out of

envy of Sir Charles's reputation; whether or not he has, or deserves to have, any real standing as a critic; or writes acceptable English; or represents, as he claims he does, "the essential Cambridge."

Dr. Leavis's Richmond Lecture, "The Significance of C. P. Snow," was delivered in the Hall of Downing College, Cambridge, on February 28 and published in the *Spectator* of March 9.* In the next week's issue of the *Spectator*, seventeen letters appeared, all defending Snow and most of them expressing anger at, or contempt for, Leavis. The following week brought fifteen more communications, of which eight expressed partisanship with Leavis; several of these deplored the tone of the previous week's correspondence. Many of the correspondents who defended Snow were of distinguished reputation; of the defenders of Leavis, the only one known to me was Mr. Geoffrey Wagner, who wrote from America to communicate his belief that the attack on Snow was much needed, for, despite a parody in *New Left Review* in which Snow appears as C. P. Sleet, despite, too, his own adverse criticism of Snow in the *Critic*, "the hosannas obediently continued on this side of the Atlantic, both from the Barzun-Trilling syndrome and the Book-of-the-Month Club, the worst of both worlds, as it were." Three of the writers of the Snow party touched upon the question of literature and science, the scientist J. D. Bernal, the historian of science Stephen Toulmin, and the literary critic G. S. Fraser. In a miasma of personality-mongering, their letters afforded a degree of relief, but they said little that was of consequence. Of the Leavis party two dons of the University of Birmingham in a joint letter touched rapidly but with some cogency on the relation between literature and science, deploring any attempt to prefer one above the other, concluding that if one must be preferred, it should be, for reasons not stated, literature.

From the *Spectator* letters, so many of them expressing small and rather untidy passions, there are no doubt conclusions to be drawn, of a sufficiently depressing sort, about the condition of cultural life at the moment. But no awareness that we may have of the generally bad state of intellectual affairs ought to blind us to the particular fault of Dr. Leavis in his treatment of Sir Charles Snow. Intelligent and serious himself, Dr. Leavis has in this instance been the cause of stupidity and triviality in other men.

There can be no two opinions about the tone in which Dr. Leavis deals with Sir Charles. It is a bad tone, an impermissible /463/ tone. It is bad in a personal sense because it is cruel—it manifestly intends to wound. It is bad intellectually because by its use Dr. Leavis has diverted attention, his own included, from the matter he sought to illuminate. The doctrine of *The Two Cultures* is a momentous one and Dr. Leavis obscures its massive significance by bringing into consideration such matters as Sir Charles's abilities as a novelist, his club membership, his opinion of his own talents, his worldly success, and his relation to worldly power. Anger, scorn, and an excessive consciousness of persons have always been elements of Dr. Leavis's thought—of the very process of his thought, not merely of his manner of expressing it. They were never exactly reassuring elements, but they could be set aside and made to seem of relatively small account in comparison with the remarkable cogency in criticism which Dr. Leavis so often achieved. But as they now appear in his valedictory address —for, in effect, that is what the Richmond Lecture was, since Dr. Leavis retires

---

*In an editorial note, Dr. Leavis is quoted as saying, "The lecture was private and representatives of the press who inquired were informed that there was no admission and that no reporting was to be permitted. The appearance in newspapers of garbled reports has made it desirable that the lecture should appear in full." /463/

this year from his university post—they cannot be easily set aside, they stand in the way of what Dr. Leavis means to say.

And, indeed, our understanding of what he means to say is to be derived less from the passionate utterance of the lecture itself than from our knowledge of the whole direction of his career in criticism. That direction was from the first determined by Dr. Leavis's belief that the human faculty above all others to which literature addresses itself is the moral consciousness, which is also the source of all successful creation, the very root of poetic genius. The extent of his commitment to this idea results in what I believe to be a fault in his critical thought—he does not give anything like adequate recognition to those aspects of art which are gratuitous, which arise from high spirits and the impulse to play. One would suppose that the moral consciousness should, for its own purposes, take account of those aspects of art and life that do not fall within its dominion. But if the intensity of Dr. Leavis's commitment to the moral consciousness contrives to produce this deficiency of understanding, it is no less responsible for the accuracy and force which we recognize as the positive characteristics of his work. For Dr. Leavis, literature is what Matthew Arnold said it is, *the criticism of life*—he can understand it in no other way. Both in all its simplicity and in all its hidden complexity, he has made Arnold's saying his own, and from it he has drawn his strength.

If, then, Dr. Leavis now speaks with a very special intensity in response to *The Two Cultures*, we must do him the justice of seeing that the Rede Lecture denies, and in an extreme way, all that he has ever believed about literature—it is, in fact, nothing less than an indictment of literature on social and moral grounds. It represents literature as constituting a danger to the national well-being, and most especially when it is overtly a criticism of life.

Not only because Charles Snow is himself a practitioner of literature but also because he is the man he is, the statement that his lecture has this purport will be shocking and perhaps it will be thought scarcely credible. And I have no doubt that, in another mood and on some other occasion, Sir Charles would be happy to assert the beneficent powers of literature. But there can be no other interpretation of his lecture than that it takes toward literature a position of extreme antagonism.

The Two Cultures begins as an objective statement of the lack of communication between scientists and literary men. This is a circumstance that must have been often observed and often deplored. Perhaps nothing in our culture is so characteristic as the separateness of the various artistic and intellectual professions. As between, say, poets and painters, or musicians and architects, there is very little discourse, and perhaps the same thing could be remarked of scientists of different interests, say biologists and physicists. But /464/ the isolation of literary men from scientists may well seem to be the most extreme of these separations, if only because it is the most significant, for a reason which Sir Charles entirely understands: the especially close though never clearly defined relation of these two professions with our social and political life.

The even-handedness with which Sir Charles at first describes the split between the two "cultures" does not continue for long. He begins by telling us that scientists and literary men are equally to blame for the separation—they are kept apart by "a gulf of mutual incomprehension," by distorted images of each other which give rise to dislike and hostility. But as Sir Charles's lecture proceeds, it becomes plain that, although the scientists do have certain crudities and limitations, they are in general in the right of things and the literary men in the wrong of them. The matter which causes the scales to shift thus suddenly is the human condition. This, Sir Charles tells us, is of its nature tragic: man dies, and he dies alone. But the awareness of the ineluctably tragic nature of human life makes a moral trap, "for it tempts one to sit back, complacent in one's unique tragedy," paying no heed to the circumstances of everyday life, which, for the larger number of human beings, are painful. It is the literary men, we are told, who are the most likely, the scientists who are the least likely, to fall into this moral trap; the scientists "are inclined to be impatient to see if something can be done: and inclined to think that it can be done, until it's proved otherwise." It is their spirit, "tough and good and determined to fight it out at the side of their brother men," which has "made scientists regard the other [i.e. the literary] culture's social attitudes as contemptible."

"This is too facile," Sir Charles says in mild rebuke of the scientists, by which he of course means that essentially they are right. There follows a brief consideration of a question raised not by Sir Charles in his own person but by "a scientist of distinction" whom he quotes: "Yeats, Pound, Wyndham Lewis, nine out of ten of those who have dominated literary sensibility in our time, weren't they not only politically silly, but politically wicked? Didn't the influence of all they represent bring Auschwitz that much nearer?" And Sir Charles in answer grants that Yeats was a magnanimous man and a great poet, but he will not, he says, defend the indefensible—"the facts . . . are broadly true." Sir Charles in general agrees, that is, that the literary sensibility of our time brought Auschwitz nearer. He goes on to say that things have changed considerably in the literary life in recent years, even if slowly, for "literature changes more slowly than science."

From the mention of Auschwitz onward, the way is open to the full assertion by Sir Charles of the virtues of the scientists. Although they are admitted to be sometimes gauche or stupidly self-assertive, although Sir Charles concedes of some of them that "the whole literature of the traditional culture doesn't seem relevant to [their] interests" and that, as a result, their "imaginative understanding" is diminished, he yet finds them to be men of a natural decency; they are free from racial feelings, they are lovers of equality, they are cooperative. And chief among their virtues, as Sir Charles describes them, is the fact that they "have the future in their bones."

Indeed, it turns out that it is the future, and not mere ignorance of each other's professional concerns, that makes the separation between the culture of science and the culture of literature. Scientists have the future in their bones. Literary men do not. Quite the contrary—"If the scientists have the future in their bones, then the traditional culture responds by wishing that the future did not exist." The future that the scientists have in their bones is understood to be nothing but a good future; it is very much like the History of the Marxists, which is always the triumph of the /465/ right, never possibly the record of defeat. In fact, to entertain the idea that the future might be bad is represented as being tantamount to moral ill-will—in a note appended to the sentence I have just quoted, Sir Charles speaks of George Orwell's *1984* as "the strongest possible wish that the future shall not exist."

It is difficult to credit the implications of this astonishing remark and to ascribe them to Sir Charles. As everyone recalls, Orwell's novel is an imagination of the condition of the world if the authoritarian tendencies which are to be observed in the present develop themselves—logically, as it were—in the future, the point being that it is quite within the range of possibility that this ultimate development should take place. In Orwell's representation of an absolute tyranny, science has a part, and a polemical partisan of science might understand this as the evidence of a literary man's malice toward science. But it is much more likely that, when Orwell imagined science as one of the instruments of repression, he meant to say that science, like everything else that is potentially good, like literature itself, can be perverted and debased to the ends of tyranny. Orwell was a man who, on the basis of actual and painful experience, tried to tell the truth about politics, even his own politics. I believe that he never gave up his commitment to socialism, but he refused to be illusioned in any way he could prevent; it lay within the reach of his mind to conceive that even an idealistic politics, perhaps especially an idealistic politics, can pervert itself. To say of such a man that he wishes that the future—the presumably good future—shall not exist is like saying that intelligence wishes that the future shall not exist.

Having characterized the culture of literature, or, as he sometimes calls it, "the traditional culture," by its hostility to the future, Sir Charles goes on to say that "it is the traditional culture, to an extent remarkably little diminished by the emergence of the scientific one, which manages the western world." This being so, it follows that the traditional culture must be strictly dealt with if the future is to be brought into being: what is called "the existing pattern" must be not merely changed but "broken." Only if this is done shall we be able to educate ourselves as we should. As for the need to educate ourselves: "To say, we have to educate ourselves or perish is perhaps a little more melodramatic than the facts warrant. To say, we have to educate ourselves or watch a steep decline in our lifetime is about right." And Sir Charles indicates our possible fate by the instance—he calls it an "historical myth"—of the Venetian Republic in its last half century. "Its citizens had become rich, as we did, by accident. They had acquired immense political skill, just as we have. A good many of them were tough-minded, realistic, patriotic men. They knew, just as clearly as we know, that the current of history had begun to flow against them. Many of them gave their minds to working out ways to keep going. It would have meant breaking the pattern into which they had been crystallized. They were fond of the pattern, just as we are fond of ours. They never found the will to break it."

I quoted without comment Sir Charles's statement of the idea on which, we may say, the whole argument of *The Two Cultures* is based: "It is the traditional culture, to an extent remarkably little diminished by the emergence of the scientific one, which manages the western world." It is a bewildering statement. In what way can we possibly understand it? That the Western world is managed by some agency which is traditional is of course comprehensible. And we can take in the idea that this agency may be described, for particular purposes of explanation, in terms of a certain set of mind, a general tendency of thought and feeling which, being pervasive, is hard to formulate, and that this is to be called "a culture." But for Sir Charles, the words "traditional" /466/ and "literary" are interchangeable, and that this culture, as we agree to call it, is *literary*, that it bears the same relation to actual literary men and their books that what is called the "scientific culture" bears to scientists and their work in laboratories, is truly a staggering thought. The actions of parliaments and congresses and cabinets in directing the massive affairs of state, the negotiations of embassies, the movement of armies and fleets, the establishment of huge scientific projects for the contrivance of armaments and of factories for the production of them, the promises made to citizens, and the choices made by voters at the polls—these, we are asked to believe, are in the charge of the culture of literature. What can this mean?

It can of course be said that literature has some part in the management of the Western world, a part which is limited but perhaps not wholly unimportant. If, for example, we compare the present condition of industrial England with the condition of industrial England in the early 19th century, we can say that the present condition is not, in human respects, anything like what men of good will might wish it to be, but that it is very much better than it was in the early years of the Industrial Revolution. And if we then ask what agencies brought about the improvement, we can say that one of them was literature. Certain literary men raised the "Condition of England Question" in a passionate and effective way and their names are still memorable to us — Coleridge, Carlyle, Mill (I take him to be a man of letters; he was certainly a good literary critic), Dickens, Ruskin, Arnold, William Morris. They made their effect only upon individuals, but the individuals they touched were numerous, and by what they said they made it ever harder for people to be indifferent to the misery around them or to the degradation of the national life in which they came to think themselves implicated. These literary men helped materially, some would say decisively, to bring about a change in the state of affairs. This is not exactly management, but it is a directing influence such as literature in the modern time often undertakes to have and sometimes does have.

Yet in Sir Charles's opinion this directing influence of the literary men of the 19th century deserves no praise. On the contrary, his description of their work is but another count in the indictment of the culture of literature. Speaking of the response which literary men made to the Industrial Revolution, he says, "Almost everywhere . . . intellectual persons did not comprehend what was happening. Certainly the writers didn't. Plenty of them shuddered away, as though the right course for a man of feeling was to contract out; some, like Ruskin and William Morris and Thoreau and Emerson and Lawrence, tried various kinds of fancies, which were not much in effect more than screams of horror. It is hard to think of a writer of high class who really stretched his imaginative sympathy, who could see at once the hideous back-streets, the smoking chimneys, the internal price — and also the prospects of life that were opening out for the poor. . . ."

Nothing could be further from the truth. No great English writer of the 19th century, once he had become aware of the Industrial Revolution, ever contracted out. This is not the place to rehearse the miseries that were acquiesced in by those who comforted the world and their own consciences with the thought of "the prospects of life that were opening out for the poor." It is enough to say that there were miseries in plenty, of a brutal and horrifying kind, by no means adequately suggested by phrases like "the hideous back-streets, the smoking chimneys, the internal price." (Auschwitz, since it has been mentioned, may be thought of as the development of the conditions of the factories and mines of the earlier Industrial Revolution.) If the writers "shuddered away," it was not in maidenly dis- /467/ gust with machines and soot; if they uttered "screams of horror," it was out of moral outrage at what man had made of man — and of women and little children. Their emotions were no different from those expressed by Karl Marx in his chapter on the Working Day, nor from those expressed in Blue Books by the factory inspectors, those remarkable men of the middle class whom Marx, in a moving passage of *Capital,* praises and wonders at for their transcendence of their class feelings.

I have mentioned Matthew Arnold among those writers who made the old conditions of the Industrial Revolution ever less possible. Like many of his colleagues in this undertaking, he did entertain "fancies" — they all found

modern life ugly and fatiguing and in some way false, and they set store by
certain qualities which are no doubt traditional to the point of being archaic.*
But Arnold's peculiar distinction as a literary critic is founded on the strong
sensitivity of his response to the modern situation. He uniquely understood
what Hegel had told the world, that the French Revolution marked an absolute
change in the condition of man. For the first time in history, Hegel said,
Reason—or Idea, or Theory, or Creative Imagination—had become decisive
in human destiny. Arnold's argument in "Literature and Science" was the
affirmation of the French Revolution; he was speaking on behalf of the illumination and refinement of that Reason by which man might shape the conditions of his own existence. This is the whole purport of his famous statement,
"Literature is the criticism of life."

That saying used to have a rough time of it, perhaps because people found
the word criticism narrow and dour and wished to believe that life was worthier
of being celebrated than criticized. But less and less, I think, will anyone find
the ground on which to quarrel with it. Whatever else we also take literature
to be, it must always, for us now, be the criticism of life.

But it would seem to be precisely the critical function of literature that
troubles Sir Charles. And perhaps that is why, despite all that he says about the
need to educate ourselves, he does not make a single substantive proposal
about education.

If we undertake to say what the purpose of modern education is, our answer
will surely be suggested by Arnold's phrase, together with the one by which
he defined the particular function of criticism: "to see the object as in itself
it really is." Whenever we undertake to pass judgment on an educational
enterprise, the import of these two phrases serves as our criterion: we ask that
education supply the means for a criticism of life and teach the student to try
to see the object as in itself it really is. Yet when Sir Charles speaks of the need
to break the "existing pattern" and to go on to a right education, he does not
touch upon any such standard of judgment. Although he would seem to be the
likeliest person in the world to speak intelligently about the instruction in
science of students who do not intend to be scientists, actually he says nothing
more on the subject than that ignorance of the Second Law of Thermodynamics is equivalent to ignorance of Shakespeare, or that the Yang-Lee experiment
at Columbia should have been a topic of general conversation at college High
Tables.

Nor does he propose anything for the education of the scientist, except, of
course, science. He does say that scientists need to be "trained not only in
scientific but in human terms," but he does not say how. Scientists—but eventually one /468/ begins to wonder if they are really scientists and not advanced
technologists and engineers—are to play a decisive part in the affairs of mankind, but nowhere does Sir Charles suggest that, if this is so, they will face
difficulties and perplexities and that their education should include the study
of books—they need not be "literary," they need not be "traditional": they
might be contemporary works of history, sociology, anthropology, psychology,
philosophy—which would raise the difficult questions and propose the tragic
complexity of the human condition, which would suggest that it is not always
easy to see the object as in itself it really is.

Well, it isn't beyond belief that a professional corps of high intellectual

*Emerson doesn't deserve Sir Charles's scorn on this point. His advice to the American scholar
was that he should respond positively to the actual and the modern, and he was inclined to take
an almost too unreserved pleasure in new forms of human energy and ingenuity. As for Thoreau,
his quarrel was not with factories but with farms—and families. /468/

quality, especially if it is charged with great responsibility, should learn to ask its own questions and go on to make its own ethos, perhaps a very good one. But Sir Charles would seem to be asking for more than the right of scientists to go their own way. What he seems to require for scientists is the right to go their own way *with no questions asked.* The culture of literature, having done its worst, must now be supplanted and is not ever to play the part of loyal opposition. How else are we to understand Sir Charles's contempt for the irresponsibility of the literary mind, his curious representation of the literary culture as having the management of the Western world, that is to say, as being answerable for all the anomalies, stupidities, and crimes of the Western world, for having made the "existing pattern" which must now be broken if the West is to survive or at least not suffer steep decline? It is manifest that the literary culture has lost the right to ask questions.

No one could possibly suppose of Charles Snow that he is a man who wants to curtail the rights of free criticism. The line which he takes in *The Two Cultures* is so far from the actuality of his temperament in this respect that we can only suppose that he doesn't mean it, not in all the extravagance of its literalness. Or we suppose that he means it at the behest of some large preoccupation of whose goodness he is so entirely convinced that he will seek to affirm it even in ways that would take him aback if the preoccupation were not in control of his thought. And this, I think, is the case. I believe that the position of *The Two Cultures* is to be explained by Sir Charles's preoccupation — it has become almost the best-known thing about him — with a good and necessary aim, with the assuring of peace, which is to say, with the compounding of the differences between the West and the Soviet Union. It is an aim which, in itself, can of course only do Sir Charles credit, yet it would seem to have implicit in it a strange desperate method of implementing itself.

For the real message of *The Two Cultures* is that an understanding between the West and the Soviet Union could be achieved by the culture of scientists, which reaches over factitious national and ideological differences. The field of agreement would be the scientists' common perception of the need for coming together to put the possibilities of the scientific revolution at the disposal of the disadvantaged of all nations. The bond between scientists, Sir Charles has told us, is virtually biological: they all have the future in their bones. Science brings men together in despite of all barriers — speaking of the way in which the very wide differences in the class origins of English scientists were overcome to make the scientific culture of England (and seeming to imply that this is a unique grace of scientists, that English men of letters never had differences of class to overcome), Sir Charles says, "Without thinking about it, they respond alike. That is what a culture means." And in the same way, "without thinking about it," the scientists of the West and the scientists of the Soviet Union may be expected to "respond alike." And, since "that is what a culture means," they will have joined together in an entity which will do what govern- /469/ ments have not done, the work of relieving the misery of the world. But in the degree to which science naturally unites men, literature separates them, and the scientists of the world cannot form this beneficent entity until we of the West break the existing pattern of our traditional culture, the literary culture, which is self-regarding in its complacent acceptance of tragedy, which is not only indifferent to human suffering but willing to inflict it, which asks rude and impertinent questions about the present and even about the future.

It is a point of view that must, I suppose, in desperate days, have a show of reason. In desperate days, it always seems wise to throw something or someone overboard, preferably Jonah or Arion, the prophet or the poet. Mr. G. S. Fraser, for example, seems to understand what Sir Charles wants, and he is rather willing to go along with him, rather open to the idea that the achievement of peace may require some adverse judgment on literature. "It does not matter," he says, "whether we save the real Cambridge within the actual Cambridge . . . ; what we want to save is our actual human world with all the spots on it. This will not be done by teaching English at universities; men like Snow, at home both in Russia and America, and in a simple blunt way trying to teach these two blunt simple giants to understand each other may in the end prove greater benefactors than Dr. Leavis."

No, the world will not be saved by teaching English at universities, nor, indeed, by any other literary activity. It is very hard to say what will save the world, and pretty surely it is no one single thing. But we can be perfectly certain that the world will not be saved by denying the actualities of the world. Among these actualities politics is one. And it can be said of *The Two Cultures* that it communicates the strongest possible wish that we should forget about politics. It mentions national politics once, speaking of it as the clog upon the activity of scientists, as the impeding circumstance in which they must work. But the point is not developed and the lecture has the effect of suggesting that the issue is not between the abilities and good intentions of scientists and the inertia or bad will of governments; the issue is represented as being between the good culture of science and the bad culture of literature.

In this denial of the actuality of politics, Sir Charles is at one with the temper of intellectuals today—we all want politics not to exist, we all want that statement of Hegel's to be absolutely and immediately true, we dream of Reason taking over the whole management of the world, and soon. No doubt a beneficent eventuality, but our impatience for it is dangerous if it leads us to deny the actuality of politics in the present. While we discuss, at Sir Charles's instance, the relative merits of scientific Philosopher Kings as against literary Philosopher Kings, politics goes on living its own autonomous life, of which one aspect is its massive resistance to Reason. What is gained by describing the resistance to Reason as other than it is, by thinking in the specious terms of two opposing "cultures"?

But of course the fact is that politics is not finally autonomous. It may be so massively resistant to Reason that we are led to think of its resistance as absolute—in bad times we conceive politics to be nothing but power. Yet it cannot be said—at least not so long as politics relies in any degree upon ideology—that politics is never susceptible to such Reason as is expressed in opinion, only that it is less susceptible in some nations and at some times than in other nations and at other times. And nowhere and at no time is politics exempt from moral judgment, whether or not that judgment is effectual. But if we make believe, as *The Two Cultures* does, that politics does not exist at all, then it cannot be the object of moral judgment. And if we deny all authority to literature, as *The Two Cultures* does, /470/ going so far as to say that the great traditional agency of moral awareness is itself immoral, then the very activity of moral judgment is impugned, except for that single instance of it which asserts the rightness of bringing the benefits of science to the disadvantaged of the world. In short, Sir Charles, seeking to advance the cause of understanding between the West and the Soviet Union, would seem to be saying that this understanding will come if we conceive both that politics cannot be judged (because it does not really exist) and that it should not be judged (because the traditional agency of judgment is irresponsible).

III

I judge *The Two Cultures* to be a book which is mistaken in a very large way
indeed. And I find the failure of Dr. Leavis's criticism of it to consist in his
addressing himself not to the full extent of its error but to extraneous matters.
From reading the Richmond Lecture one gains the impression that the substance of the Rede Lecture is extremely offensive to Dr. Leavis, that all his
sensibilities are outraged by it: we conclude that Sir Charles wants something
which is very different from what Dr. Leavis wants, and that Dr. Leavis thinks
that what Sir Charles wants is crude and vulgar. But we can scarcely suppose
from Dr. Leavis's response that what Sir Charles says has a very wide reference
—for all we can tell, he might have been proposing a change in the university
curriculum which Dr. Leavis is repelling with the violence and disgust that
are no doubt often felt though not expressed at meetings of curriculum committees. For Dr. Leavis, who has always attached great importance to educational matters, the proposed change is certainly important beyond the university. He understands it both as likely to have a bad effect on the national
culture and as being the expression of something already bad in the national
culture. But this, we suppose, he would feel about any change in the curriculum.

In short, Dr. Leavis, in dealing with the Rede Lecture, has not seen the
object as in itself it really is, just as Sir Charles, in dealing with the culture
of literature in its relation to politics, has not seen the object as in itself it
really is.

An example of the inadequacy of Dr. Leavis's criticism of *The Two Cultures*
is his response to what Sir Charles says, in concert with the distinguished
scientist, about the political posture of the great writers of the modern period.
That statement, if we stop short of its mention of Auschwitz—which makes
a most important modification—certainly does have a color of truth. It is one
of the cultural curiosities of the first three decades of the 20th century that,
while the educated people, the readers of books, tended to become ever more
liberal and radical in their thought, there is no literary figure of the very
first rank (although many of the next rank) who, in his work, makes use of
or gives credence to liberal or radical ideas. I remarked on this circumstance
in an essay of 1946. "Our educated class," I said, "has a ready if mild suspicious-
ness of the profit motive, a belief in progress, science, social legislation,
planning, and international cooperation, perhaps especially where Russia
is in question. These beliefs do great credit to those who hold them. Yet it
is a comment, if not on our beliefs then on our way of holding them, that not
a single first-rate writer has emerged to deal with these ideas, and the emotions
that are consonant with them, in a great literary way. . . . If we name those
writers who, by the general consent of the most, serious criticism; by consent
too of the very class of educated people of which we speak, are thought of as
the monumental figures of our time, we see that to these writers the liberal
ideology has been at best a matter of indifference. Proust, Joyce, Lawrence,
Yeats, Mann [as novelist], Kafka, Rilke, Gide [also as /471/ novelist]—all of
them have their own love of justice and the good life, but in not one of them
does it take the form of a love of the ideas and emotions which liberal democracy, as known by our educated class, has declared respectable." To which it
can be added that some great writers have in their work given credence or
utterance to conservative and even reactionary ideas, and that some in their
personal lives maintained a settled indifference to all political issues, or a dis-

dain of them. No reader is likely to derive political light either from the works or the table-talk of a modern literary genius, and some readers (of weak mind) might even be led into bad political ways.

If these writers are to be brought to the bar of judgment, anyone who speaks as their advocate is not, as Sir Charles says, defending the indefensible. The advocacy can be conducted in honest and simple ways. It is not one of these ways to say that literature is by its nature or by definition innocent—it is powerful enough for us to suppose that it has the possibility of doing harm. But the ideational influence of literature is by no means always as direct as, for polemical purposes, people sometimes say it is. As against the dismay of Sir Charles and the distinguished scientist at the reactionary tendencies of modern literary geniuses, there is the fact—a bald one—that the English poets who learned their trade from Yeats and Eliot, or even from Pound, have notably had no sympathy with the social ideas and attitudes of their poetical masters.

Every university teacher of literature will have observed the circumstance that young people who are of radical social and political opinion are virtually never troubled by the opposed views or the settled indifference of the great modern writers. This is not because the young exempt the writer from dealing with the serious problems of living, or because they see him through a mere aesthetic haze. It is because they know—and quite without instruction—that, in D. H. Lawrence's words, they are to trust the tale and not the teller of the tale. They perceive that the tale is always on the side of their own generous impulses. They know that, if the future is in the bones of anyone, it is in the bones of the literary genius, and exactly because the present is in his bones, exactly because the past is in his bones. They know that if a work of literature has any true artistic existence, it has value as a criticism of life; in whatever complex way it has chosen to speak, it is making a declaration about the qualities that life should have, about the qualities life does not have but should have. They feel, I think, that it is simply not possible for a work of literature that comes within the borders of greatness *not* to ask for more energy and fineness of life, and, by its own communication of awareness, bring these qualities into being. And if, in their experience of such a work, they happen upon an expression of contempt for some idea which they have connected with political virtue, they are not slow to understand that it is not the idea in its ideal form that is being despised, but the idea as it passes current in specious form, among certain and particular persons. I have yet to meet the student committed to an altruistic politics who is alienated from Stephen Daedalus by that young man's disgust with political idealism, just as I have yet to meet the student from the most disadvantaged background who feels debarred from what Yeats can give him by the poet's slurs upon shopkeepers or by anything else in his inexhaustible fund of snobbery.

If ever a man was qualified to state the case for literature, and far more persuasively than I have done, it is Dr. Leavis His career as a critic and a teacher has been devoted exactly to the exposition of the idea that literature presents to us "the possibilities of life," the qualities of energy and fineness that life might have. And it is, of course, the intention of the Richmond Lecture to say just this in answer to /472/ Sir Charles's indictment. Yet something checks Dr. Leavis. When it is a question of the defense, not of literature in general, but of modern literature, he puts into countervailing evidence nothing more than a passage in which Lawrence says something, in a wry and grudging way, on behalf of social equality. This does not meet the charge; against it Sir Charles might cite a dozen instances in which Lawrence utters what Sir Charles—and perhaps even Dr. Leavis himself—would consider "the most imbecile expressions of anti-social feeling."

There is only one feasible approach to the anti-social utterances of many modern writers, and that is to consider whether their expressions of anti-social feeling are nothing but imbecile. It is the fact, like it or not, that a characteristic cultural enterprise of our time has been the questioning of society itself, not its particular forms and aspects but its very essence. To this extreme point has the criticism of life extended itself. Of the ways of dealing with this phenomenon, that of horror and dismay, such as Sir Charles's, is perhaps the least useful. Far better, it seems to me, is the effort to understand what this passionate hostility to society implies, to ask whether it is a symptom, sufficiently gross, of the decline of the West, or whether it is not perhaps an act of critical energy on the part of the West, an act of critical energy on the part of society itself—the effort of society to identify in itself that which is but speciously good, the effort to understand afresh the nature of the life it is designed to foster. I would not anticipate the answer, but these questions make, I am sure, the right way to come at the phenomenon.

It is not the way that Dr. Leavis comes at the phenomenon, despite his saying that the university study of literature must take its stand on the "intellectual-cultural frontier." Of the two D. H. Lawrences, the one who descended from the social-minded 19th century and who did, in some sort, affirm the social idea, and the other, for whom the condition of salvation was the total negation of society, Dr. Leavis can be comfortable only with the former. For the fact is that his commitment to the intellectual-cultural frontier is sincere but chiefly theoretical; he has, as is well known, sympathy with very few modern writers, and he therefore cannot in good grace come to their defense against Sir Charles's characterization of them.

Mr. Walter Allen, writing in the *New York Times Book Review,* has accurately remarked on "the common areas of agreement" between Dr. Leavis and Sir Charles. "One would expect . . . that Snow would be sympathetic to Leavis's emphasis on the all-importance of the moral center of literature," Mr. Allen says. "Both have attacked experiment in literature. Neither of them, to put it into crude shorthand, are Flaubert-and-Joyce men." The similarities go further. In point of social background the two men are not much apart, at least to the untutored American eye. Both spring from the provincial middle class in one or another of its strata, and whatever differences there may have been in the material advantages that were available or lacking to one or the other, neither was reared in the assumption of easy privilege. From these origins they derived, we may imagine, their strong sense of quotidian actuality and a respect for those who discharge the duties it imposes, and a high regard for the domestic affections, a quick dislike of the frivolous and merely elegant. Neither, as I have suggested, has any least responsiveness to the tendencies of modern thought or literature which are existential or subversive. A lively young person of advanced tastes would surely say that if ever two men were committed to England, Home, and Duty, they are Leavis and Snow—he would say that in this they are as alike as two squares.

There is one other regard, an especially significant one, in which they are similar. This is their feeling about social class. One of the chief interests of Sir Charles's /473/ novels is their explicitness about class as a determinative of the personal life, and in this respect *The Two Cultures* is quite as overt as the novels—its scientists make a new class by virtue of their alienation from the old class attitudes, and Sir Charles's identification of literary men with the traditional culture which supposedly manages the Western world implies that they are in effect the representatives of an aristocratic ruling class, decadent but still powerful. The work of Dr. Leavis is no less suffused by the idea of social class, even though its preoccupation with the subject is far less explicit. To my recollection, Dr. Leavis does not make use of any of the words which denote the distinctions of English society—he does not refer to an aristocracy, a gentry, an upper-middle or lower-middle or working class. For him a class defines itself by its idea of itself—that is, by its tastes and style. Class is for him a cultural entity. And when he conceives of class power, as he often does, it is not economic or political power but, rather, cultural power that he thinks of. It is true that cultural power presents itself to his mind as being in some way suggestive of class power, but the actualities of power or influence are for him always secondary to the culture from which they arose or to which they give rise.

And indeed, no less than Sir Charles, Dr. Leavis is committed to the creation of a new class. This, we might even say, is the whole motive of his work. The social situation he would seem to assume is one in which there is a fair amount of mobility which is yet controlled and limited by the tendency of the mobile people to allow themselves to be absorbed into one of the traditional classes. As against the attraction exerted by a quasi-aristocratic, metropolitan upper-middle class, Dr. Leavis has taken it to be his function to organize the mobile people, those of them who are gifted and conscious, into a new social class formed on the basis of its serious understanding of and response to literature, chiefly English literature. In this undertaking he has by no means been wholly unsuccessful. One has the impression that many of the students he has trained think of themselves, as they take up their posts in secondary schools and universities, as constituting at least a social cadre.

The only other time I wrote about Dr. Leavis I remarked that the Cromwellian Revolution had never really come to an end in England and that Dr. Leavis was one of the chief colonels of the Roundhead party. His ideal readers are people who "are seriously interested in literature," and it is on their behalf that he wages war against a cultural-social class which, when it concerns itself with literature, avows its preference for the qualities of grace, lightness, and irony, and deprecates an overt sincerity and seriousness. "To a polished nation," said Gibbon, "poetry is an amusement of the fancy, not a passion of the soul," and all through his career it is against everything that Gibbon means by a polished nation and might mean by a polished class that Dr. Leavis has set his face. Bloomsbury has been his characteristic antagonist. But now, in Charles Snow, he confronts an opponent who is as Roundhead as himself, and as earnest and *intentional.*

To this confrontation Dr. Leavis is not adequate. It is not an adequate response to the massive intention of *The Two Cultures* for Dr. Leavis to meet Sir Charles's cultural preferences with his own preferences; or to seek to discredit Sir Charles's ideas chiefly by making them out to be vulgar ideas or outmoded (Wellsian) ideas; or to offer, as against Sir Charles's vision of a future made happier by science, the charms of primitive peoples "with their marvellous arts and skills and vital intelligence." I do not mean to say that Dr. Leavis does not know where Sir Charles goes wrong in the details of his argument—he is as clear as we expect him to be in rebuking that quite massive /474/ blunder about the Victorian writers. Nor, certainly, do I mean that Dr. Leavis does not know what the great fundamental mistake of Sir Charles's position is—he does, and he can be eloquent in asserting against a simplistic confidence in a scientific "future" the need of mankind, in the face of a rapid advance of science and technology, "to be in full intelligent possession of its full humanity (and 'possession' here means, not confident ownership of that which belongs to *us*—our property, but a basic living deference towards that to which, opening as it does into the unknown and itself immeasurable, we know we belong)." But such moments of largeness do not save the Richmond Lecture from its general aspect of dealing with an issue that is essentially parochial. For example, of the almost limitless political implications of Sir Charles's position it gives no evidence of awareness. And if we undertake to find a reason for the inadequacy of Dr. Leavis's response, we will find, I think, that it is the same as the reason which accounts for Sir Charles having been in the first place so wholly mistaken in what he says—both men set too much store by the idea of *culture* as a category of thought.

The concept of culture is an idea of great attractiveness and undoubted usefulness. We may say that it begins in the assumption that all human expressions or artifacts are indicative of some considerable tendencies in the life of social groups or sub-groups, and that what is indicative is also causative—all cultural facts have their consequences. To think in cultural terms is to consider human expressions not only in their overt existence and avowed intention, but in, as it were, their secret life, taking cognizance of the desires and impulses which lie behind the open formulation. In the judgments which we make when we think in the category of culture we rely to a very large extent upon the style in which an expression is made, believing that style will indicate, or betray, what is not intended to be expressed. The aesthetic mode is integral to the idea of culture, and our judgments of social groups are likely to be made chiefly on an aesthetic basis—we like or do not like what we call their life-styles, and even when we judge moralities, the criterion by which we choose between two moralities of, say, equal strictness or equal laxness is likely to be an aesthetic one.

The concept of culture affords to those who use it a sense of the liberation of their thought, for they deal less with abstractions and mere objects, more with the momentous actualities of human feelings as these shape and condition the human community, as they make and as they indicate the quality of man's existence. Not the least of the attractions of the cultural mode of thought are the passions which attend it—because it assumes that all things are causative or indicative of the whole of the cultural life, it proposes to us those intensities of moralized feeling which seem appropriate to our sense that all that is good in life is at stake in every cultural action. An instance of mediocrity or failure in art or thought is not only what it is but also a sin, deserving to be treated as such. These passions are vivifying; they have the semblance of heroism.

And if we undertake to say what were the circumstances that made the cultural mode of thought as available and as authoritative as it now is, we must refer to Marx, and to Freud, and to the general movement of existentialism, to all that the tendencies of modernity imply of the sense of contingency in life, from which we learn that the one thing that can be disputed, and that is worth disputing, is preference or taste. The Rede Lecture and the Richmond Lecture exemplify the use to which the idea of culture can be put in shaking the old certainties of class, in contriving new social groups on the basis of taste. All this does indeed give the cultural mode of thought a very considerable authority. Yet sometimes we /475/ may wonder if it is wholly an accident that so strong an impulse to base our sense of life, and our conduct of the intellectual life, chiefly upon the confrontations of taste should have developed in an age dominated by advertising, the wonderful and terrible art which teaches us that we define ourselves and realize our true being by choosing the right style. In our more depressed moments we might be led to ask whether there is a real difference between being The Person Who defines himself by his commitment to one or another idea of morality, politics, literature, or city-planning, and being The Person Who defines himself by wearing trousers without pleats.

We can, I suppose, no more escape from the cultural mode of thought than we can escape from culture itself. Yet perhaps we must learn to cast a somewhat colder eye upon it for the sake of whatever regard we have for the intellectual life, for the possibility of rational discourse. Sir Charles envisages a new and very powerful social class on the basis of a life-style which he imputes to a certain profession in contrast with the life-style he imputes to another profession, and he goes on from there to deny both the reality of politics and the possibility of its being judged by moral standards. Dr. Leavis answers him with a passion of personal scorn which obscures the greater part of the issue and offers in contradiction truth indeed but truth so hampered and hidden by the defenses of Dr. Leavis's own choice in life-styles that it looks not much different from a prejudice. And the *Spectator* correspondents exercise their taste in life-styles and take appropriate sides. It is at such a moment that our dispirited minds yearn to find comfort and courage in the idea of Mind, that faculty whose ancient potency our commitment to the idea of culture denies. To us today, Mind must inevitably seem but a poor gray thing, for it always sought to detach itself from the passions (but not from the emotions, Spinoza said, and explained the difference) and from the conditions of time and place. Yet it is salutary for us to contemplate it, whatever its grayness, because of the bright belief that was once attached to it, that it was the faculty which belonged not to professions, or to social classes, or to cultural groups, but to Man, and that it was possible for men, and becoming to them, to learn its proper use, for it was the means by which they could communicate with each other.

It was on this belief that science based its early existence, and it gave to the men who held it a character which is worth remarking. Sir Charles mentions Faraday among those scientists who overrode the limitations of social class to form the "scientific culture" of England. This is true only so far as it can be made consonant with the fact that Faraday could not have imagined the idea of a "scientific culture" and would have been wholly repelled by it. It is told of Faraday that he refused to be called a *physicist;* he very much disliked the new name as being too special and particular and insisted on the old one, *philosopher,* in all its spacious generality: we may suppose that this was his way of saying that he had not overridden the limiting conditions of class only to submit to the limitations of profession. The idea of Mind which had taught the bookbinder's apprentice to embark on his heroic enterprise of self-instruction also taught the great scientist to place himself beyond the specialness of interest which groups prescribe for their members. Every personal episode in Tyndall's classic account of his master, *Faraday as a Researcher,* makes it plain that Faraday undertook to be, in the beautiful lost sense of the word, a *disinterested* man. From his belief in Mind, he derived the certitude that he had his true being not as a member of this or that profession or class, but as — in the words of a poet of his time — "a man speaking to men."

No one now needs to be reminded of what may befall the idea of Mind in the /476/ way of excess and distortion. The literature of the 19th century never wearied of telling us just this, of decrying the fatigue and dessication of spirit which result from an allegiance to Mind that excludes impulse and will, and desire and preference. It was, surely, a liberation to be made aware of this, and then to go on to take serious account of those particularities of impulse and will, of desire and preference, which differentiate individuals and groups —to employ what I have called the cultural mode of thought. We take it for granted that this, like any other mode of thought, has its peculiar dangers, but there is cause for surprise and regret that it should be Sir Charles Snow and Dr. Leavis who have jointly demonstrated how far the cultural mode of thought can go in excess and distortion. /477/

PART II

The Debate
in Historical
Perspective

The issues with which this book is concerned began to assume clear form near the beginning of the seventeenth century—the age of Harvey, Boyle, Newton, and a host of other thinkers who profoundly influenced the development of modern science. During the first two decades of this century Sir Francis Bacon devoted his energies to the cause of scientific progress, analyzing the forces that had retarded the advance of science and setting forth his conception of the program to be followed. Bacon was unexcelled as a propagandist, and the scientists who followed him were glad to quote the great Lord Chancellor against their critics, many of whom regarded the rise of science as a threat to traditional ways of thought and entrenched academic disciplines.

The opening selections of Part II have been chosen to illustrate significant aspects of Bacon's writings on science: the missionary zeal with which he approached his chosen task; his rejection of the authority and the methods of the "Ancients," especially the method of deductive logic deriving from Aristotle; his insistence on the necessity of induction—an approach to knowledge based upon the patient accumulation of verifiable facts; and his anticipation of the quarters from which opposition to his program might be expected. The selections by Bacon are concluded by an excerpt from New Atlantis, *one of his later works, in which he cast his hopes into a piece of Utopian science fiction.*

Bacon labored to make the world safe for the fledgling natural sciences; in his examination of the various branches of learning he reported "no deficience" in poetry. By the early years of the nineteenth century, however, when the next two selections were written, the position of science was secure, and that of poetry had become somewhat ambiguous. Thomas Love Peacock's The Four Ages of Poetry *ironically characterizes an attitude, widespread among men of his time, that poetry is trivial, primitive, or childish, in contrast to the mature and "civilized" discipline of the sciences. The poet William Wordsworth, however, voices a calm confidence in the enduring capacity of poetry to absorb and make relevant to the human emotions all the unsettling discoveries of an expanding science.*

The next selections date from the middle of the nineteenth century. John Ruskin's writings represent a climax to the expressions of dismay, voiced especially by the English Romantics, elicited by the effects of the Industrial Revolution. New methods of production had brought with them changing values and a widespread dislocation of social and personal relationships. The factory, and the factory-engendered slum, had defaced the English countryside and deformed the minds and bodies of a whole new class of men, women, and children that had been called into being to serve the expanding industries. Ruskin failed to appreciate many of the possibilities latent in the new technology. His praise of the virtues of manual labor should be read in the context of C. P. Snow's condemnation of literary men as "natural Luddites." But Ruskin foresaw with terrible clarity certain social effects of mechanization that have come to fruition in our own time and have provided the subject for many painful diagnoses.

In the classic debate between Matthew Arnold and Thomas Henry Huxley which concludes Part II, the controversy over the relative importance to education of science and the humanities appears couched in terms that closely anticipate its modern form. Both Arnold, the poet and literary critic, and Huxley, the man of science, were men of powerful and sensitive intelligence, and both had absorbed the best elements in a common intellectual heritage. Neither was prepared to disparage the value of the studies that the other recommended. The rift between the "two cultures" did not seem to them so wide as it appears to many of today's writers. Yet to Arnold "humane letters," and to Huxley natural science, appeared to constitute the more valuable education if a choice between the two disciplines had to be made. Increasingly, in the pattern of contemporary education, this has become a necessary choice. Many of the other writers represented in this book, either directly or by implication, carry the reader back to the issues as they were defined in the Arnold-Huxley debate.

Sir Francis Bacon

THE NEW SCIENCE

Francis Bacon (1561–1626) began his preparation for a public career by reading law at Gray's Inn. His election to the House of Commons in 1584 was followed by a distinguished Parliamentary career. Under James I, Bacon rose rapidly in public office; in 1617 he was made Lord Keeper of the Great Seal, and in 1618, Lord Chancellor—the highest appointive offices in the realm. Bacon's fall was even more rapid than his rise. In 1621 he was charged with, and confessed to, the taking of bribes—not an uncommon practice of judges in his day—and his public career came to an end. Elements of mystery still surround the circumstances of Bacon's disgrace.

His enforced retirement enabled Bacon to polish and add to the already vast body of his writings. These include legal studies, historical writings, and the famous Essays *(first published in 1597). But Bacon's strongest claim to permanent significance rests upon his works in natural history and the philosophy of science—especially* The Advancement of Learning *(1605) and* The New Organon *(1620).*

from FILUM LABYRINTHI*

Francis Bacon thought in this manner. The knowledge whereof the world is now possessed, especially that of nature, extendeth not to magnitude and certainty of works. The Physician pronounceth many diseases incurable, and faileth oft in the rest. The Alchemists wax old and die in hopes. The Magicians perform nothing that is permanent and profitable. The Mechanics take small light from natural philosophy, and do but spin on their own little threads. Chance sometimes discovereth inventions; but that worketh not in years, but ages. So he saw well, that the inventions known are very unperfect; and that new are not like to be brought to light but in great length of time; and that those which are, came not to light by philosophy. /496/

from THE GREAT INSTAURATION

For the end which this science of mine proposes is the invention not of arguments but of arts; not of things in accordance with principles, but of principles themselves; not of probable reasons, but of designations and directions for works. And as the intention is different, so accordingly is the effect; the effect of the one being to overcome an opponent in argument, of the other to command nature in action.

In accordance with this end is also the nature and order of the demonstrations. For in the ordinary logic almost all the work is spent about the syllogism. Of induction the logicians seem hardly to have taken any serious thought, but they pass it by with a slight notice, and hasten on to the formulae of disputation. I on the contrary reject demonstration by syllogism, as acting too confusedly, and letting nature slip out of its hands. For although no one can doubt that things which agree in a middle term agree with one another (which is a proposition of mathematical certainty), yet it leaves an opening for deception; which is

From *The Works of Francis Bacon*, ed. James Spedding, R. L. Ellis, and D. D. Heath (London: Longmans, 1857–1874), Vol. III, pp. 496–504.
Filum Labyrinthi is translated as "The Clue to the Maze"—*Editors' note.*
From *The Works of Francis Bacon*, Vol. IV, pp. 7–33.

this. The syllogism consists of propositions; propositions of words; and words are the tokens and signs of notions. Now if the very notions of the mind (which are as the soul of words and the basis of the whole structure) be improperly and overhastily abstracted from facts, vague, not sufficiently definite, faulty in short in many ways, the whole edifice tumbles. I therefore reject the syllogism; and that not only as regards principles (for to principles the logicians themselves do not apply it) but also as regards middle propositions; which, though obtainable no doubt by the syllogism, are, when so obtained, barren of works, remote from practice, and altogether unavailable for the active department of the sciences. Although therefore I leave to the syllogism and these famous and boasted modes of demonstration their jurisdiction over popular arts and such as are matter of opinion (in which department I leave all as it is), yet in dealing with the nature of things I use induction throughout, and that in the minor propositions as well as the major. For I consider induction to be that form of demonstration which upholds the sense, and closes with nature, /24/ and comes to the very brink of operation, if it does not actually deal with it. /25/

. . . Those . . . who aspire not to guess and divine, but to discover and know; who propose not to devise mimic and fabulous worlds of their own, but to examine and dissect the nature of this very world itself; must go to facts themselves for everything. Nor can the place of this labour and search and worldwide perambulation be supplied by any genius or meditation or argumentation; no, not if all men's wits could meet in one. This therefore we must have, or the business must be for ever abandoned. But up to this day such has been the condition of men in this matter, that it is no wonder if nature will not give herself into their hands.

For first, the information of the sense itself, sometimes failing, sometimes false; observation, careless, irregular, and led by chance; tradition, vain and fed on rumour; practice, slavishly bent upon its work; experiment, blind, stupid, vague, and prematurely broken off; lastly, natural history trivial and poor; — all these have contributed to supply the understanding with very bad materials for philosophy and the sciences.

Then an attempt is made to mend the matter by a preposterous subtlety and winnowing of argument. But this comes too late, the case being already past remedy; and is far from setting the business right or sifting away the errors. The only hope therefore of any greater increase or progress lies in a reconstruction of the sciences.

Of this reconstruction the foundation must be laid in natural history, and that of a new kind and gathered on a new principle. For it is in vain that you polish the mirror if there are no images to be reflected; and it is as necessary that the intellect should be supplied with fit matter to work upon, as with safeguards to guide its working. But my history differs from that in use (as my logic does) in many things, — in end and office, in mass and composition, in subtlety, in selection also and setting forth, with a view to the operations which are to follow.

For first, the object of the natural history which I propose /28/ is not so much to delight with variety of matter or to help with present use of experiments, as to give light to the discovery of causes and supply a suckling philosophy with its first food. For though it be true that I am principally in pursuit of works and the active department of the sciences, yet I wait for harvest-time, and do not attempt to mow the moss or to reap the green corn. For I well know that axioms once rightly discovered will carry whole troops of works along with them, and produce them, not here and there one, but in clusters. And that unseasonable and puerile hurry to snatch by way of earnest at the first works which come within reach, I utterly condemn and reject, as an Atalanta's apple that hinders the race. Such then is the office of this natural history of mine. /29/

from THE NEW ORGANON

Be it remembered then that I am far from wishing to /41/ interfere with the philosophy which now flourishes, or with any other philosophy more correct and complete than this which has been or may hereafter be propounded. For I do not object to the use of this received philosophy, or others like it, for supplying matter for disputations or ornaments for discourse, — for the professor's lecture and for the business of life. Nay more, I declare openly that for these uses the philosophy which I bring forward will not be much available. It does not lie in the way. It cannot be caught up in passage. It does not flatter the understanding by conformity with preconceived notions. Nor will it come down to the apprehension of the vulgar except by its utility and effects.

Let there be therefore (and may it be for the benefit of both) two streams and two dispensations of knowledge; and in like manner two tribes or kindreds of students in philosophy — tribes not hostile or alien to each other, but bound together by mutual services; — let there in short be one method for the cultivation, another for the invention, of knowledge.

And for those who prefer the former, either from hurry or from considerations of business or for want of mental power to take in and embrace the other (which must needs be most men's case), I wish that they may succeed to their desire in what they are about, and obtain what they are pursuing. But if any man there be who, not content to rest in and use the knowledge which has already been discovered, aspires to penetrate further; to overcome, not an adversary in argument, but nature in action; to seek, not pretty and probable conjectures, but certain and demonstrable knowledge; — I invite all such to join themselves, as true sons of knowledge, with me, that passing by the outer courts of nature, which numbers have trodden, we may find a way at length into her inner chambers. And to make my meaning clearer and to familiarise the thing by giving it a name, I have chosen to call one of these methods or ways *Anticipation of the Mind,* the other *Interpretation of Nature.* /42/

. . . [I]n the customs and institutions of schools, academies, colleges, and similar bodies destined for the abode of learned men and the cultivation of learning, everything is found adverse to the progress of science. For the lectures and exercises there are so ordered, that to think or speculate on anything out of the common way can hardly occur to any man. And if one or two have the boldness to use any liberty of judgment, they must undertake the task all by themselves; they can have no advantage from the company of others. And if they can endure this also, they will find their industry and largeness of mind no slight hindrance to their fortune. For the studies of men in these places are confined and as it were imprisoned in the writings of certain authors, from whom if any man dissent he is straightway arraigned as a turbulent person and an innovator. But surely there is a great distinction between matters of state and the arts; for the danger from new motion and from new light is not the same. In matters of state a change even for the better is distrusted, because it unsettles what is established; these things resting on authority, consent, fame and opinion, not on demonstration. But arts and sciences should be like mines, where the noise of new works /89/ and further advances is heard on every side. But though the matter be so according to right reason, it is not so acted on in practice; and the points above mentioned in the administration and government of learning put a severe restraint upon the advancement of the sciences.

Nay, even if that jealousy were to cease, still it is enough to check the growth of science, that efforts and labours in this field go unrewarded. For it does not rest with the same persons to cultivate sciences and to reward them. The growth of them comes from great wits; the prizes and rewards of them are in the hands of the people, or of great persons, who are but in a very few cases even moderately learned. Moreover this kind of progress is not only unrewarded with prizes and substantial benefits; it has not even the advantage of popular applause. For it is a greater matter than the generality of men can take in, and is apt to be overwhelmed and extinguished by the gales of popular opinions. And it is nothing strange if a thing not held in honour does not prosper. . . . /90/

It remains for me to say a few words touching the excellency of the end in view. Had they been uttered earlier, they might have seemed like idle wishes; but now that hopes have been raised and unfair prejudices removed, they may perhaps have greater weight. Also if I had finished all myself, and had no occasion to call in others to help and take part in the work, I should even now have abstained from such language, lest it might be taken as a proclamation of my own deserts. But since I want to quicken the industry and rouse and kindle the zeal of others, it is fitting that I put men in mind of some things.

In the first place then, the introduction of famous discoveries appears to hold by far the first place among human actions; and this was the judgment of the former ages. For to the authors of inventions they awarded divine honours; while to those who did good service in the state (such as founders of cities and empires, legislators, saviours of their country from long endured evils, quellers of tyrannies, and the like) they decreed no higher honours than heroic. And certainly if a man rightly compare the two, he will find that this judgment of antiquity was just. For the benefits of discoveries may extend to the whole race of man, civil benefits only to particular places; the latter last not beyond a few ages, the former through all time. Moreover the reformation of a state in civil matters is seldom brought in without violence and confusion; but discoveries carry blessings with them, and confer benefits without causing harm or sorrow to any. . . . /113/

Again, let a man only consider what a difference there is between the life of men in the most civilised province of Europe, and in the wildest and most barbarous districts of New India; he will feel it be great enough to justify the saying that "man is a god to man," not only in regard of aid and benefit, but also by a comparison of condition. And this difference comes not from soil, not from climate, not from race, but from the arts.

Again, it is well to observe the force and virtue and consequences of discoveries; and these are to be seen nowhere more conspicuously than in those three which were unknown to the ancients, and of which the origin, though recent, is obscure and inglorious; namely, printing, gunpowder, and the magnet. For these three have changed the whole face and state of things throughout the world; the first in literature, the second in warfare, the third in navigation; whence have followed innumerable changes; insomuch that no empire, no sect, no star seems to have exerted greater power and influence in human affairs than these mechanical discoveries.

Further, it will not be amiss to distinguish the three kinds and as it were grades of ambition in mankind. The first is of those who desire to extend their own power in their native country; which kind is vulgar and degenerate. The second is of those who labour to extend the power of their country and its dominion among men. This certainly has more dignity, though not less covetousness. But if a man endeavour to establish and extend the power and dominion of the human race itself over the universe, his ambition (if ambition it can be called) is without doubt both a more wholesome thing and a more noble than the other two. Now the empire of man over things depends wholly on the arts and sciences. For we cannot command nature except by obeying her. /114/

from NEW ATLANTIS

Bacon's New Atlantis *records the experiences of a group of voyagers in the south seas who are blown off their course and land on a previously undiscovered island. In the culminating episode of the work the narrator is admitted to the presence of the master of Salomon's House, who explains to him the activities of this scientific foundation.*

. . . He was set upon a low throne richly adorned, and a rich cloth of state over his head, of blue satin embroidered. He was alone, save that he had two pages of honour, on either hand one, finely attired in white. His undergarments were the like that we saw him wear in the chariot; but instead of his gown, he had on him a mantle with a cape, of the same fine black, fastened about him. When we came in, as we were taught, we bowed low at our first entrance; and when we were come near his chair, he stood up, holding forth his hand ungloved, and in posture of blessing; and we every one of us stooped down, and kissed the hem of his tippet. That done, the rest departed, and I remained. Then he warned the pages forth of the room, and caused me to sit down beside him, and spake to me thus in the Spanish tongue:

"God bless thee, my son; I will give thee the greatest jewel I have. For I will impart unto thee, for the love of God and men, a relation of the true state of Salomon's House. Son, to make you know the true state of Salomon's House, I will keep this order. First, I will set forth unto you the end of our foundation. Secondly, the preparations and instruments we have for our works. Thirdly, the several employments and functions whereto our fellows are assigned. And fourthly, the ordinances and rites which we observe.

"The End of our Foundation is the knowledge of Causes, and secret motions of things; and the enlarging of the bounds of Human Empire, to the effecting of all things possible.

"The Preparations and Instruments are these. We have large and deep caves of several depths: the deepest are sunk six hundred fathom; and some of them are digged and made under great hills and mountains: so that if you reckon together the depth of the hill and the depth of the cave, they are (some of them) above three miles deep. For we find that the depth of a hill, and the depth of a cave from the flat, is the same thing; both remote alike from the sun and heaven's beams, and from the open air. These caves we call the Lower Region. And we use them for all coagulations, indurations, refrigerations, and conservations of bodies. We use them like- /156/ wise for the imitation of natural mines; and the producing also of new artificial metals, by compositions and materials which we use, and lay there for many years. We use them also sometimes, (which may seem strange,) for curing of some diseases, and for prolongation of life in some hermits that choose to live there, well accommodated of all things necessary; and indeed live very long; by whom also we learn many things.

"We have burials in several earths, where we put divers cements, as the Chineses do their porcellain. But we have them in greater variety, and some of them more fine. We have also great variety of composts, and soils, for the making of the earth fruitful.

"We have high towers; the highest about half a mile in height; and some of them likewise set upon high mountains; so that the vantage of the hill with the tower is in the highest of them three miles at least. And these places we call the Upper Region: accounting the air between the high places and the low, as a Middle Region. We use these towers, according to their several heights and situations, for insolation, refrigeration, conservation; and for the view of divers meteors; as winds, rain, snow, hail; and some of the fiery meteors also. And upon them, in some places, are dwellings of hermits, whom we visit sometimes, and instruct what to observe.

"We have great lakes both salt and fresh, whereof we have use for the fish and fowl. We use them also for burials of some natural bodies: for we find a difference in things buried in earth or in air below the earth, and things buried in water. We have also pools, of which some do strain fresh water out of salt; and others by art do turn fresh water into salt. We have also some rocks in the midst of the sea, and some bays upon the shore, for some works wherein is required the air and vapour of the sea. We have likewise violent streams and cataracts, which serve us for many motions: and likewise engines for multiplying and enforcing of winds, to set also on going divers motions.

"We have also a number of artificial wells and fountains, /157/ made in imitation of the natural sources and baths; as tincted upon vitriol, sulphur, steel, brass, lead, nitre, and other minerals. And again we have little wells for infusions of many things, where the waters take the virtue quicker and better than in vessels or basons. And amongst them we have a water which we call Water of Paradise, being, by that we do to it, made very sovereign for health, and prolongation of life.

"We have also great and spacious houses, where we imitate and demonstrate meteors; as snow, hail, rain, some artificial rains of bodies and not of water, thunders, lightnings; also generations of bodies in air; as frogs, flies, and divers others.

"We have also certain chambers, which we call Chambers of Health, where we qualify the air as we think good and proper for the cure of divers diseases, and preservation of health.

"We have also fair and large baths, of several mixtures, for the cure of diseases, and the restoring of man's body from arefaction: and others for the confirming of it in strength of sinews, vital parts, and the very juice and substance of the body.

"We have also large and various orchards and gardens, wherein we do not so much respect beauty, as variety of ground and soil, proper for divers trees and herbs: and some very spacious, where trees and berries are set whereof we make divers kinds of drinks, besides the vineyards. In these we practise likewise all conclusions of grafting and inoculating, as well of wild-trees as fruit-trees, which produceth many effects. And we make (by art) in the same orchards and gardens, trees and flowers to come earlier or later than their seasons; and to come up and bear more speedily than by their natural course they do. We make them also by art greater much than their nature; and their fruit greater and sweeter and of differing taste, smell, colour, and figure, from their nature. And many of them we so order, as they become of medicinal use.

"We have also means to make divers plants rise by mixtures of earths without seeds; and likewise to make divers new /158/ plants, differing from the vulgar; and to make one tree or plant turn into another.

"We have also parks and inclosures of all sorts of beasts and birds, which we use not only for view or rareness, but likewise for dissections and trials; that thereby we may take light what may be wrought upon the body of man. Wherein we find many strange effects; as continuing life in them, though divers parts, which you account vital, be perished and taken forth; resuscitating of some that seem dead in appearance; and the like. We try also all poisons and other medicines upon them, as well of chirurgery as physic. By art likewise, we make them greater or taller than their kind is; and contrariwise dwarf them, and stay their growth: we make them more fruitful and bearing than their kind is; and contrariwise barren and not generative. Also we make them differ in colour, shape, activity, many ways. We find means to make commixtures and copulations of different kinds; which have produced many new kinds, and them not barren, as the general opinion is. We make a number of kinds of serpents, worms, flies, fishes, of putrefaction; whereof some are advanced (in effect) to be perfect creatures, like beasts or birds; and have sexes, and do propagate. Neither do we this by chance, but we know beforehand of what matter and commixture what kind of those creatures will arise. . . . /159/

"We have dispensatories, or shops of medicines. Wherein you may easily think, if we have such variety of plants and living creatures more than you have in Europe, (for we know what you have,) the simples, drugs, and ingredients of medicines, must likewise be in so much the greater variety. We have them likewise of divers ages, and long fermentations. And for their preparations, we have not only all manner of exquisite distillations and separations, and especially by gentle heats and percolations through divers strainers, yea and substances; but /160/ also exact forms of composition, whereby they incorporate almost, as they were natural simples.

"We have also divers mechanical arts, which you have not; and stuffs made by them; as papers, linen, silks, tissues; dainty works of feathers of wonderful lustre; excellent dyes, and many others; and shops likewise, as well for such as are not brought into vulgar use amongst us as for those that are. For you must know that of the things before recited, many of them are grown into use throughout the kingdom; but yet if they did flow from our invention, we have of them also for patterns and principals.

"We have also furnaces of great diversities, and that keep great diversity of heats, fierce and quick; strong and constant; soft and mild; blown, quiet; dry, moist; and the like. But above all, we have heats in imitation of the sun's and heavenly bodies' heats, that pass divers inequalities and (as it were) orbs, progresses, and returns, whereby we produce admirable effects. Besides, we have heats of dungs, and of bellies and maws of living creatures, and of their bloods and bodies; and of hays and herbs laid up moist; of lime unquenched; and such like. Instruments also which generate heat only by motion. And farther, places for strong insolations; and again, places under the earth, which by nature or art yield heat. These divers heats we use, as the nature of the operation which we intend requireth.

"We have also perspective-houses, where we make demonstrations of all lights and radiations; and of all colours; and out of things uncoloured and transparent, we can represent unto you all several colours; not in rain-bows, as it is in gems and prisms, but of themselves single. We represent also all multi-plications of light, which we carry to great distance, and make so sharp as to discern small points and lines; also all colorations of light: all delusions and deceits of the sight, in figures, magnitudes, motions, colours: all demonstra-tions of shadows. We find also divers means, yet unknown to you, /161/ of producing of light originally from divers bodies. We procure means of seeing objects afar off; as in the heaven and remote places; and represent things near as afar off, and things afar off as near; making feigned distances. We have also helps for the sight, far above spectacles and glasses in use. We have also glasses and means to see small and minute bodies perfectly and distinctly; as the shapes and colours of small flies and worms, grains and flaws in gems, which cannot otherwise be seen; observations in urine and blood, not other-wise to be seen. We make artificial rain-bows, halos, and circles about light. We represent also all manner of reflexions, refractions, and multiplications of visual beams of objects. . . . /162/

"We have also engine-houses, where are prepared engines and instruments for all sorts of motions. There we imitate and practise to make swifter motions than any you have, either out of your muskets or any engine that you have; and to make them and multiply them more easily, and with small force, by wheels and other means: and to make them stronger, and more violent than yours are; exceeding your greatest cannons and basilisks. We represent also ordnance and instruments of war, and engines of all kinds: and likewise new mixtures and compositions of gun-powder, wildfires burning in water, and unquenchable. Also fire-works of all variety both for pleasure and use. We imitate also flights of birds; we have some degrees of flying in the air; we have ships and boats for going underwater, and brooking of seas; also swimming-girdles and /163/ supporters. We have divers curious clocks, and other like motions of return, and some perpetual motions. We imitate also motions of living creatures, by images of men, beasts, birds, fishes, and serpents. We have also a great number of other various motions, strange for equality, fineness, and subtilty.

"We have also a mathematical house, where are represented all instruments, as well of geometry as astronomy, exquisitely made.

"We have also houses of deceits of the senses; where we represent all manner of feats of juggling, false apparitions, impostures, and illusions; and their fallacies. And surely you will easily believe that we that have so many things truly natural which induce admiration, could in a world of particulars deceive the senses, if we would disguise those things and labour to make them seem more miraculous. But we do hate all impostures and lies: insomuch as we have severely forbidden it to all our fellows, under pain of ignominy and fines, that they do not shew any natural work or thing, adorned or swelling; but only pure as it is, and without all affectation of strangeness.

"These are (my son) the riches of Salomon's House." /164/

William Wordsworth

PREFACE TO LYRICAL BALLADS

William Wordsworth (1770–1850) was born at Cockermouth, Cumberland, in the northern part of England's Lake District. This beautiful country with its mountains, meadows, streams, and lakes deeply affected Wordsworth's thinking and poetry. After graduating from Cambridge and spending a year in Revolutionary France, he formed the friendship with Coleridge which led in 1798 to their joint publication of Lyrical Ballads. *In style and subject matter this collection was a revolutionary departure from the poetic practice of the time. In the decade 1797–1807, Wordsworth experienced his greatest creative period. After 1807 a noticeable decline in his power as a poet took place, although he continued to write voluminously and to grow in reputation. He received various honors until his death in 1850, among them, his appointment as Poet Laureate in 1843.*

The famous Preface was written in 1800 for the second edition of Lyrical Ballads. *It was enlarged in 1802 and revised in later editions. The selection below comes from the enlarged Preface of 1802.*

. . . Aristotle, I have been told, has said, that Poetry is the most philosophic of all writing: it is so: its object is truth, not individual and local, but general, and operative; not standing upon external /394/ testimony, but carried alive into the heart by passion; truth which is its own testimony, which gives competence and confidence to the tribunal to which it appeals, and receives them from the same tribunal. Poetry is the image of man and nature. The obstacles which stand in the way of the fidelity of the Biographer and Historian, and of their consequent utility, are incalculably greater than those which are to be encountered by the Poet who comprehends the dignity of his art. The Poet writes under one restriction only, namely, the necessity of giving immediate pleasure to a human Being possessed of that information which may be expected from him, not as a lawyer, a physician, a mariner, an astronomer, or a natural philosopher, but as a Man. Except this one restriction, there is no object standing between the Poet and the image of things; between this, and the Biographer and Historian, there are a thousand.

Nor let this necessity of producing immediate pleasure be considered as a degradation of the Poet's art. It is far otherwise. It is an acknowledgement of the beauty of the universe, an acknowledgement the more sincere, because not formal, but indirect; it is a task light and easy to him who looks at the world in the spirit of love: further, it is a homage paid to the native and naked dignity of man, to the grand elementary principle of pleasure, by which he knows, and feels, and lives, and moves. We have no sympathy but what is propagated by pleasure: I would not be misunderstood; but wherever we sympathize with pain, it will be found that the sympathy is produced and carried on by subtle combinations with pleasure. We have no knowledge, that is, no general principles drawn from the contemplation of particular facts, but what has been built up by pleasure, and exists in us by pleasure alone. The Man of science, the Chemist and Mathematician, whatever difficulties and disgusts they may have had to struggle with, know and feel this. However painful may be the objects

From Preface to *Lyrical Ballads,* in *The Poetical Works of William Wordsworth,* eds. Ernest de Selincourt and Helen Darbishire (Oxford: The Clarendon Press, 1952), Vol. II, pp. 384–404.

with which the Anatomist's knowledge is connected, he feels that his knowledge is pleasure; and where he has no pleasure he has no knowledge. What then does the Poet? He considers man and the objects that surround him as acting and reacting upon each other, so as to produce an infinite complexity of pain and pleasure; he considers man in his own nature and in his ordinary life as contemplating this with a certain quantity of immediate knowledge, with certain convictions, intuitions, and deductions, which from habit acquire the quality of intuitions; he considers him as looking upon this complex scene of ideas and sensations, and finding everywhere /395/ objects that immediately excite in him sympathies which, from the necessities of his nature, are accompanied by an overbalance of enjoyment.

To this knowledge which all men carry about with them, and to these sympathies in which, without any other discipline than that of our daily life, we are fitted to take delight, the Poet principally directs his attention. He considers man and nature as essentially adapted to each other, and the mind of man as naturally the mirror of the fairest and most interesting properties of nature. And thus the Poet, prompted by this feeling of pleasure, which accompanies him through the whole course of his studies, converses with general nature, with affections akin to those, which, through labour and length of time, the Man of science has raised up in himself, by conversing with those particular parts of nature which are the objects of his studies. The knowledge both of the Poet and the Man of science is pleasure; but the knowledge of the one cleaves to us as a necessary part of our existence, our natural and unalienable inheritance; the other is a personal and individual acquisition, slow to come to us, and by no habitual and direct sympathy connecting us with our fellow-beings. The Man of science seeks truth as a remote and unknown benefactor; he cherishes and loves it in his solitude: the Poet singing a song in which all human beings join with him, rejoices in the presence of truth as our visible friend and hourly companion. Poetry is the breath and finer spirit of all knowledge; it is the impassioned expression which is in the countenance of all Science. Emphatically may it be said of the Poet, as Shakespeare hath said of man, "that he looks before and after." He is the rock of defence for human nature; an upholder and preserver, carrying everywhere with him relationship and love. In spite of difference of soil and climate, of language and manners, of laws and customs: in spite of things silently gone out of mind, and things violently destroyed; the Poet binds together by passion and knowledge the vast empire of human society, as it is spread over the whole earth, and over all time. The objects of the Poet's thoughts are everywhere; though the eyes and senses of man are, it is true, his favourite guides, yet he will follow wheresoever he can find an atmosphere of sensation in which to move his wings. Poetry is the first and last of all knowledge – it is as immortal as the heart of man. If the labours of Men of science should ever create any material revolution, direct or indirect, in our condition, and in the impressions which we habitually receive, the Poet will sleep then no more than at present; he will be ready to follow the steps of the Man of science, not only in those general indirect effects, but he will be at his side, carrying sensation into the midst of the objects of the science itself. The remotest discoveries of the Chemist, the Botanist, or /396/ Mineralogist, will be as proper objects of the Poet's art as any upon which it can be employed, if the time should ever come when these things shall be familiar to us, and the relations under which they are contemplated by the followers of these respective sciences shall be manifestly and palpably material to us as enjoying and suffering beings. If the time should ever come when what is now called science, thus familiarized to men, shall be ready to put on, as it were, a form of flesh and blood, the Poet will lend his divine spirit to aid the transfiguration, and will welcome the Being thus produced, as a dear and genuine inmate of the household of man. . . . /397/

Thomas Love Peacock

THE FOUR AGES OF POETRY

Thomas Love Peacock (1785–1866) was for a long time a businessman employed by the East India Company. He had a flair for writing novels that are a curious blend of satire and romance. The best of these include Headlong Hall *(1816),* Melincourt *(1817),* Nightmare Abbey *(1818), and* Crochet Castle *(1831). His most important prose work, apart from his fiction, is* The Four Ages of Poetry *(1820), a witty attack on Romantic poetry. Peacock was himself a poet, and his attack was ironic, intended more to poke fun at the excesses of the Romantic poets of his day than to attack poetry in general. This work gave rise to Shelley's classic essay,* The Defense of Poetry, *written in 1821. Shelley, who was a close friend of Peacock, saw the intention of* The Four Ages of Poetry, *but at the same time he realized that the attitude it expressed was similar to that held by many people of the time.*

A poet in our times is a semi-barbarian in a civilized community. He lives in the days that are past. His ideas, thoughts, feelings, associations, are all with barbarous manners, obsolete customs, and exploded superstitions. The march of his intellect is like that of a crab, backward. The brighter the light diffused around him by the progress of reason, the thicker is the darkness of antiquated barbarism, in which he buries himself like a mole, to throw up the barren hillocks of his Cimmerian labours. The philosophic mental tranquillity which looks round with an equal eye on all external things, collects a store of ideas, discriminates their relative value, assigns to all their proper place, and from the materials of useful knowledge thus collected, appreciated, and arranged, forms new combinations that impress the stamp of their power and utility on the real business of life, is diametrically the reverse of that frame of mind which poetry inspires, or from which poetry can emanate. The highest inspirations of poetry are resolvable into three ingredients: the rant of unregulated passion, the whining of exaggerated feeling, and the cant of factitious sentiment: and can therefore serve only to ripen a splendid lunatic like Alexander, a puling driveller like Werter, or a morbid dreamer like Wordsworth. It can never make a philosopher, nor a statesman, nor in any class of life an useful or rational man. It cannot claim the slightest share in any /335/ one of the comforts and utilities of life of which we have witnessed so many and so rapid advances. But though not useful, it may be said it is highly ornamental, and deserves to be cultivated for the pleasure it yields. Even if this be granted, it does not follow that a writer of poetry in the present state of society is not a waster of his own time, and a robber of that of others. Poetry is not one of those arts which, like painting, require repetition and multiplication, in order to be diffused among society. There are more good poems already existing than are sufficient to employ that portion of life which any mere reader and recipient

From "The Four Ages of Poetry," in *The Works of Thomas Love Peacock*, ed. Henry Cole (London: Richard Bentley and Son, 1875), Vol. III, pp. 324–338.

of poetical impressions should devote to them, and these having been produced in poetical times, are far superior in all the characteristics of poetry to the artificial reconstructions of a few morbid ascetics in unpoetical times. To read the promiscuous rubbish of the present time to the exclusion of the select treasures of the past, is to substitute the worse for the better variety of the same mode of enjoyment.

But in whatever degree poetry is cultivated, it must necessarily be to the neglect of some branch of useful study: and it is a lamentable spectacle to see minds, capable of better things, running to seed in the specious indolence of these empty aimless mockeries of intellectual exertion. Poetry was the mental rattle that awakened the attention of intellect in the infancy of civil society: but for the maturity of mind to make a serious business of the playthings of its childhood, is as absurd as for a full-grown man to rub his gums with coral, and cry to be charmed to sleep by the jingle of silver bells.

As to that small portion of our contemporary poetry, which is neither descriptive, nor narrative, nor dramatic, and which, for want of a better name, may be called ethical, the most distinguished portion of it, consisting merely of querulous, egotistical rhapsodies, to express the writer's high dissatisfaction with the world and every thing in it, serves only to confirm what has been said of the semi-barbarous character of poets, who from singing dithyrambics and "Io Triumphe," while society was savage, grow rabid, and out of their element, as it becomes polished and enlightened.

Now when we consider that it is not the thinking and studious, and scientific and philosophical part of the community, not to those whose minds are bent on the pursuit and promotion of permanently useful ends and aims, that /336/ poets must address their minstrelsy, but to that much larger portion of the reading public, whose minds are not awakened to the desire of valuable knowledge, and who are indifferent to any thing beyond being charmed, moved, excited, affected, and exalted: charmed by harmony, moved by sentiment, excited by passion, affected by pathos, and exalted by sublimity: harmony, which is language on the rack of Procrustes; sentiment, which is canting egotism in the mask of refined feeling; passion, which is the commotion of a weak and selfish mind; pathos, which is the whining of an unmanly spirit; and sublimity, which is the inflation of an empty head: when we consider that the great and permanent interests of human society become more and more the main spring of intellectual pursuit; that in proportion as they become so, the subordinacy of the ornamental to the useful will be more and more seen and acknowledged; and that therefore the progress of useful art and science, and of moral and political knowledge, will continue more and more to withdraw attention from frivolous and unconducive, to solid and conducive studies: that therefore the poetical audience will not only continually diminish in the proportion of its number to that of the rest of the reading public, but will also sink lower and lower in the comparison of intellectual acquirement: when we consider that the poet must still please his audience, and must therefore continue to sink to their level, while the rest of the community is rising above it: we may easily conceive that the day is not distant, when the degraded state of every species of poetry will be as generally recognized as that of dramatic poetry has long been: and this not from any decrease either of intellectual power, or intellectual acquisition, but because intellectual power and intellectual acquisition have turned themselves into other and better channels, and have abandoned the cultivation and the fate of poetry to the degenerate fry of modern rhymesters, and their olympic judges, the magazine critics, who continue to debate and promulgate oracles about poetry, as if it were still what it was in the Homeric age, the all-in-all of intellectual progression, and as if there were no such things in existence as mathematicians, astronomers, chemists, moralists, metaphysicians, historians, politicians, and political econo-mists, who have built into the upper air of intelligence a pyramid, from the summit of which they see the modern Parnassus far beneath them, and, know- /337/ ing how small a place it occupies in the comprehensiveness of their prospect, smile at the little ambition and the circumscribed perceptions with which the drivellers and mountebanks upon it are contending for the poetical palm and the critical chair. /338/

John Ruskin

ON MACHINE LABOR

John Ruskin (1819–1900) was an English essayist, critic, and reformer. The son of a wealthy wine merchant, he had the means to enable him to spend his life traveling, lecturing, and writing. His literary production was immense. In the early part of his career Ruskin dealt mainly with the aesthetics of painting and architecture in such works as Modern Painters *(1843–1860),* The Seven Lamps of Architecture *(1849), and* The Stones of Venice *(1851–1853). With these and other writings he made himself the leading art critic of his time. In the latter part of his career, however, Ruskin turned to social criticism. The change is foreshadowed in his famous chapter in* The Stones of Venice, *"The Nature of Gothic," a part of which is printed below. Ruskin was appalled by the human misery created by industrialism—the squalor of the cities, the sufferings of workmen created by* laissez faire *capitalism, and the enslavement of men to machines. In* Unto This Last *(1862),* The Crown of Wild Olives *(1866),* Munera Pulveris *(1872), and* Fors Clavigera *(1871–1884), he dwelt on these prob-lems. Ruskin's contemporaries did not give much ear to his ideas; some were outraged by them. These works, however, later exerted a considerable influence on the thinking of the British Labour Party and on such individuals as William Morris, G. B. Shaw, and D. H. Lawrence.*

from THE NATURE OF GOTHIC

And now, reader, look round this English room of yours, about which you have been proud so often, because the work of it was so good and strong, and the ornaments of it so finished. Examine again all those accurate mouldings, and perfect polishings, and unerring adjustments of the seasoned wood and tempered steel. Many a time you have exulted over them, and thought how great England was, because her slightest work was done so thoroughly. Alas! if read rightly, these perfectnesses are signs of a slavery in our England a thousand times more bitter and more degrading than that of the scourged African, or helot Greek. Men may be beaten, chained, tormented, yoked like cattle, slaughtered like summer flies, and yet remain in one sense, and the best sense, free. But to smother their souls with them, to blight and hew into rotting pollards the suckling branches of their human intelligence, to make the flesh and skin which, after the worm's work on it, is to see God, into leathern thongs

From *The Works of John Ruskin*, eds. E. T. Cook and Alexander Wedderburn (Library Edition; London: George Allen, 1903–1912), Vol. X, *The Stones of Venice*, pp. 180–269.

to yoke machinery with,—this is to be slave-masters indeed; and there might be more freedom in England, though her feudal lords' lightest words were worth men's lives, and though the blood of the vexed husbandman dropped in the furrows of her fields, than there is while the animation of her multitudes is sent like fuel to feed the factory smoke, and the strength of them is given daily to be wasted into the fineness of a web, or racked into the exactness of a line.

And, on the other hand, go forth again to gaze upon the old cathedral front, where you have smiled so often at the fantastic ignorance of the old sculptors: examine once more those ugly goblins, and formless monsters, and stern statues, anatomiless and rigid; but do not mock at them, for they are signs of the life and liberty of every workman who /193/ struck the stone; a freedom of thought, and rank in scale of being, such as no laws, no charters, no charities can secure; but which it must be the first aim of all Europe at this day to regain for her children.

Let me not be thought to speak wildly or extravagantly. It is verily this degradation of the operative into a machine, which, more than any other evil of the times, is leading the mass of the nations everywhere into vain, incoherent, destructive struggling for a freedom of which they cannot explain the nature to themselves. Their universal outcry against wealth, and against nobility, is not forced from them either by the pressure of famine, or the sting of mortified pride. These do much, and have done much in all ages; but the foundations of society were never yet shaken as they are at this day. It is not that men are ill fed, but that they have no pleasure in the work by which they make their bread, and therefore look to wealth as the only means of pleasure. It is not that men are pained by the scorn of the upper classes, but they cannot endure their own; for they feel that the kind of labour to which they are condemned is verily a degrading one, and makes them less than men. Never had the upper classes so much sympathy with the lower, or charity for them, as they have at this day, and yet never were they so much hated by them: for, of old, the separation between the noble and the poor was merely a wall built by law; now it is a veritable difference in level of standing, a precipice between upper and lower grounds in the field of humanity, and there is pestilential air at the bottom of it. I know not if a day is ever to come when the nature of right freedom will be understood, and when men will see that to obey another man, to labour for him, yield reverence to him or to his place, is not slavery. . . . /194/ [I]n all ages and all countries, reverence has been paid and sacrifice made by men to each other, not only without complaint, but rejoicingly; and famine, and peril, and sword, and all evil, and all shame, have been borne willingly in the causes of masters and kings; for all these gifts of the heart ennobled the men who gave, not less than the men who received them, and nature prompted, and God rewarded the sacrifice. But to feel their souls withering within them, unthanked, to find their whole being sunk into an unrecognized abyss, to be counted off into a heap of mechanism numbered with its wheels, and weighed with its hammer strokes—this, nature bade not,—this, God blesses not,—this, humanity for no long time is able to endure. /195/

We have much studied and much perfected, of late, the great civilized invention of the division of labour; only we give it a false name. It is not, truly speaking, the labour that is divided; but the men:—Divided into mere segments of men—broken into small fragments and crumbs of life; so that all the little piece of intelligence that is left in a man is not enough to make a pin, or a nail, but exhausts itself in making the point of a pin or the head of a nail. Now it is a good and desirable thing, truly, to make many pins in a day; but if we could only see with what crystal sand their points were polished,—sand of human soul, much to be magnified before it can be discerned for what it is—we should think there might be some loss in it also. And the great cry that rises from all our manufacturing cities, louder than their furnace blast, is all in very deed for this,—that we manufacture everything there except men; we blanch cotton, and strengthen steel, and refine sugar, and shape pottery; but to brighten, to strengthen, to refine, or to form a single living spirit, never enters into our estimate of advantages. And all the evil to which that cry is urging our myriads can be met only in one way: not by teaching nor preaching, for to teach them is but to show them their misery, and to preach to them, if we do nothing more than preach, is to mock at it. It can be met only by a right understanding, on the part of all classes, of what kinds of labour are good for men, raising them, and making them happy; by a determined sacrifice of such convenience, or beauty, or cheapness as is to be got only by the degradation of the workman; and by equally determined demand for the products and results of healthy and ennobling labour. /196/

from THE FUTURE OF ENGLAND

. . . What faculty have you? What can you do best? Can you drive a nail into wood? Go and mend the parish fences. Can you lay a brick? Mend the walls of the cottages where the wind comes in. Can you lift a spadeful of earth? Turn this field up three feet deep all over. Can you only drag a weight with your shoulders? Stand at the bottom of this hill and help up the overladen horses. Can you weld iron and chisel stone? Fortify this wreck-strewn coast into a harbour; and change these shifting sands into fruitful ground. Wherever death was, bring life; that is to be your work; that your parish refuge; that your education. So and no otherwise can we meet existent distress. But for the continual education of the whole people, and for their future happiness, they must have such consistent employment as shall develop all the powers of the fingers, and the limbs, and the brain: and that development is only to be obtained by hand-labour, of which you have these four great divisions—hand-labour on the earth, hand-labour on the sea, hand-labour in art, hand-labour in war. Of the last two of these I cannot speak to-night, and of the first two only with extreme brevity.

Hand-labour on the earth, the work of the husbandman and of the shepherd;—to dress the earth and to keep the flocks of it—the first task of man, and the final one—the education always of noblest lawgivers, kings and teachers; the education of Hesiod, of Moses, of David; of all the true strength of Rome; and all its tenderness: the pride of Cincinnatus, and the inspiration of Virgil. Hand-labour on the earth, and the harvest of it brought forth with singing:—not steam-piston labour on the earth, and the harvest of it brought forth with steam-whistling. You will have no prophet's voice accompanied by that shepherd's pipe, and pastoral symphony. Do you know that lately, in Cumberland, in the chief pastoral district of England,—in Wordsworth's own home,—a procession of /508/ villagers on their festa day provided for themselves, by way of music, a steam-plough whistling at the head of them?

Give me patience while I put the principle of machine labour before you, as clearly and in as short compass as possible; it is one that should be known at this juncture. Suppose a farming proprietor needs to employ a hundred men on his estate, and that the labour of these hundred men is enough, but not more than enough, to till all his land, and to raise from it food for his own family, and for the hundred labourers. He is obliged under such circumstances, to maintain all the men in moderate comfort, and can only by economy accumulate much for himself. But, suppose he contrive a machine that will easily do the work of fifty men, with only one man to watch it. This sounds like a great advance in civilisation. The farmer of course gets his machine made, turns off the fifty men, who may starve or emigrate at their choice, and now he can keep half of the produce of his estate, which formerly went to feed them, all to himself. That is the essential and constant operation of machinery among us at this moment. . . . /509/

He has got his machine made, which goes creaking, screaming, and occasionally exploding, about modern Arcadia. He has turned off his fifty men to starve. Now, at some distance from his own farm, there is another on which the labourers were working for their bread in the same way, by tilling the land. The machinist sends over to these, saying— "I have got food enough for you without your digging or ploughing any more. I can maintain you in other occupations instead of ploughing that land; if you rake in its gravel you will find some hard stones—you shall grind those on mills till they glitter; then, my wife shall wear a necklace of them. Also, if you turn up the meadows below you will find some fine white clay, of which you shall make a porcelain service for me: and the rest of the farm I want for pasture for horses for my carriage—and you shall groom them, and some of you ride behind the carriage with staves in your hands, and I will keep you much fatter for doing that than you can keep yourselves by digging."

Well—but it is answered, are we to have no diamonds, nor china, nor pictures, nor footmen, then—but all to be farmers? I am not saying what we ought to do, I want only to show you with perfect clearness first what we *are doing;* and that, I repeat, is the upshot of machine-contriving in this country. . . . /510/

That is one effect of machinery; but at all events, if we have thus lost in men, we have gained in riches; instead of happy human souls, we have at least got pictures, china, horses, and are ourselves better off than we were before. But very often, and in much of our machine-contriving, even *that* result does not follow. We are not one whit the richer for the machine, we only employ it for our amusement. For observe, our gaining in riches depends on the men who are out of employment consenting to be starved, or sent out of the country. But suppose they do not consent passively to be starved; but some of them become criminals, and have to be taken charge of and fed at a much greater cost than if they were at work, and others, paupers, rioters, and the like,—then you attain the real outcome of modern wisdom and ingenuity. You had your hundred men honestly at country work; but you don't like the sight of human beings in your fields; you like better to see a smoking kettle. You pay, as an amateur, for that pleasure, and you employ your fifty men in picking oakum, or begging, rioting, and thieving.

By hand-labour, therefore, and that alone, we are to till the ground. By hand-labour also to plough the sea; both for food, and in commerce, and in war: not with floating kettles there neither, but with hempen bridle, and the winds of heaven in harness. That is the way the power of Greece rose on her Egean, the power of Venice on her Adria, of Amalfi in her blue bay, of the Norman sea-riders from the North Cape to Sicily: — so, your own dominion also of the past. Of the past, mind you. On the Baltic and the Nile, your power is already departed.* By /511/ machinery you would advance to discovery; by machinery you would carry your commerce; — you would be engineers instead of sailors; and instantly in the North seas you are beaten among the ice, and before the very Gods of Nile, beaten among the sand. Agriculture, then, by the hand or by the plough drawn only by animals; and shepherd and pastoral husbandry, are to be the chief schools of Englishmen. And this most royal academy of all academies you have to open over all the land, purifying your heaths and hills, and waters, and keeping them full of every kind of lovely natural organism, in tree, herb, and living creature. All land that is waste and ugly, you must redeem into ordered fruitfulness; all ruin, desolateness, imperfectness of hut or habitation, you must do away with; and throughout every village and city of your English dominion, there must not be a hand that cannot find a helper, nor a heart that cannot find a comforter. /512/

Thomas Henry Huxley

SCIENCE AND CULTURE

Thomas Henry Huxley (1825–1895), a brilliant English biologist and lecturer, was a vigorous spokesman for science in the nineteenth century. With a lucid expository style, he made the results of new scientific discoveries intelligible in lectures to both workmen and students. He was one of the first, though with some reservations, to accept Darwin's theory of evolution, and as "Darwin's Bulldog" he vigorously defended the theory against attacks by English churchmen. He also helped to forward the cause of popular education and, especially, to bring about the acceptance of natural science as an essential component of a liberal education. Many like Arnold felt, however, that he did so at too great an expense to traditional humanistic studies.

Mr. Arnold tells us that the meaning of culture is "to know the best that has been thought and said in the world." It is the criticism of life contained in literature. That criticism regards "Europe as being, for intellectual and spiritual purposes, one great confederation, bound to a joint action and working to a common result; and whose members have, for their common outfit, a knowledge of Greek, Roman, and Eastern /142/ antiquity, and of one another. Special, local, and temporary advantages being put out of account, that modern nation will in the intellectual and spiritual sphere make most progress, which most thoroughly carries out this programme. And what is that but saying that we too, all of us, as individuals, the more thoroughly we carry it out, shall make the more progress?"

We have here to deal with two distinct propositions. The first, that a criticism of life is the essence of culture; the second, that literature contains the materials which suffice for the construction of such criticism.

---

* Here and in the remarks which follow, Ruskin refers to an abortive expedition to the Baltic during the Crimean War, to the failure of English polar expeditions, and to the victory of French engineering in the building of the Suez Canal — *Editors' note.*

From "Science and Culture," in *Collected Essays* (New York: D. Appleton and Company, 1898), Vol. III, *Science and Education*, pp. 134–159.

I think that we must all assent to the first proposition. For culture certainly means something quite different from learning or technical skill. It implies the possession of an ideal, and the habit of critically estimating the value of things by comparison with a theoretic standard. Perfect culture should supply a complete theory of life, based upon a clear knowledge alike of its possibilities and of its limitations.

But we may agree to all this, and yet strongly dissent from the assumption that literature alone is competent to supply this knowledge. After having learnt all that Greek, Roman, and Eastern antiquity have thought and said, and all that modern literature have to tell us, it is not self-evident that we have laid a sufficiently broad /143/ and deep foundation for that criticism of life, which constitutes culture.

Indeed, to any one acquainted with the scope of physical science, it is not at all evident. Considering progress only in the "intellectual and spiritual sphere," I find myself wholly unable to admit that either nations or individuals will really advance, if their common outfit draws nothing from the stores of physical science. I should say that an army, without weapons of precision and with no particular base of operations, might more hopefully enter upon a campaign on the Rhine, than a man, devoid of a knowledge of what physical science has done in the last century, upon a criticism of life.

When a biologist meets with an anomaly, he instinctively turns to the study of development to clear it up. The rationale of contradictory opinions may with equal confidence be sought in history.

It is, happily, no new thing that Englishmen should employ their wealth in building and endowing institutions for educational purposes. But, five or six hundred years ago, deeds of foundation expressed or implied conditions as nearly as possible contrary to those which have been thought expedient by Sir Josiah Mason. That is to say, physical science was practically ignored, while a certain literary training was enjoined as a means to the acquirement of knowledge which was essentially theological. /144/

The reason of this singular contradiction between the actions of men alike animated by a strong and disinterested desire to promote the welfare of their fellows, is easily discovered.

At that time, in fact, if any one desired knowledge beyond such as could be obtained by his own observation, or by common conversation, his first necessity was to learn the Latin language, inasmuch as all the higher knowledge of the western world was contained in works written in that language. Hence, Latin grammar, with logic and rhetoric, studied through Latin, were the fundamentals of education. With respect to the substance of the knowledge imparted through this channel, the Jewish and Christian Scriptures, as interpreted and supplemented by the Romish Church, were held to contain a complete and infallibly true body of information.

Theological dicta were, to the thinkers of those days, that which the axioms and definitions of Euclid are to the geometers of these. The business of the philosophers of the middle ages was to deduce from the data furnished by the theologians, conclusions in accordance with ecclesiastical decrees. They were allowed the high privilege of showing, by logical process, how and why that which the Church said was true, must be true. And if their demonstrations fell short of or exceeded this limit, the Church was maternally ready to check their /145/ aberrations; if need were by the help of the secular arm.

Between the two, our ancestors were furnished with a compact and complete

criticism of life. They were told how the world began and how it would end;
they learned that all material existence was but a base and insignificant blot
upon the fair face of the spiritual world, and that nature was, to all intents
and purposes, the play-ground of the devil; they learned that the earth is
the centre of the visible universe, and that man is the cynosure of things
terrestrial; and more especially was it inculcated that the course of nature had
no fixed order, but that it could be, and constantly was, altered by the agency
of innumerable spiritual beings, good and bad, according as they were moved
by the deeds and prayers of men. The sum and substance of the whole doctrine
was to produce the conviction that the only thing really worth knowing in this
world was how to secure that place in a better which, under certain conditions,
the Church promised.

Our ancestors had a living belief in this theory of life, and acted upon it
in their dealings with education, as in all other matters. Culture meant saint-
liness—after the fashion of the saints of those days; the education that led
to it was, of necessity, theological; and the way to theology lay through Latin.

That the study of nature—further than was re- /146/ quisite for the satisfaction of everyday wants—should have any bearing on human life was far from
the thoughts of men thus trained. Indeed, as nature had been cursed for
man's sake, it was an obvious conclusion that those who meddled with nature
were likely to come into pretty close contact with Satan. And, if any born
scientific investigator followed his instincts, he might safely reckon upon
earning the reputation, and probably upon suffering the fate, of a sorcerer.

Had the western world been left to itself in Chinese isolation, there is no
saying how long this state of things might have endured. But, happily, it was
not left to itself. Even earlier than the thirteenth century, the development
of Moorish civilisation in Spain and the great movement of the Crusades had
introduced the leaven which, from that day to this, has never ceased to work.
At first, through the intermediation of Arabic translations, afterwards by the
study of the originals, the western nations of Europe became acquainted with
the writings of the ancient philosophers and poets, and, in time, with the
whole of the vast literature of antiquity.

Whatever there was of high intellectual aspiration or dominant capacity in
Italy, France, Germany, and England, spent itself for centuries in taking
possession of the rich inheritance left by the dead civilisations of Greece
and Rome. Marvellously aided by the invention of printing, /147/ classical
learning spread and flourished. Those who possessed it prided themselves on
having attained the highest culture then within the reach of mankind.

And justly. For, saving Dante on his solitary pinnacle, there was no figure
in modern literature at the time of the Renascence to compare with the men
of antiquity; there was no art to compete with their sculpture; there was no
physical science but that which Greece had created. Above all, there was no
other example of perfect intellectual freedom—of the unhesitating acceptance
of reason as the sole guide to truth and the supreme arbiter of conduct.

The new learning necessarily soon exerted a profound influence upon
education. The language of the monks and schoolmen seemed little better
than gibberish to scholars fresh from Virgil and Cicero, and the study of
Latin was placed upon a new foundation. Moreover, Latin itself ceased to
afford the sole key to knowledge. The student who sought the highest thought
of antiquity, found only a second-hand reflection of it in Roman literature,
and turned his face to the full light of the Greeks. And after a battle, not

altogether dissimilar to that which is at present being fought over the teaching of physical science, the study of Greek was recognized as an essential element of all higher education.

Thus the Humanists, as they were called, won /148/ the day; and the great reform which they effected was of incalculable service to mankind. But the Nemesis of all reformers is finality; and the reformers of education, like those of religion, fell into the profound, however common, error of mistaking the beginning for the end of the work of reformation.

The representatives of the Humanists, in the nineteenth century, take their stand upon classical education as the sole avenue to culture, as firmly as if we were still in the age of Renascence. Yet, surely, the present intellectual relations of the modern and the ancient worlds are profoundly different from those which obtained three centuries ago. Leaving aside the existence of a great and characteristically modern literature, of modern painting, and, especially, of modern music, there is one feature of the present state of the civilised world which separates it more widely from the Renascence, than the Renascence was separated from the middle ages.

This distinctive character of our own times lies in the vast and constantly increasing part which is played by natural knowledge. Not only is our daily life shaped by it, not only does the prosperity of millions of men depend upon it, but our whole theory of life has long been influenced, consciously or unconsciously, by the general conceptions of the universe, which have been forced upon us by physical science. /149/

In fact, the most elementary acquaintance with the results of scientific investigation shows us that they offer a broad and striking contradiction to the opinion so implicitly credited and taught in the middle ages.

The notions of the beginning and the end of the world entertained by our forefathers are no longer credible. It is very certain that the earth is not the chief body in the material universe, and that the world is not subordinated to man's use. It is even more certain that nature is the expression of a definite order with which nothing interferes, and that the chief business of mankind is to learn that order and govern themselves accordingly. Moreover this scientific "criticism of life" presents itself to us with different credentials from any other. It appeals not to authority, nor to what anybody may have thought or said, but to nature. It admits that all our interpretations of natural fact are more or less imperfect and symbolic, and bids the learner seek for truth not among words but among things. It warns us that the assertion which outstrips evidence is not only a blunder but a crime.

The purely classical education advocated by the representatives of the Humanists in our day, gives no inkling of all this. A man may be a better scholar than Erasmus, and know no more of the chief causes of the present intellectual fermentation than Erasmus did. Scholarly and /150/ pious persons, worthy of all respect, favor us with allocutions upon the sadness of the antagonism of science to their mediaeval way of thinking, which betray an ignorance of the first principles of scientific investigation, an incapacity for understanding what a man of science means by veracity, and an unconsciousness of the weight of established scientific truths, which is almost comical.

There is no great force in the *tu quoque* argument, or else the advocates of scientific education might fairly enough retort upon the modern Humanists that they may be learned specialists, but that they possess no such sound foundation for a criticism of life as deserves the name of culture. And, indeed, if we were disposed to be cruel, we might urge that the Humanists have brought this reproach upon themselves, not because they are too full of the spirit of the ancient Greek, but because they lack it.

The period of the Renascence is commonly called that of the "Revival of Letters," as if the influences then brought to bear upon the mind of Western Europe had been wholly exhausted in the field of literature. I think it is very commonly forgotten that the revival of science, effected by the same agency, although less conspicuous, was not less momentous.

In fact, the few and scattered students of nature of that day picked up the clue to her secrets exactly as it fell from the hands of the /151/ Greeks a thousand years before. The foundations of mathematics were so well laid by them, that our children learn their geometry from a book written for the schools of Alexandria two thousand years ago. Modern astronomy is the natural continuation and development of the work of Hipparchus and of Ptolemy; modern physics of that of Democritus and of Archimedes; it was long before modern biological science outgrew the knowledge bequeathed to us by Aristotle, by Theophrastus, and by Galen.

We cannot know all the best thoughts and sayings of the Greeks unless we know what they thought about natural phaenomena. We cannot fully apprehend their criticism of life unless we understand the extent to which that criticism was affected by scientific conceptions. We falsely pretend to be the inheritors of their culture, unless we are penetrated, as the best minds among them were, with an unhesitating faith that the free employment of reason, in accordance with scientific method, is the sole method of reaching truth.

Thus I venture to think that the pretensions of our modern Humanists to the possession of the monopoly of culture and to the exclusive inheritance of the spirit of antiquity must be abated, if not abandoned. But I should be very sorry that anything I have said should be taken to imply a desire on my part to depreciate the value of classical education, as it might be and as it some- /152/ times is. The native capacities of mankind vary no less than their opportunities; and while culture is one, the road by which one man may best reach it is widely different from that which is most advantageous to another. Again, while scientific education is yet inchoate and tentative, classical education is thoroughly well organized upon the practical experience of generations of teachers. So that, given ample time for learning and estimation for ordinary life, or for a literary career, I do not think that a young Englishman in search of culture can do better than follow the course usually marked out for him, supplementing its deficiencies by his own efforts.

But for those who mean to make science their serious occupation; or who intend to follow the profession of medicine; or who have to enter early upon the business of life; for all these, in my opinion, classical education is a mistake; and it is for this reason that I am glad to see "mere literary education and instruction" shut out from the curriculum of Sir Josiah Mason's College, seeing that its inclusion would probably lead to the introduction of the ordinary smattering of Latin and Greek.

Nevertheless, I am the last person to question the importance of genuine literary education, or to suppose that intellectual culture can be complete without it. An exclusively scientific training will bring about a mental twist as surely as an /153/ exclusively literary training. The value of the cargo does not compensate for a ship's being out of trim; and I should be very sorry to think that the Scientific College would turn out none but lop-sided men.

There is no need, however, that such a catastrophe should happen. Instruction in English, French, and German is provided, and thus the three greatest literatures of the modern world are made accessible to the student.

French and German, and especially the latter language, are absolutely indispensable to those who desire full knowledge in any department of science. But even supposing that the knowledge of these languages acquired is not more than sufficient for purely scientific purposes, every Englishman has, in his native tongue, an almost perfect instrument of literary expression; and, in his own literature, models of every kind of literary excellence. If an Englishman cannot get literary culture out of his Bible, his Shakespeare, his Milton, neither, in my belief, will the profoundest study of Homer and Sophocles, Virgil and Horace, give it to him.

Thus, since the constitution of the College makes sufficient provision for literary as well as for scientific education, and since artistic instruction is also contemplated, it seems to me that a fairly complete culture is offered to all who are willing to take advantage of it. /154/

Matthew Arnold

LITERATURE AND SCIENCE

Matthew Arnold (1822–1888) was an English poet, critic, and classical scholar. Arnold's poetry, the bulk of which was written during the first half of his career, has earned him a place as one of the leading poets of the nineteenth century. But he is perhaps more famous as a critic of literature, society, and religion. During the latter half of his career he virtually gave up writing poetry in order to deal in prose with the social and cultural problems of his day. In this period he produced such classic works as the first series of Essays in Criticism *(1865),* Culture and Anarchy *(1869),* Literature and Dogma *(1873), and* Discourses in America *(1885).*

"Literature and Science," a reply to the argument of Huxley's Science and Culture, *was first read at Cambridge in 1882 as the Rede Lecture (cf. C. P. Snow's* The Two Cultures, *the Rede Lecture for 1959). During the following year Arnold used a modified version as one of a repertory of three lectures delivered during a tour of America. It was subsequently published in* Discourses in America.

. . . 'An intelligent man,' says Plato, 'will prize those studies which result in his soul getting soberness, righteousness, and wisdom, and will less value the others.' I cannot consider *that* a bad description of the aim of education, and of the motives which should govern us in the choice of studies, whether we are preparing ourselves for a hereditary seat in the English House of Lords or for the pork trade in Chicago.

Still I admit that Plato's world was not ours, that his scorn of trade and handicraft is fantastic, that he had no conception of a great industrial community such as that of the United States, and that such a community must and will shape its education to suit its own needs. If the usual education handed down to it from the past does not suit it, it will certainly before long drop this and try another. The usual education in the past has been mainly literary. The question

From "Literature and Science," in *The Works of Matthew Arnold* (London: Macmillan and Co., Ltd., 1903–1904), Vol. IV, *Discourses in America*, pp. 317–348.

is whether the studies which were long supposed to be the best for all of us are practically the best now; whether others are not better. The tyranny of the past, many think, weighs on us injuriously in the predominance given to letters in education. The question is raised whether, to meet the needs of our modern life, the predominance ought not now to pass from letters to science; and naturally the question is nowhere /320/ raised with more energy than here in the United States. The design of abasing what is called 'mere literary instruction and education,' and of exalting what is called 'sound, extensive, and practical scientific knowledge,' is, in this intensely modern world of the United States, even more perhaps than in Europe, a very popular design, and makes great and rapid progress.

I am going to ask whether the present movement for ousting letters from their old predominance in education, and for transferring the predominance in education to the natural sciences, whether this brisk and flourishing movement ought to prevail, and whether it is likely that in the end it really will prevail. An objection may be raised which I will anticipate. My own studies have been almost wholly in letters, and my visits to the field of the natural sciences have been very slight and inadequate, although those sciences have always strongly moved my curiosity. A man of letters, it will perhaps be said, is not competent to discuss the comparative merits of letters and natural science as means of education. To this objection I reply, first of all, that his incompetence, if he attempts the discussion but is really incompetent for it, will be abundantly visible; nobody will be taken in; he will have plenty of sharp observers and critics to save mankind from that danger. But the line I am going to follow is, as you will soon discover, so extremely simple, that perhaps it may be followed /321/ without failure even by one who for a more ambitious line of discussion would be quite incompetent.

Some of you may possibly remember a phrase of mine which has been the object of a good deal of comment; an observation to the effect that in our culture, the aim being *to know ourselves and the world,* we have, as the means to this end, *to know the best which has been thought and said in the world.* A man of science, who is also an excellent writer and the very prince of debaters, Professor Huxley, in a discourse at the opening of Sir Josiah Mason's college at Birmingham, laying hold of this phrase, expanded it by quoting some more words of mine, which are these: 'The civilised world is to be regarded as now being, for intellectual and spiritual purposes, one great confederation, bound to a joint action and working to a common result; and whose members have for their proper outfit a knowledge of Greek, Roman, and Eastern antiquity, and of one another. Special local and temporary advantages being put out of account, that modern nation will in the intellectual and spiritual sphere make most progress, which most thoroughly carries out this programme.'

Now on my phrase, thus enlarged, Professor Huxley remarks that when I speak of the above-mentioned knowledge as enabling us to know ourselves and the world, I assert *literature* to /322/ contain the materials which suffice for thus making us know ourselves and the world. But it is not by any means clear, says he, that after having learnt all which ancient and modern literatures have to tell us, we have laid a sufficiently broad and deep foundation for that criticism of life, that knowledge of ourselves and the world, which constitutes culture. On the contrary, Professor Huxley declares that he finds himself 'wholly unable to admit that either nations or individuals will really advance, if their outfit draws nothing from the stores of physical science. An army without weapons of precision, and with no particular base of operations, might more hopefully enter upon a campaign on the Rhine, than a man, devoid of a knowledge of what physical science has done in the last century, upon a criticism of life.'

This shows how needful it is for those who are to discuss any matter together, to have a common understanding as to the sense of the terms they employ, — how needful, and how difficult. What Professor Huxley says, implies just the reproach which is so often brought against the study of *belles lettres,* as they are called: that the study is an elegant one, but slight and ineffectual; a smattering of Greek and Latin and other ornamental things, of little use for any one whose object is to get at truth, and to be a practical man. So, too, M. Renan talks of the 'superficial humanism' of a school- /323/ course which treats us as if we were all going to be poets, writers, preachers, orators, and he opposes this humanism to positive science, or the critical search after truth. And there is always a tendency in those who are remonstrating against the predominance of letters in education, to understand by letters *belles lettres,* and by *belles lettres* a superficial humanism, the opposite of science or true knowledge.

But when we talk of knowing Greek and Roman antiquity, for instance, which is the knowledge people have called the humanities, I for my part mean a knowledge which is something more than a superficial humanism, mainly decorative. 'I call all teaching *scientific*,' says Wolf, the critic of Homer, 'which is systematically laid out and followed up to its original sources. For example: a knowledge of classical antiquity is scientific when the remains of classical antiquity are correctly studied in the original languages.' There can be no doubt that Wolf is perfectly right; that all learning is scientific which is systematically laid out and followed up to its original sources, and that a genuine humanism is scientific.

When I speak of knowing Greek and Roman antiquity, therefore, as a help to knowing ourselves and the world, I mean more than a knowledge of so much vocabulary, so much grammar, so many portions of authors in the Greek and Latin languages, I mean knowing the Greeks /324/ and Romans, and their life and genius, and what they were and did in the world; what we get from them, and what is its value. That, at least, is the ideal; and when we talk of endeavouring to know Greek and Roman antiquity, as a help to knowing ourselves and the world, we mean endeavouring so to know them as to satisfy this ideal, however much we may still fall short of it.

The same also as to knowing our own and other modern nations, with the like aim of getting to understand ourselves and the world. To know the best that has been thought and said by the modern nations, is to know, says Professor Huxley, 'only what modern *literatures* have to tell us; it is the criticism of life contained in modern literature.' And yet 'the distinctive character of our times,' he urges, 'lies in the vast and constantly increasing part which is played by natural knowledge.' And how, therefore, can a man, devoid of knowledge of what physical science has done in the last century, enter hopefully upon a criticism of modern life?

Let us, I say, be agreed about the meaning of the terms we are using. I talk of knowing the best which has been thought and uttered in the world; Professor Huxley says this means knowing *literature*. Literature is a large word; it may mean everything written with letters or printed in a book. Euclid's *Elements* and /325/ Newton's *Principia* are thus literature. All knowledge that reaches us through books is literature. But by literature Professor Huxley means *belles lettres*. He means to make me say, that knowing the best which has been thought and said by the modern nations is knowing their *belles lettres* and no more. And this is no sufficient equipment, he argues, for a criticism of modern life. But as I do not mean, by knowing ancient Rome, knowing merely more or less of Latin *belles lettres,* and taking no account of Rome's military, and political, and legal, and administrative work in the world; and as, by knowing ancient Greece, I understand knowing her as the giver of Greek art, and the guide to a free and right use of reason and to scientific method, and the founder of our mathematics and physics and astronomy and biology, — I understand knowing her as all this, and not merely knowing certain Greek poems, and histories, and treatises, and speeches, — so as to the knowledge of modern nations also. By knowing modern nations, I mean not merely knowing their *belles lettres,* but knowing also what has been done by such men as Copernicus, Galileo, Newton, Darwin. 'Our ancestors learned,' says Professor Huxley, 'that the earth is the centre of the visible universe, and that man is the cynosure of things terrestrial; and more especially was it inculcated that the course of nature had no fixed order, but that it could be, and constantly, was /326/ altered.' But for us now, continues Professor Huxley, 'the notions of the beginning and the end of the world entertained by our forefathers are no longer credible. It is very certain that the earth is not the chief body in the material universe, and that the world is not subordinated to man's use. It is even more certain that nature is the expression of a definite order, with which nothing interferes.' 'And yet,' he cries, 'the purely classical education advocated by the representatives of the humanists in our day gives no inkling of all this!'

In due place and time I will just touch upon that vexed question of classical education; but at present the question is as to what is meant by knowing the best which modern nations have thought and said. It is not knowing their *belles lettres* merely which is meant. To know Italian *belles lettres* is not to know Italy, and to know English *belles lettres* is not to know England. Into knowing Italy and England there comes a great deal more, Galileo and Newton amongst it. The reproach of being a superficial humanism, a tincture of *belles lettres,* may attach rightly enough to some other disciplines; but to the particular discipline recommended when I proposed knowing the best that has been thought and said in the world, it does not apply. In that best I certainly include what in modern times has been thought and said by the great observers and knowers of nature. /327/

There is, therefore, really no question between Professor Huxley and me as to whether knowing the great results of the modern scientific study of nature is not required as a part of our culture, as well as knowing the products of literature and art. But to follow the processes by which those results are reached, ought, say the friends of physical science, to be made the staple of education for the bulk of mankind. And here there does arise a question between those whom Professor Huxley calls with playful sarcasm 'the Levites of culture,' and those whom the poor humanist is sometimes apt to regard as its Nebuchadnezzars.

The great results of the scientific investigation of nature we are agreed upon knowing, but how much of our study are we bound to give to the processes by which those results are reached? The results have their visible bearing on human life. But all the processes, too, all the items of fact, by which those results are reached and established, are interesting. All knowledge is interesting to a wise man, and the knowledge of nature is interesting to all men. It is very interesting to know, that, from the albuminous white of the egg, the chick in the egg gets the materials for its flesh, bones, blood, and feathers; while, from the fatty yolk of the egg, it gets the heat and energy which enable it at length to break its shell and begin the world. It is less interesting, perhaps, but still it is interesting, to /328/ know that when a taper burns, the wax is converted into carbonic acid and water. Moreover, it is quite true that the habit of dealing with facts, which is given by the study of nature, is, as the friends of physical science praise it for being, an excellent discipline. The appeal, in the study of nature, is constantly to observation and experiment; not only is it said that the thing is so, but we can be made to see that it is so. Not only does a man tell us that when a taper burns the wax is converted into carbonic acid and water, as a man may tell us, if he likes, that Charon is punting his ferry-boat on the river Styx, or that Victor Hugo is a sublime poet, or Mr. Gladstone the most admirable of statesmen; but we are made to see that the conversion into carbonic acid and water does actually happen. This reality of natural knowledge it is, which makes the friends of physical science contrast it, as a knowledge of things, with the humanist's knowledge, which is, say they, a knowledge of words. And hence Professor Huxley is moved to lay it down that, 'for the purpose of attaining real culture, an exclusively scientific education is at least as effectual as an exclusively literary education.' And a certain President of the Section for Mechanical Science in the British Association is, in Scripture phrase, 'very bold,' and declares that if a man, in his mental training, 'has substituted literature and history for natural science, he has chosen the less useful alternative.' /329/ But whether we go these lengths or not, we must all admit that in natural science the habit gained of dealing with facts is a most valuable discipline, and that every one should have some experience of it.

More than this, however, is demanded by the reformers. It is proposed to make the training in natural science the main part of education, for the great majority of mankind at any rate. And here, I confess, I part company with the friends of physical science, with whom up to this point I have been agreeing. In differing from them, however, I wish to proceed with the utmost caution and diffidence. The smallness of my own acquaintance with the disciplines of natural science is ever before my mind, and I am fearful of doing these disciplines an injustice. The ability and pugnacity of the partisans of natural science make them formidable persons to contradict. The tone of tentative inquiry, which befits a being of dim faculties and bounded knowledge, is the tone I would wish to take and not to depart from. At present it seems to me, that those who are for giving to natural knowledge, as they call it, the chief place in the education of the majority of mankind, leave one important thing out of their account: the constitution of human nature. But I put this forward on the strength of some facts not at all recondite, very far from it; facts capable of being stated in the simplest possible fashion, and /330/ to which, if I so state them, the man of science will, I am sure, be willing to allow their due weight.

Deny the facts altogether, I think, he hardly can. He can hardly deny, that when we set ourselves to enumerate the powers which go to the building up of human life, and say that they are the power of conduct, the power of intellect and knowledge, the power of beauty, and the power of social life and manners, —he can hardly deny that this scheme, though drawn in rough and plain lines enough, and not pretending to scientific exactness, does yet give a fairly true representation of the matter. Human nature is built up by these powers; we have the need for them all. When we have rightly met and adjusted the claims of them all, we shall then be in a fair way for getting soberness and righteousness, with wisdom. This is evident enough, and the friends of physical science would admit it.

But perhaps they may not have sufficiently observed another thing: namely, that the several powers just mentioned are not isolated, but there is, in the generality of mankind, a perpetual tendency to relate them one to another in divers ways. With one such way of relating them I am particularly concerned now. Following our instinct for intellect and knowledge, we acquire pieces of knowledge; and presently, in the generality of men, there arises the desire to relate these pieces of knowledge to our sense for conduct, /331/ to our sense for beauty,—and there is weariness and dissatisfaction if the desire is baulked. Now in this desire lies, I think, the strength of that hold which letters have upon us.

All knowledge is, as I said just now, interesting; and even items of knowledge which from the nature of the case cannot well be related, but must stand isolated in our thoughts, have their interest. Even lists of exceptions have their interest. If we are studying Greek accents, it is interesting to know that *pais* and *pas*, and some other monosyllables of the same form of declension, do not take the circumflex upon the last syllable of the genitive plural, but vary, in this respect, from the common rule. If we are studying physiology, it is interesting to know that the pulmonary artery carries dark blood and the pulmonary vein carries bright blood, departing in this respect from the common rule for the division of labour between the veins and the arteries. But every one knows how we seek naturally to combine the pieces of our knowledge together, to bring them under general rules, to relate them to principles; and how unsatisfactory and tiresome it would be to go on for ever learning lists of exceptions, or accumulating items of fact which must stand isolated.

Well, that same need of relating our knowledge, which operates here within the sphere of our knowledge itself, we shall find operating, /332/ also, outside that sphere. We experience, as we go on learning and knowing,—the vast majority of us experience,—the need of relating what we have learnt and known to the sense which we have in us for conduct, to the sense which we have in us for beauty.

A certain Greek prophetess of Mantineia in Arcadia, Diotima by name, once explained to the philosopher Socrates that love, and impulse, and bent of all kinds, is, in fact, nothing else but the desire in men that good should for ever be present to them. This desire for good, Diotima assured Socrates, is our fundamental desire, of which fundamental desire every impulse in us is only some one particular form. And therefore this fundamental desire it is, I suppose,—this desire in men that good should be for ever present to them,— which acts in us when we feel the impulse for relating our knowledge to our sense for conduct and to our sense for beauty. At any rate, with men in general the instinct exists. Such is human nature. And the instinct, it will be admitted, is innocent, and human nature is preserved by our following the lead of its innocent instincts. Therefore, in seeking to gratify this instinct in question, we are following the instinct of self-preservation in humanity.

But, no doubt, some kinds of knowledge cannot be made to directly serve the instinct in question, cannot be directly related to the sense /333/ for beauty, to the sense for conduct. These are instrument-knowledges; they lead on to other knowledges, which can. A man who passes his life in instrument-knowledges is a specialist. They may be invaluable as instruments to something beyond, for those who have the gift thus to employ them; and they may be disciplines in themselves wherein it is useful for every one to have some school-ing. But it is inconceivable that the generality of men should pass all their mental life with Greek accents or with formal logic. My friend Professor Sylvester, who is one of the first mathematicians in the world, holds transcen-dental doctrines as to the virtue of mathematics, but those doctrines are not for common men. In the very Senate House and heart of our English Cam-bridge I once ventured, though not without an apology for my profaneness, to hazard the opinion that for the majority of mankind a little of mathematics, even, goes a long way. Of course this is quite consistent with their being of immense importance as an instrument to something else; but it is the few who have the aptitude for thus using them, not the bulk of mankind.

The natural sciences do not, however, stand on the same footing with these instrument-knowledges. Experience shows us that the generality of men will find more interest in learning that, when a taper burns, the wax is converted into carbonic acid and water, or in /334/ learning the explanation of the phenomenon of dew, or in learning how the circulation of the blood is carried on, than they find in learning that the genitive plural of *pais* and *pas* does not take the circumflex on the termination. And one piece of natural knowledge is added to another, and others are added to that, and at last we come to propositions so interesting as Mr. Darwin's famous proposition that 'our ancestor was a hairy quadruped furnished with a tail and pointed ears, prob-ably arboreal in his habits.' Or we come to propositions of such reach and magnitude as those which Professor Huxley delivers, when he says that the notions of our forefathers about the beginning and the end of the world were all wrong, and that nature is the expression of a definite order with which nothing interferes.

Interesting, indeed, these results of science are, important they are, and we should all of us be acquainted with them. But what I now wish you to mark is, that we are still, when they are propounded to us and we receive them, we are still in the sphere of intellect and knowledge. And for the generality of men there will be found, I say, to arise, when they have duly taken in the proposition that their ancestor was 'a hairy quadruped furnished with a tail and pointed ears, probably arboreal in his habits,' there will be found to arise an invincible desire to relate this proposition to the sense in us for /335/ conduct, and to the sense in us for beauty. But this the men of science will not do for us, and will hardly even profess to do. They will give us other pieces of knowledge, other facts, about other animals and their ancestors, or about plants, or about stones, or about stars; and they may finally bring us to those great 'general conceptions of the universe, which are forced upon us all,' says Professor Huxley, 'by the progress of physical science.' But still it will be *knowledge* only which they give us; knowledge not put for us into relation with our sense for conduct, our sense for beauty, and touched with emotion by being so put; not thus put for us, and therefore, to the majority of mankind, after a certain while, unsatisfying, wearying.

Not to the born naturalist, I admit. But what do we mean by a born natu-ralist? We mean a man in whom the zeal for observing nature is so uncom-monly strong and eminent, that it marks him off from the bulk of mankind. Such a man will pass his life happily in collecting natural knowledge and reasoning upon it, and will ask for nothing, or hardly anything, more. I have heard it said that the sagacious and admirable naturalist whom we lost not very long ago, Mr. Darwin, once owned to a friend that for his part he did not experience the necessity for two things which most men find so necessary to them—religion and poetry; /336/ science and the domestic affections, he thought, were enough. To a born naturalist, I can well understand that this should seem so. So absorbing is his occupation with nature, so strong his love for his occupation, that he goes on acquiring natural knowledge and reasoning upon it, and has little time or inclination for thinking about getting it related to the desire in man for conduct, the desire in man for beauty. He relates it to them for himself as he goes along, so far as he feels the need; and he draws from the domestic affections all the additional solace necessary. But then Darwins are extremely rare. Another great and admirable master of natural knowledge, Faraday, was a Sandemanian. That is to say, he related his knowledge to his instinct for conduct and to his instinct for beauty, by the aid of that respectable Scottish sectary, Robert Sandeman. And so strong, in general, is the demand of religion and poetry to have their share in a man, to associate themselves with his knowing, and to relieve and rejoice it, that, probably, for one man amongst us with the disposition to do as Darwin did in this respect, there are at least fifty with the disposition to do as Faraday.

Education lays hold upon us, in fact, by satisfying this demand. Professor Huxley holds up to scorn mediæval education, with its neglect of the knowledge of nature, its poverty even of literary studies, its formal logic devoted to /337/ 'showing how and why that which the Church said was true must be true.' But the great mediæval Universities were not brought into being, we may be sure, by the zeal for giving a jejune and contemptible education. Kings have been their nursing fathers, and queens have been their nursing mothers, but not for this. The mediæval Universities came into being, because the supposed knowledge, delivered by Scripture and the Church, so deeply engaged men's hearts, by so simply, easily, and powerfully relating itself to their desire for conduct, their desire for beauty. All other knowledge was dominated by this supposed knowledge and was subordinated to it, because of the surpassing strength of the hold which it gained upon the affections of men, by allying itself profoundly with their sense for conduct, their sense for beauty.

But now, says Professor Huxley, conceptions of the universe fatal to the notions held by our forefathers have been forced upon us by physical science. Grant to him that they are thus fatal, that the new conceptions must and will soon become current everywhere, and that everyone will finally perceive them to be fatal to the beliefs of our forefathers. The need of humane letters, as they are truly called, because they serve the paramount desire in men that good should be for ever present to them, — the need of humane letters, to establish a relation between /338/ the new conceptions, and our instinct for beauty, our instinct for conduct, is only the more visible. The Middle Age could do without humane letters, as it could do without the study of nature, because its supposed knowledge was made to engage its emotions so powerfully. Grant that the supposed knowledge disappears, its power of being made to engage the emotions will of course disappear along with it, — but the emotions themselves, and their claim to be engaged and satisfied, will remain. Now if we find by experience that humane letters have an undeniable power of engaging the emotions, the importance of humane letters in a man's training becomes not less, but greater, in proportion to the success of modern science in extirpating what it calls 'mediæval thinking.'

Have humane letters, then, have poetry and eloquence, the power here attributed to them of engaging the emotions, and do they exercise it? And if they have it and exercise it, *how* do they exercise it, so as to exert an influence upon man's sense for conduct, his sense for beauty? Finally, even if they can and do exert an influence upon the senses in question, how are they to relate to them the results, — the modern results, — of natural science? All these questions may be asked. First, have poetry and eloquence the power of calling out the emotions? The appeal is to experience. Experience shows that for the vast majority of men, for mankind in general, /339/ they have the power. Next, do they exercise it? They do. But then, *how* do they exercise it so as to affect man's sense for conduct, his sense for beauty? And this is perhaps a case for applying the Preacher's words: 'Though a man labour to seek it out, yet he shall not find it; yea, farther, though a wise man think to know it, yet shall he not be able to find it.'[1] Why should it be one thing, in its effect upon the emotions, to say, 'Patience is a virtue,' and quite another thing, in its effect upon the emotions, to say with Homer.

$$\tau\lambda\eta\tau\grave{o}\nu\ \gamma\grave{\alpha}\rho\ Mo\hat{\imath}\rho\alpha\iota\ \theta\upsilon\mu\grave{o}\nu\ \theta\acute{\epsilon}\sigma\alpha\nu\ \grave{\alpha}\nu\theta\rho\acute{\omega}\pi o\iota\sigma\iota\nu-^{2}$$

'for an enduring heart have the destinies appointed to the children of men'? Why should it be one thing, in its effect upon the emotions, to say with the philosopher Spinoza, *Felicitas in eo consistit quod homo suum esse conservare potest* — 'Man's happiness consists in his being able to preserve his own essence,' and quite another thing, in its effect upon the emotions, to say with the Gospel, 'What is a man advantaged, if he gain the whole world, and lose himself, forfeit himself?' How does this difference of effect arise? I cannot tell, and I am not much concerned to know; the important thing is that it does arise, and that we can profit by it. But how, finally, are poetry and eloquence to exercise the power of relating the modern /340/ results of natural science to man's instinct for conduct, his instinct for beauty? And here again I answer that I do not know *how* they will exercise it, but that they can and will exercise it I am sure. I do not mean that modern philosophical poets and modern philosophical moralists are to come and relate for us, in express terms, the results of modern scientific research to our instinct for conduct, our instinct for beauty. But I mean that we shall find, as a matter of experience, if we know the best that has been thought and uttered in the world, we shall find that the art and poetry and eloquence of men who lived, perhaps, long ago, who had the most limited natural knowledge, who had the most erroneous conceptions about many important matters, we shall find that this art, and poetry, and eloquence, have in fact not only the power of refreshing and delighting us, they have also the power, — such is the strength and worth, in essentials, of their authors' criticism of life, — they have a fortifying, and elevating, and quickening, and suggestive power, capable of wonderfully helping us to relate the results of modern science to our need for conduct, our need for beauty. Homer's conceptions of the physical universe were, I imagine, grotesque; but really, under the shock of hearing from modern science that 'the world is not subordinated to man's use, and that man is not the cynosure of things terrestrial,' I could, for my own part, /341/ desire no better comfort than Homer's line which I quoted just now,

$$\tau\lambda\eta\tau\grave{o}\nu\ \gamma\grave{\alpha}\rho\ Mo\hat{\imath}\rho\alpha\iota\ \theta\upsilon\mu\grave{o}\nu\ \theta\acute{\epsilon}\sigma\alpha\nu\ \grave{\alpha}\nu\theta\rho\acute{\omega}\pi o\iota\sigma\iota\nu-$$

'for an enduring heart have the destinies appointed to the children of men'!

And the more that men's minds are cleared, the more that the results of science are frankly accepted, the more that poetry and eloquence come to be received and studied as what in truth they really are, — the criticism of

1. Ecclesiastes, viii. 17. /340/
2. *Iliad*, xxiv. 49. /340/

life by gifted men, alive and active with extraordinary power at an unusual number of points; — so much the more will the value of humane letters, and of art also, which is an utterance having a like kind of power with theirs, be felt and acknowledged, and their place in education be secured.

Let us therefore, all of us, avoid indeed as much as possible any invidious comparison between the merits of humane letters, as means of education, and the merits of the natural sciences. But when some President of a Section for Mechanical Science insists on making the comparison, and tells us that 'he who in his training has substituted literature and history for natural science has chosen the less useful alternative,' let us make answer to him that the student of humane letters only, will, at least, know also the great general conceptions brought in by modern physical science; for science, as Professor Huxley says, forces them upon us all. But the /342/ student of the natural sciences only, will, by our very hypothesis, know nothing of humane letters; not to mention that in setting himself to be perpetually accumulating natural knowledge, he sets himself to do what only specialists have in general the gift for doing genially. And so he will probably be unsatisfied, or at any rate incomplete, and even more incomplete than the student of humane letters only.

I once mentioned in a school-report, how a young man in one of our English training colleges having to paraphrase the passage in *Macbeth* beginning,

Can'st thou not minister to a mind diseased?

turned this line into, 'Can you not wait upon the lunatic?' And I remarked what a curious state of things it would be, if every pupil of our national schools knew, let us say, that the moon is two thousand one hundred and sixty miles in diameter, and thought at the same time that a good paraphrase for

Can'st thou not minister to a mind diseased? —

was, 'Can you not wait upon the lunatic?' If one is driven to choose, I think I would rather have a young person ignorant about the moon's diameter, but aware that 'Can you not wait upon the lunatic?' is bad, than a young person whose education had been such as to manage things the other way. /343/

Or to go higher than the pupils of our national schools. I have in my mind's eye a member of our British Parliament who comes to travel here in America, who afterwards relates his travels, and who shows a really masterly knowledge of the geology of this great country and of its mining capabilities, but who ends by gravely suggesting that the United States should borrow a prince from our Royal Family, and should make him their king, and should create a House of Lords of great landed proprietors after the pattern of ours; and then America, he thinks, would have her future happily and perfectly secured. Surely, in this case, the President of the Section for Mechanical Science would himself hardly say that our member of Parliament, by concentrating himself upon geology and mineralogy, and so on, and not attending to literature and history, had 'chosen the more useful alternative.'

If then there is to be separation and option between humane letters on the one hand, and the natural sciences on the other, the great majority of mankind, all who have not exceptional and overpowering aptitudes for the study of nature, would do well, I cannot but think, to choose to be educated in humane letters rather than in the natural sciences. Letters will call out their being at more points, will make them live more. /344/

PART III

Contemporary
Attitudes

Ways of Knowing

The selections in this first section of Part III mainly concern science and the arts as modes of knowledge. In the first essay Stuart Chase explains what science is and what it does. The other spokesmen for science, John R. Baker and Bertrand Russell, discuss the intrinsic values of science and in doing so tell us much about the ways of scientific thinking. Both insist that usefulness and material value are by no means the only or most significant values of science. They point to intrinsic elements: to the optimism and the cumulative character of scientific thought (elements they deny the arts) and to the aesthetic satisfactions derived from giving order and harmony to what was previously disordered. Still another value, developed by Russell, is the detachment or impersonality of scientific method in the search for truth.

Because of the dominance of scientific thinking in modern times, those who speak for the arts are concerned to establish the validity of the arts (especially poetry) by explaining how art has meaning. In doing this, they sometimes contrast the artistic way of knowing with the scientific way. Thus John Ciardi analyzes the difference between a poetic and a scientific knowledge of a horse. Archibald MacLeish argues that poetry, which presents the concrete, deals with knowledge equally as well as science—deals, indeed, with "a kind of knowledge of which science is not capable." Finally, Maxwell Anderson, with energetic optimism, points to the artist's "faith in the human race and its gradual acquisition of wisdom." Contrary to Baker and Russell, he sees the arts as evidence of cumulative moral and intellectual progress.

Stuart Chase

WHAT SCIENCE IS

Stuart Chase (1888–   ), an American economist of great energies and wide interests, has written numerous books concerning economic and social problems. In his first important work, The Tragedy of Waste *(1925), he deals with the misuse of money, manpower, and natural resources, a theme which recurs in such works as* Rich Land, Poor Land *(1936) and* Idle Money, Idle Men *(1940). In* The Proper Study of Mankind *(1948; rev. ed. in consulation with Edmund de S. Brunner, 1956) and* Roads to Agreement *(in collaboration with his wife, Marian Tyler,. 1951) he has concerned himself with the field of social science. Chase has also dealt with the problems of semantics in* The Tyranny of Words *(1938) and* The Power of Words *(with Marian Tyler, 1954).*

From *The Proper Study of Mankind*, rev. ed., in consultation with Edmund de S. Brunner (New York: Harper & Brothers, 1956).

What Is "Science"?

The scientific method tells us not how things *ought* to behave, but how they do in fact behave. Today it is universally applied to problems connected with matter and energy, and occasionally applied to many other sorts of problems, as we shall see. It is the only method yet discovered which produces knowledge that stays put, at least until a closer fit to reality is found. One can think of scientific achievement as a storehouse with many well-filled shelves, their contents neatly classified and ready for use by any qualified student. An engineer could not build a bridge without going to the storehouse for the equations of stress and strain. A doctor could not write a prescription without referring to carefully tested knowledge on the shelves. Engineers in a dozen countries are now drawing on recent deposits of knowledge to build their first atomic power plants.

"Some people . . . say that social science isn't science. Some say that astrology is a science, and so is dowsing. Some speak of the science of boxing; while if you call a person a "scientist" in certain of our sunnier states, he may think you mean a Christian Scientist.

"Science" is a roomy term, covering a wide range of subject matter and behavior. There is no one proper meaning. For instance, *Webster's New World Dictionary*, 1953, gives six different meanings:

1. Knowledge as opposed to intuition.
2. Systematized knowledge derived from observation and experiment.
3. A branch of knowledge—as the science of music.
4. A branch of natural science—as physics or chemistry.
5. Skill, based on training—as the science of boxing.
6. Christian Science.

The two-volume *Oxford Dictionary* explains how "science" formerly applied to philosophy, and was often synonymous with the "seven liberal arts" of grammar, logic, rhetoric, arith- /5/ metic, music, geometry, and astronomy. About 100 years ago the concept of the "exact sciences" came in, referring to astronomy, physics, and the natural sciences; but the other meanings still have plenty of life in them.

If we select "exact science," and add the idea of the "scientific method" or the "scientific attitude" in approaching a given problem, we shall come close to what is meant by "science" in this book.[1]

Morris R. Cohen, in his *Logic and Scientific Method*, examines the various techniques for discovering truth, and finds none but the scientific method free from human caprice and wishful thinking. None of the others, he says, is flexible enough to admit an error. "What is called the scientific method differs radically from these, by encouraging and developing the *utmost possible doubt*, so that what is left after such doubt is always supported by the best available evidence." As new evidence comes in, new doubts may arise and must be taken into account. "It is the essence of the scientific method to make them an integral part of the knowledge so far attained."

Science as thus defined—corresponding to Webster's second definition—is

1. *The American College Dictionary* defines social science as: "The group of studies seeking to establish a science of the social life of human groups." Increasingly one hears the term "the behavioral sciences." /6/

dynamic, open at the top, and thus able to come ever closer to the truth. It has abandoned absolutes in favor of relationships and probabilities. Nothing in modern science can be dogmatically taken as 100 percent true, though quite a few things may be 99.999. . . . For a long time physicists regarded Newton's laws of gravitation as 100 percent so — Absolute Space, Absolute Time, Absolute Motion. Einstein's principles of relativity shattered these absolutes. Newton was not wrong in terrestrial areas, but his laws did not always apply in astronomical areas. Einstein found a closer fit to the space-time world. Presently some genius may discover a still closer fit.

Einstein's work gives us a clear idea of three cardinal steps in exact science: /6/

First, he was worried and curious about the relation between matter and energy, and got together the knowledge already available.

Second, he assembled his thoughts in the language of mathematics and came out with a startling hypothesis governing the conversion of matter into energy.

Third, he proposed various experiments to verify the hypothesis, such as the bending of light rays as they passed the sun in an eclipse.

The experiments were performed and in due course relativity was put in the storehouse of knowledge, later to be abundantly verified by the Manhattan Project. If the experimental results had been persistently negative, the theory would have gone into the wastebasket, together with thousands of other brilliant theories which have not survived the test of verification.

Human emotions are excluded as far as possible from scientific discipline. Alone among man's activities, science can resolve problems independently of our desires and wills. Scientific method, as Morris Cohen said, is systematic doubt. To fudge an experiment, to slant a conclusion, to report anything but the whole truth as one knows it alone in the night, brings ignominy and oblivion. There can be no secret processes, no patent medicines, no private understandings or payoffs on the side. The calculations must be laid on the table, face up, for all the world to see. In this sense, science is perhaps the most *moral* of all man's disciplines. It will be corrupted and debased if ever its direction falls permanently into the hands of national governments and ideologists. It is as international as the north wind.

One comforting thing about adopting the scientific attitude is that you no longer need try to save face when you find that you are wrong. You expect to be wrong a good part of the time. Ehrlich was wrong 605 times before he found the famous specific "606" for venereal disease.

A rough test of science is the amount of argument a conclusion generates. Men used to argue violently about the composition of water, and about the nature of heat. Today they know /7/ the answers and arguments are stilled. An argument may answer a debater or a politician, but it will never answer an experiment. An experiment can be answered only by a more careful experiment.

Finding a Pattern

Another broad definition of science is *finding a pattern in a set of phenomena.* Once the pattern is determined, prediction becomes possible. Failing prediction, we are still in the pre-scientific stage. One of the earliest scientific patterns was the movement of the stars across the heavens. For millennia men had watched them in wonder and perplexity; but some 5,000 years ago a few of the more curious among the watchers began to name them, trace their courses, and predict when they would return.

Mendeleev's Periodic Table is another revealing example of finding a pattern, this one in the atomic weights of the various elements, and with it predicting new elements which no one had ever found on earth. Presently they were found, each in its proper place. Another pattern is the Reproductive Index whereby future population curves can be predicted.

Observation, whether in astronomy or sociology, identifies the pattern and checks it. Prediction then becomes possible. The magnetic compass, for instance, can be relied on to tell us which way is north. Next we invariably inquire: *Why?* Finding an answer is the next long step in science. The planets move so and so, we can plot them to the second. *Why* do they move that way? This is a much harder question. Nobody even suspected why planets moved the way they did until Newton worked out the laws of gravitation. Nobody yet knows much about the magnetic field governing the compass.

Patterns of Human Behavior

A good deal of natural science, and more social science, is still in the prediction stage. If this occurs, then that will follow. The *understanding* stage, finding the why, is far advanced in /8/ physics, just beginning in sociology. But the difference is in degree, not in kind. Scientists can find patterns in the behavior of people as well as in the behavior of electrons. On this level of discussion, there is no difference between social science and natural science. On this level we define social science as *the use of the scientific method to answer questions about human behavior.* Science ·goes with the method, not with the subject matter.

If the whys are carried far enough, they take us into the realm of unanswerable questions, where no operations can be performed to obtain an answer. Some questions, formerly supposed unanswerable, have yielded to new techniques of investigation, which themselves have uncovered still newer and more baffling problems. Many are likely to remain forever closed to human understanding. We shall have more to say about this later.

"The social realm," said the great sociologist Emile Durkheim, "is a natural realm which differs from the others only by a greater complexity. Now it is impossible that nature should differ radically from itself in one case and the other in regard to which is most essential. The fundamental relations that exist between things . . . cannot be essentially dissimilar in the different realms."

The informal picture I carry around in my mind of a social scientist is that of a man with a notebook watching people behave. He may be watching a town meeting in New England, a religious riot in India, a nursery school in Pasadena, a Japanese internment camp. Perhaps my most vivid picture is of the man with the notebook at the Hawthorne plant of the Western Electric Company, finding out in a world-famous experiment what makes workers work.

The scientific investigator puts down what he sees, not what he wants to see. He puts it down in such a way that other observers can verify his findings. Without a situation where the findings of one observer can be checked by other competent observers and agreement reached, we must surrender the idea of the scientific method. /9/

John Ciardi

HOW DOES A POEM MEAN?

John Ciardi (1916–   ) is an American poet, critic, translator, and editor who has published various volumes of poetry, among them Homeward to America *(1940),* Live Another Day *(1951),* I Marry You *(1958), and* 39 Poems *(1959). He is also well known for his translation of the* Inferno *of Dante (1954) and for* How Does a Poem Mean? *(1959), a critical anthology. His reviews and critical articles on poetry for the* Saturday Review, *for which he is poetry editor, have attracted attention and controversy.*

"Bitzer," said Thomas Gradgrind, "your definition of a horse."

"Quadruped. Gramnivorous. Forty teeth, namely twenty-four grinders, four eye-teeth, and twelve incisive. Sheds coat in the spring; in marshy countries sheds hoofs too. Hoofs hard, but requiring to be shod with iron. Age known by marks in mouth." Thus (and much more) Bitzer.

"Now girl number twenty," said Mr. Gradgrind, "you know what a horse is."

Charles Dickens, *Hard Times*

The School of Hard Facts over which Mr. Gradgrind presided was a school of fixed answers. Mr. Gradgrind would have agreed with a recent anthologist who wrote that the inspection of a poem should be as certain as a chemical analysis. Mr. Gradgrind would have assured himself that he was a first-class critic, of poetry as of horses. "Now girl number twenty," he would have said looking up from his analysis, "you know what a poem is."

Today, a century later than Mr. Gradgrind's School of Hard Facts, the idea is still current that the methods of measurement evolved by the physical sciences can be applied to all human processes. And there still lingers the belief that a dictionary definition is a satisfactory description of an idea or of an experience.

There are many grounds on which dictionary definitions can be disputed, but only one need concern us here. Bitzer's definition of a horse was a dictionary definition. Note that it is put almost exclusively in terms of classification. In those terms, it may do as a table of physical characteristics of *Equus caballus.* But what can it possibly say of the experience one has had of the living animal? No horseman ever rode a "gramnivorous quadruped." No gambler ever bet on one. No sculptor ever dreamed one out of a block of stone. For horseman, gambler, and sculptor are involved in a living relation to a living animal, *and the kind of relation is expressed in the language each has evolved for his experience.* ("A good winded bay," says the horseman, "but he has a mouth like iron and won't answer to the bit. He's had bad schooling." Or the gambler: "A good four-year-old. Better than his performance to date. And a good mudder. He's due to win, especially on a wet track. And at nice odds." Or the sculptor: "The set of the stone suggested a rearing posture: the line of force curving down the haunches repeated in the straining line of the neck with the mouth held hard-down by the bit.") Whatever the "gramnivorous quad- /665/

From *How Does a Poem Mean?* Part Three of *An Introduction to Literature,* gen. ed. Gordon N. Ray (Boston: Houghton Mifflin Company, 1959), pp. 663-1022.

ruped" may be to the biologist, these three ways of speaking are three experiences of the living horse. As Tip O'Neill once wrote in a fine sarcastic
line: "There's not a wedding in the world that's worth a running horse." Now
try the line revised: "There is not a marriage ceremony in existence worthy
of comparison with a gramnivorous quadruped of the genus *Equus caballus*
in rapid motion."

The point is that *the language of experience is not the language of classification.*
A boy burning with ambition to become a jockey does not study a text on zoology. He watches horses, he listens to what is said by those who have spent their
lives around horses, he rides them, trains them, feeds them, curries them, pets
them. He lives with intense feelings toward them. He may never learn how
many incisors a horse has, nor how many yards of intestines. What does it
matter? He is concerned with a *feel*, a response-to, a sense of the character
and reaction of the living animal. And zoology cannot give him that. Not all
the anatomizing of all the world's horses could teach a man horse-sense. /666/

John R. Baker

THE APPRECIATION OF SCIENCE
AS AN END IN ITSELF

*John Randal Baker (1900 –   ) is a Fellow of the Royal Society and a Reader
in Cytology at Oxford University. His works include* Sex in Man and Animals *(1926),*
The Scientific Life *(1942),* Science and the Planned State *(1945), and* Principles
of Biological Microtechnique *(1958).*

We must now analyse the immaterial or spiritual values of science.

The history of science suggests that many great investigators have accepted
the value of science as an end in itself as something so obvious as not to require
analysis. Einstein has well expressed what are probably the inarticulate feelings of many people who value science as an end. "The satisfaction of physical
needs," he writes, "is indeed the indispensable precondition of a satisfactory
existence, but in itself it is not enough. In order to be content, men must also
have the possibility of developing their intellectual and artistic powers to
whatever extent accords with their personal characteristics and abilities."

There are reasons for thinking that science is potentially the greatest achievement of the human mind. Optimists may look for that greatest achievement
in ethical perfection. They may be right and I hope they are; but life among
savages has shown me that if civilization and religion have improved men
morally, then the improvement that has occurred has been too small to give
reason for much optimism about the future. In most intellectual fields we cannot look forward with confidence of progress. There is no reason to suppose
that the historians of the future will tower above those of the present /29/
day. Philosophy has given the world some of its greatest geniuses, but the
history of the subject contradicts the idea of a gradual approximation towards
a consensus of opinion on philosophical subjects. We cannot guess the future
of music, but at least it may be said that the world to-day has no composer
who will bear comparison with the geniuses of the past. It is sometimes argued

From *Science and the Planned State* (New York: The Macmillan Company, 1945).

that geniuses are not recognized in their own times, and that we may even now have a genius of musical composition in our midst; but the fallacy of this argument is apparent to anyone who is acquainted with the history of music. The same considerations apply to pictorial art, and there is no sure ground for thinking that we are merely experiencing a phase of relative inactivity which will be followed by a new outburst of progress. In science, on the contrary, the present state of affairs and the prospect for the future are both very good. The standard of excellence is as high as ever it was. We have genius to rank with the greatest of all time (in physics alone we have Bohr, Dirac, Einstein and Schrödinger, and have only recently lost Rutherford and J. J. Thomson). If science be left free to expand, its expansion is inevitable, for science grows by accretion.

The unimportant composer or artist does nothing permanent to make his subject greater. The unimportant scientific research worker, on the contrary, places his brick firmly in position, and on it every subsequent worker in the same field — geniuses included — will build again. The knowledge that every step forward is an advance in a gigantic undertaking is an inspiration to the scientist, for he may legitimately feel that he is playing his part in the greatest adventure of the human mind. This knowledge is one of the supreme values of science to the investigator.

It is impossible to read the biographies of the greatest scientists without realizing the high value which they have attributed to science apart from its material benefits, but they seldom analyse their appreciation very explicitly. It is unquestionable that a pleasurable excitement in approaching the /30/ unfamiliar is a part of the reason for their appreciation, an attitude of mind which is shared with the geographical explorer. A pleasure in finding order where previously disorder seemed to reign is another component of the scientific attitude. This has been stated quite unequivocally by the Danish genius of physics, Niels Bohr, who writes that the deepest foundation of science is "the abiding impulse in every human being to seek order and harmony behind the manifold and the changing in the existing world." T. H. Huxley wrote in his *Method and Results* that the research worker is inspired by "the supreme delight of extending the realm of law and order ever farther towards the unattainable goals of the infinitely great and the infinitely small, between which our little race of life is run." Some scientists, again, are animated by a component of that special awareness of the natural environment and feeling of community with nature and joy in natural beauty which also animate the poet and artist in their respective fields. This was clearly understood by the great German scientist, Alexander Humboldt, who wrote of "that important stage of our communion with the external world, when the enjoyment arising from a knowledge of the laws, and the mutual connexion of phenomena, associates itself with the charm of a simple contemplation of nature."

Humboldt was a person of extraordinarily wide interests. As a young man he was a successful mining technologist, but his passion for travel drew him into wider and wider fields of study until it might be said of him that if ever there was such a person as a general scientist, it was he. Few men, if any, have ever made such substantial contributions to so many diverse branches of science; and it was not only science that engaged his attention, for he was also a diplomat of high rank and a political economist. The extraordinary breadth of outlook of this great man enabled him to see science as a whole, and he expressed very vividly what he saw. In thirteen words of the utmost simplicity he expressed a truth which our modern materialists cannot shake:

"other interests," he wrote, /31/ "besides the material wants of life, occupy the minds of men." He instanced the "desire of embellishing life by augmenting the mass of ideas, and by multiplying means for their generalization. . . . The higher enjoyments yielded by the study of nature depend upon the correctness and the depth of our views, and upon the extent of the subjects that may be comprehended in a single glance." These words are strikingly similar to those written by the philosopher, Alexander, not much less than a century later: "The greatest truths are perhaps those which being simple in themselves illuminate a large and complex body of knowledge." Such truths, when grasped, unquestionably bring pleasure to the mind; and it would be fantastic to deny the existence of this kind of pleasure or to assess it lower than crude or material kinds. "In considering the study of physical phenomena," said Humboldt, "we find its noblest and most important result to be a knowledge of the chain of connexion, by which all natural forces are linked together, and made mutually dependent upon each other; and it is the perception of these relations that exalts our views and ennobles our enjoyments."

The enjoyments appear subjectively to be of the same kind as those caused by the perception of artistic beauty, combined with wonder or even a pleasurable astonishment. Professor J. B. S. Haldane has stressed the value of beauty in science in a particularly concrete way. "As a result of Faraday's work," he wrote, "you are able to listen to the wireless. But more than that, as a result of Faraday's work scientifically educated men and women have an altogether richer view of the world: for them, apparently empty space is full of the most intricate and beautiful patterns. So Faraday gave the world not only fresh wealth but fresh beauty." These simple words express a profound truth, which can be denied only as a tone-deaf man can deny the spiritual value of music. They are a distinguished investigator's flat contradiction of the materialist concept of science. Darwin expresses his feelings of beauty and wonder in the final words of *The Origin of Species:* "There /32/ is grandeur in this view of life, with its several powers, having been originally breathed by the Creator into a few forms or into one; and that, whilst this planet has gone cycling on according to the fixed law of gravity, from so simple a beginning endless forms most beautiful and most wonderful have been, and are being evolved."

The finding of a kind of wonder or awe in the majesty and apparently infinite complexity of the universe has led some of the greatest scientists— among them Boyle, Hooke, Newton, and Trembley—to ascribe the value of science to its giving us an insight into the mind of God. The great Swiss-born American zoologist, Louis Agassiz, for instance, expressed this idea unequivocally: "If I mistake not, the great object of our museums should be to exhibit the whole animal kingdom as a manifestation of the Supreme Intellect." This seems to be related to the subtler feeling of some of the greatest mathematicians that mathematical reality lies outside human beings, and that in their apparently creative work they are actually only observing and recording.

The scientist is able to construct a sort of scale of scientific values and to decide that one thing or theory is relatively trivial and another relatively important, quite apart from any question of practical applications. There is, as Poincaré has well said, "une hiérarchie des faits." Most scientists will agree that certain discoveries or propositions are more important because more widely significant than others, though around any particular level on the scale of values there may be disagreement. Thus, every scientist will agree that the discovery of atoms and of cells was important, and that the discovery of a new species of beetle, not markedly unusual in any way, is unimportant. So also with theories and "laws." A law, says Poincaré, "sera d'autant plus précieuse qu'elle sera plus générale." Professor G. H. Hardy has shown how mathematicians value their ideas by generality and depth, and how they universally value general and deep theorems above mere isolated curiosities, such as the fact that 8712 and 9801 /33/ are the only four-figure numbers that are integral multiples of themselves written backwards (8712 = 2178 × 4 and 9801 = 1089 × 9). A general theorem is one of wide significance, and a deep theorem one requiring a first understanding of a simpler theorem. Both these ideas are continually being used, consciously or unconsciously, whenever one scientist says that another has done a "good" bit of work.

The existence of amateur scientists is a proof that science is appreciated as an end. The amateur plays a smaller part in scientific research than he did in the eighteenth and nineteenth centuries, but excellent work is still done by amateurs in geology and biology. Apart from those who are sufficiently interested to rank as amateur scientists, there is a mass of people who possess the same sort of feelings as the great investigator but in lesser degree. For instance, a markedly strange animal of any kind arouses great public interest in both savage and civilized communities, and no sharp dividing line can be drawn between this sort of interest and that which inspires the zoologist, though the latter's interest is of course greater and more lasting. One has only to think of the interest taken by the most diverse people in the microscopical discoveries of van Leeuwenhoek to realize how widespread is an interest in unfamiliar natural objects. When it was discovered by Abraham Trembley almost exactly two hundred years ago that an organism exists (we now call it *Hydra*) which feeds like an animal but buds like a plant, and reorganizes itself into two or more individuals if cut into bits with scissors, the interest aroused was such that polyps became, in the words of an anonymous eighteenth-century writer, "à la mode." Interest in the unfamiliar is abundantly illustrated by the history of science. Even in modern times, when people tend to be less enthusiastic than they were two or three centuries ago, the discovery of a living fish belonging to a group thought to have been extinct for some sixty million years caused great excitement, and a popular weekly journal devoted a large double page entirely to the event. /34/

Just as the unfamiliar attracts the interest of both layman and scientist, so also does the orderly. In a low form one sees the appreciation of the orderly exhibited in a collection of butterflies systematically arranged by a collector who understands little of the life-processes of what he collects. No sharp line of separation can be drawn between the simple arrangement of natural objects in an orderly fashion and the systematic presentations of natural knowledge by great scientists. I found this out many years ago when demonstrating to a class of students preparing for the final Honours examination in zoology at Oxford. We were studying the anatomy of certain marine worms, and I noticed that one of the women-students had a book beside her, open at a coloured plate showing the external characters of some of the animals that we were studying. The book was unfamiliar to me and I stooped down to look at it. The name gave me a surprise that I have not forgotten. I learnt a useful lesson in modesty that day, which I should be happy to share with any scientist who thinks himself a different kind of being from the layman. The student, preparing for the highest examination in zoology at a great university, was using *The Seashore shown to the Children.*

There is a widespread belief in the "worth-whileness" of finding out. The community as a whole appears to approve of the setting apart of a limited number of talented people for the express purpose of discovery, without requiring that all research should be directed towards material ends. The public expects as almost a matter of course that some one or other should concern himself with all branches of natural knowledge. This was forcibly brought home to me some years ago when I was one of the three or four people in the world who were making systematic studies of the causes of breeding seasons. When I remarked to non-scientific friends that the environmental causes which regulate the breeding seasons of animals were not known — that no one knew what makes the blackbird breed in early spring — I was met by frank /35/ incredulity. "Oh, *some one* knows," I was assured; "the experts *must* know." It seemed intolerable that a community which maintains people expressly for the purpose of getting all sorts of knowledge should not be able to obtain information on such a very straightforward and familiar subject.

There is one particular kind of knowledge which both the scientist and the layman place high up on the scale of values. This is the knowledge that throws light on man's place in the universe. The discoveries of Copernicus and Darwin caused a ferment of excitement which shook and changed the outlook of the whole civilized world, quite apart from any application to material human welfare. Again, one's whole outlook on the universe is changed and broadened by the knowledge that great groups of animals, some of them of gigantic bulk, have arisen in the distant past, evolved, persisted for millions of years, and then become totally extinct millions of years before man, or even his ape-like ancestors, appeared on earth. /36/

Maxwell Anderson

WHATEVER HOPE WE HAVE

Maxwell Anderson (1888–1959) won success with his first play, written in collaboration with Laurence Stallings, What Price Glory? *(1924). During the next thirty years he wrote numerous plays which brought him fame as one of America's leading dramatists. In 1933 he won the Pulitzer Prize for Drama with* Both Your Houses, *and in 1936 and 1937 he was awarded the Drama Critics' Award for* Winterset *and* High Tor. *Among his other well-known plays are* Key Largo *(1939),* Anne of the Thousand Days *(1947), and* The Bad Seed *(1954).*

There is always something slightly embarrassing about the public statements of writers and artists, for they should be able to say whatever they have to say in their work, and let it go at that. Moreover, the writer or artist who brings a message of any importance to his generation will find it impossible to reduce that message to a bald statement, or even a clearly scientific statement, because the things an artist has to communicate can be said only in symbols, in the symbols of his art. The work of art is a hieroglyph, and the artist's endeavor is to set forth his vision of the world in a series of picture writings which convey meanings beyond the scope of direct statement. There is reason for believing that there is no other way of communicating new concepts save the artist's way, no other way save the artist's way of illuminating new pathways in the mind. Even the mathematician leaves the solid plane of the multiplica- /36/ tion table and treads precariously among symbols when he advances toward ideas previously unattained.

But I am not reaching for such ideas at the moment. I am writing this for the young people of this country who may at this moment be trying to decide what to do with their lives. Shall it be business, politics, law, science, or any of the subheads under these? Shall it be something that vaguely comes under the label of "the arts," and which our civilization only in rare cases encourages? Shall it be the army, the navy, the university? Shall it be exploration or invention? I am not unprejudiced in this matter and I wish to state a case.

Let me begin then with a picture of the earth as I see it. The human race, some two billion strong, finds itself embarked on a curious voyage among the stars, riding a planet which must have set out from somewhere and must be going somewhere, but which was cut adrift so long ago that its origin is a matter of speculation and its future beyond prophecy. Our planet is of limited area, and our race is divided into rival nations and cultures that grow and press on one another, fighting for space and the products of the ground. We are ruled by men like ourselves, men of limited intelligence, with no foreknowledge of what is to come, and hampered by the constant necessity of maintaining themselves in power by placating our immediate selfish demands. There have been men among us from time to time who had more wisdom than the majority, and who laid down precepts for the conduct of a man's /37/ brief life. Some of them claimed inspiration from beyond our earth, from spirits or forces which we cannot apprehend with our five senses. Some of them speak of gods that govern our destinies, but no one of them has had proof of his inspiration or of the existence of a god. Nevertheless there have been wise men among them, and we have taken their precepts to heart and taken their gods and their inspiration for granted.

Each man and woman among us, with a short and harried life to live, must decide for himself what attitude he will take toward the shifting patterns of government, justice, religion, business, morals, and personal conduct. We are hampered as well as helped in these decisions by every prejudice of ancestry and race, but no man's life is ready-made for him. Whether he chooses to conform or not to conform, every man's religion is his own, every man's politics is his own, every man's vice or virtue is his own, for he alone makes decisions for himself. Every other freedom in this world is restricted, but the individual mind is free according to its strength and desire. The mind has no master save the master it chooses.

And each must make his choices, now as always, without sufficient knowledge and without sufficient wisdom, without certainty of our origin, without certainty of what undiscovered forces lie beyond known scientific data, without certainty of the meaning of life, if it has a meaning, and without an inkling of our racial destiny. In matters of daily and yearly living, we have a few, often fallible, rules of thumb to guide /38/ us, but on all larger questions the darkness and silence about us is complete.

Or almost complete. Complete save for an occasional prophetic voice, an occasional gleam of scientific light, an occasional extraordinary action which may make us doubt that we are utterly alone and completely futile in this incomprehensible journey among the constellations. From the beginning of our story men have insisted, despite the darkness and silence about them, that they had a destiny to fulfill — that they were part of a gigantic scheme which was understood somewhere, though they themselves might never understand it. There are no proofs of this. There are only indications — in the idealism of children and young men, in the sayings of such teachers as Christ and Buddha, in the vision of the world we glimpse in the hieroglyphics of the masters of the great arts, and in the discoveries of pure science, itself an art, as it pushes away the veils of fact to reveal new powers, new laws, new mysteries, new goals for the eternal dream. The dream of the race is that it may make itself better and wiser than it is, and every great philosopher or artist who has ever appeared among us has turned his face away from what man is toward whatever seems to him most godlike that man may become. Whether the steps proposed are immediate or distant, whether he speaks in the simple parables of the New Testament or the complex musical symbols of Bach and Beethoven, the message is always to the effect that men are not essentially as they are but as they imagine and /39/ as they wish to be. The geologists and anthropologists, working hand in hand, tracing our ancestry to a humble little animal with a rudimentary forebrain which grew with use and need, reinforce the constant faith of prophet and artist. We need more intelligence and more sensitivity if ever an animal needed anything. Without them we are caught in a trap of selfish interest, international butchery, and a creed of survival that periodically sacrifices the best to the worst, and the only way out that I can see is a race with a better brain and superior inner control. The artist's faith is simply a faith in the human race and its gradual acquisition of wisdom.

Now it is always possible that he is mistaken or deluded in what he believes about his race, but I myself accept his creed as my own. I make my spiritual code out of my limited knowledge of great music, great poetry, and great plastic and graphic arts, including with these, not above them, such wisdom as the Sermon on the Mount and the last chapter of Ecclesiastes. The test of a man's inspiration for me is not whether he spoke from a temple or the stage of a theater, from a martyr's fire or a garden in Hampstead. The test of a message is its continuing effect on the minds of men over a period of generations. The world we live in is given meaning and dignity, is made an endurable habitation, by the great spirits who have preceded us and set down their records of nobility or torture or defeat in blazons and symbols which we can understand. I accept these not only as prophecy, but as direct motivation to- /40/ ward some far goal of racial aspiration. He who meditates with Plato, or finds himself shaken by Lear's "five-fold never" over Cordelia, or climbs the steep and tragic stairway of symphonic music, is certain to be better, both intellectually and morally, for the experience. The nobler a man's interests the better citizen he is. And if you ask me to define nobility, I can answer only by opposites, that it is not buying and selling, or betting on the races. It might be symbolized by such a figure as a farmer boy in western Pennsylvania plowing corn through a long afternoon and saying over and over to himself certain musical passages out of Marlowe's *Doctor Faustus*. He might plow his corn none too well, he might be full of what we used to call original sin, but he carries in his brain a catalytic agent the presence of which fosters ripening and growth. It may be an impetus that will advance him or his sons an infinitesimal step along the interminable ascent.

The ascent, if we do climb, is so slow, so gradual, so broken, that we can see little or no evidence of it between the age of Homer and our own time. The evidence we have consists in a few mountain peaks of achievement, the age of Pericles, the centuries of Dante and Michelangelo, the reign of Elizabeth in England, the century and a half of music in Germany, peaks and highlands from which the masters seem to have looked forward into the distance far beyond our plodding progress. Between these heights lie long valleys of mediocrity and desolation, and, artistically at least, we appear to be miles beneath the upper levels /41/ traversed behind us. It must be our hope as a nation that either in pure art or in pure science we may arrive at our own peak of achievement, and earn a place in human history by making one more climb above the clouds.

The individual, the nation, and the race are all involved together in this effort. Even in our disillusioned era, when fixed stars of belief fall from our sky like a rain of meteors, we find that men cling to what central verities they can rescue or manufacture, because without a core of belief neither man nor nation has courage to go on. This is no figure of speech, no sanctimonious adjuration—it is a practical, demonstrable fact which all men realize as they add to their years. We must have a personal, a national, and a racial faith, or we are dry bones in a death valley, waiting for the word that will bring us life. Mere rationalism is mere death. Mere scientific advance without purpose is an advance toward the waterless mirage and the cosmic scavengers. The doctrine of Machiavelli is a fatal disease to the citizen or the state. The national conscience is the sum of personal conscience, the national culture the sum of personal culture—and the lack of conscience is an invitation to destruction, the lack of culture an assurance that we shall not even be remembered.

No doubt I shall be accused of talking a cloudy philosophy, of mixed metaphors and fantasy, but unless I misread my history, the artist has usually been wiser even about immediate aims than the materialist or the enthusiast for sweeping political reform. The /42/ artist is aware that man is not perfect, but that he seeks perfection. The materialist sees that men are not perfect, and erects his philosophy on their desire for selfish advantage. He fails quickly always, because men refuse to live by bread alone. The utopian sees that men seek perfection and sets out to achieve it or legislate it into existence. He fails because he cannot build an unselfish state out of selfish citizens, and he who asks the impossible gets nothing. The concepts of truth and justice are variables approaching an imaginary limit which we shall never see; nevertheless, those who have lost their belief in truth and justice and no longer try for them are traitors to the race, traitors to themselves, advocates of the dust.

To my mind a love of truth and justice is bound up in men with a belief in their destiny; and the belief in their destiny is of one piece with national and international culture. The glimpse of the godlike in man occasionally vouchsafed in a work of art or prophecy is the vital spark in a world that would otherwise stand stock-still or slip backward down the grade, devoid of motive power.

For national growth and unity the artist's vision is the essential lodestone without which there is no coherence. A nation is not a nation until it has a culture which deserves and receives affection and reverence from the people themselves. Our culture in this country has been largely borrowed or sectional or local; what we need now to draw us together and make us a nation is a flowering of the national arts, a flowering /43/ of the old forms in this new soil, a renaissance of our own. If we want to live, or deserve to live, as a force or in history, we must somehow encourage the artists who appear among us, and we must encourage excellence among them. How to go about it is a problem entirely unsolved. I wish I could believe that prizes, or critics, or governmental endowments were effective stimulants toward effort or excellence in any artistic field. They may be occasionally, but the greatest achievements have occurred in the absence of endowments, or professional critics or prizes, seemingly as the result of a feverish desire for accomplishment in any single art, permeating a whole society during a period long enough to allow for more than one generation of devotees. Probably an artist can ask nothing better than a free society which likes his work and is willing to pay for it.

Looking ahead, I have no more than a hope that our nation will sometime take as great a place in the cultural history of the world as has been taken by Greece or Italy or England. So far we have, perhaps, hardly justified even the hope. But what hope there is for us lies in our nascent arts, for if we are to be remembered as more than a mass of people who lived and fought wars and died, it is for our arts that we will be remembered. The captains and the kings depart; the great fortunes wither, leaving no trace; inherited morals dissipate as rapidly as inherited wealth; the multitudes blow away like locusts; the records and barriers go down. The rulers, too, are forgotten unless /44/ they have had the forethought to surround themselves with singers and makers, poets and artificers in things of the mind.

This is not immortality, of course. So far as I know there is no immortality. But the arts make the longest reach toward permanence, create the most enduring monuments, project the farthest, widest, deepest influence of which human prescience and effort are capable. The Greek religion is gone, but Aeschylus remains. Catholicism shrinks back toward the papal state, but the best of medieval art perishes only where its pigments were perishable. The Lutheranism of Bach retains little content for us, but his music is indispensable. And there is only one condition that makes possible a Bach, an Aeschylus, or a Michelangelo—it is a national interest in and an enthusiasm for the art he practices. The supreme artist is only the apex of a pyramid; the pyramid itself must be built of artists and art-lovers, apprentices and craftsmen so deeply imbued with a love for the art they follow or practice that it has become for them a means of communication with whatever has been found highest and most admirable in the human spirit. To the young people of this country I wish to say: if you practice an art, be proud of it, and make it proud of you; if you now hesitate on the threshold of your maturity, wondering what rewards you should seek, wondering perhaps whether there are any rewards beyond the opportunity to feed and sleep and breed, turn to the art which has moved you most readily, take what part in it you can, as par- /45/ ticipant, spectator, secret practitioner, or hanger-on and waiter at the door. Make your living any way you can, but neglect no sacrifice at your chosen altar. It may break your heart, it may drive you half mad, it may betray you into unrealizable ambitions or blind you to mercantile opportunities with its wandering fires. But it will fill your heart before it breaks it; it will make you a person in your own right; it will open the temple doors to you and enable you to walk with those who have come nearest among men to what men may sometime be. If the time arrives when our young men and women lose their extravagant faith in the dollar and turn to the arts, we may then become a great nation, nurturing great artists of our own, proud of our own culture and unified by that culture into a civilization worthy of our unique place on this rich and lucky continent—and worth remembering, perhaps, when our wealth and our luck run out. /46/

Bertrand Russell

SCIENCE AS AN ELEMENT IN CULTURE

Bertrand Russell (1872 –   ) ranks among the most distinguished philosophers and mathematicians of the twentieth century. He has published books of very great importance in the fields of mathematical theory, "pure" philosophy, and the history of philosophy. He has also reached a wide audience with his witty, urbane, and penetrating essays on ethical, sociological, and educational problems. He has attracted international attention as a champion of pacifist causes. In 1950 he was awarded the Nobel Prize for Literature.

I

Science, to the ordinary reader of newspapers, is represented by a varying selection of sensational triumphs, such as wireless telegraphy and aeroplanes, radio-activity and the marvels of modern alchemy. It is not of this aspect of science that I wish to speak. Science, in this aspect, consists of detached up-to-date fragments, interesting only until they are replaced by something newer and more up-to-date, displaying nothing of the systems of patiently constructed knowledge out of which, almost as a casual incident, have come the practically useful results which interest the man in the street. The increased command over the forces of nature which is derived from science is undoubtedly an amply sufficient reason for encouraging scientific research, but this reason has been so often urged and is so easily appreciated that other reasons, to my mind quite as important, are apt to be overlooked. It is with these other reasons, especially with the intrinsic value of a scientific habit of mind in forming our outlook on the world, that I shall be concerned in what follows.

The instance of wireless telegraphy will serve to illustrate the difference between the two points of view. Almost all the serious intellectual labour required for the possibility of this invention is due to three men — Faraday, Maxwell, and Hertz. In alternating layers of experiment and theory these three men built up the modern theory of electromagnetism, and demonstrated the identity of light with electromagnetic waves. The system which they discovered is one of profound intellectual interest, bringing together and unifying an endless variety of apparently detached phenomena, and displaying a cumulative mental power which cannot but afford delight to every generous spirit. The mechanical details which remained to be adjusted in order to utilise their discoveries for a practical system of telegraphy demanded, no doubt, very considerable ingenuity, but had not that broad sweep and that universality which could give them intrinsic interest as an object of disinterested contemplation.

From the point of view of training the mind, of giving that well-informed, impersonal outlook which /202/ constitutes culture in the good sense of this much-misused word, it seems to be generally held indisputable that a literary education is superior to one based on science. Even the warmest advocates of science are apt to rest their claims on the contention that culture ought to be sacrificed to utility. Those men of science who respect culture, when they

From *The New Statesman*. Part I is reprinted from the May 24, 1913, issue, pp. 202–204; and Part II from the May 31, 1913, issue, pp. 234–236.

associate with men learned in the classics, are apt to admit, not merely politely, but sincerely, a certain inferiority on their side, compensated doubtless by the services which science renders to humanity, but none the less real. And so long as this attitude exists among men of science, it tends to verify itself: the intrinsically valuable aspects of science tend to be sacrificed to the merely useful, and little attempt is made to preserve that leisurely, systematic survey by which the finer quality of mind is formed and nourished.

But even if there be, in present fact, any such inferiority as is supposed in the educational value of science, this is, I believe, not the fault of science itself, but the fault of the spirit in which science is taught. If its full possibilities were realised by those who teach it, I believe that its capacity of producing those habits of mind which constitute the highest mental excellence would be at least as great as that of literature, and more particularly of Greek and Latin literature. In saying this I have no wish whatever to disparage a classical education. I have not myself enjoyed its benefits, and my knowledge of Greek and Latin authors is derived almost wholly from translations. But I am firmly persuaded that the Greeks fully deserve all the admiration that is bestowed upon them, and that it is a very great and serious loss to be unacquainted with their writings. It is not by attacking them, but by drawing attention to neglected excellences in science, that I wish to conduct my argument.

One defect, however, does seem inherent in a purely classical education — namely, a too exclusive emphasis on the past. By the study of what is absolutely ended and can never be renewed a habit of criticism towards the present and the future is engendered. The qualities in which the present excels are qualities to which the study of the past does not direct attention, and to which, therefore, the student of Greek civilisation may easily become blind. In what is new and growing there is apt to be something crude, insolent, even a little vulgar, which is shocking to the man of sensitive taste; quivering from the rough contact, he retires to the trim gardens of a polished past, forgetting that they were reclaimed from the wilderness by men as rough and earth-soiled as those from whom he shrinks in his own day. The habit of being unable to recognise merit until it is dead is too apt to be the result of a purely bookish life, and a culture based wholly on the past will seldom be able to pierce through everyday surroundings to the essential splendour of contemporary things, or to the hope of still greater splendour in the future.

"My eyes saw not the men of old;
And now their age away has rolled.
I weep — to think I shall not see
The heroes of posterity."

So says the Chinese poet; but such impartiality is rare in the more pugnacious atmosphere of the West, where the champions of past and future fight a never-ending battle, instead of combining to seek out the merits of both.

This consideration, which militates not only against the exclusive study of the classics, but against every form of culture which has become static, traditional, and academic, leads inevitably to the fundamental question: What is the true end of education? But before attempting to answer this question it will be well to define the sense in which we are to use the word "education." For this purpose I shall distinguish the sense in which I mean to use it from two others, both perfectly legitimate, the one broader and the other narrower than the sense in which I mean to use the word.

In the broader sense, education will include not only what we learn through instruction, but all that we learn through personal experience — the formation of character through the education of life. Of this aspect of education, vitally important as it is, I will say nothing, since its consideration would introduce topics quite foreign to the question with which we are concerned.

In the narrower sense, education may be confined to instruction, the imparting of definite information on various subjects, because such information, in and for itself, is useful in daily life. Elementary education — reading, writing, and arithmetic — is almost wholly of this kind. But instruction, necessary as it is, does not *per se* constitute education in the sense in which I wish to consider it.

Education, in the sense in which I mean it, may be defined as *the formation, by means of instruction, of certain mental habits and a certain outlook on life and the world*. It remains to ask ourselves, what mental habits, and what sort of outlook, can be hoped for as the result of instruction? When we have answered this question we can attempt to decide what science has to contribute to the formation of the habits and outlook which we desire.

Our whole life is built about a certain number — not a very small number — of primary instincts and impulses. Only what is in some way connected with these instincts and impulses appears to us desirable or important; there is no faculty, whether "reason" or "virtue" or whatever it may be called, that can take our active life and our hopes and fears outside the region controlled by these first movers of all desire. Each of them is like a queen-bee, aided by a hive of workers gathering honey; but when the queen is gone the workers languish and die, and the cells remain empty of their expected sweetness. So with each primary impulse in civilised man: it is surrounded and protected by a busy swarm of attendant derivative desires, which store up in its service whatever honey the surrounding world affords. But if the queen-impulse dies, the death-dealing influence, though retarded a little by habit, spreads slowly through all the subsidiary impulses, and a whole tract of life becomes inexplicably colourless. What was formerly full of zest, and so obviously worth doing that it raised no questions, has now grown dreary and purposeless: /203/ with a sense of disillusion we inquire the meaning of life, and decide, perhaps, that all is vanity. The search for an outside meaning that can *compel* an inner response must always be disappointed: all "meaning" must be at bottom related to our primary desires, and when they are extinct no miracle can restore to the world the value which they reflected upon it.

The purpose of education, therefore, cannot be to create any primary impulse which is lacking in the uneducated; the purpose can only be to enlarge the scope of those that human nature provides, by increasing the number and variety of attendant thoughts, and by showing where the most permanent satisfaction is to be found. Under the impulse of a Calvinistic horror of the "natural man," this obvious truth has been too often misconceived in the training of the young; "nature" has been falsely regarded as excluding all that is best in what is natural, and the endeavour to teach virtue has led to the production of stunted and contorted hypocrites instead of full-grown human beings. From such mistakes in education a better psychology or a kinder heart is beginning to preserve the present generation; we need, therefore, waste no more words on the theory that the purpose of education is to thwart or eradicate nature.

But although nature must supply the initial force of desire, nature is not, in the civilised man, the spasmodic, fragmentary, and yet violent set of impulses that it is in the savage. Each impulse has its constitutional ministry of thought and knowledge and reflection, through which possible conflicts of impulses are foreseen, and temporary impulses are controlled by the unifying impulse which may be called wisdom. In this way education destroys the crudity of instinct, and increases through knowledge the wealth and variety of the individual's contacts with the outside world, making him no longer an isolated fighting unit, but a citizen of the universe, embracing distant countries, remote regions of space, and vast stretches of past and future within the circle of his interests. It is this simultaneous softening in the insistence of desire and enlargement of its scope that is the chief moral end of education.

Closely connected with this moral end is the more purely intellectual aim of education, the endeavour to make us see and imagine the world in an objective manner, as far as possible as it is in itself, and not merely through the distorting medium of personal desire. The complete attainment of such an objective view is no doubt an ideal, indefinitely approachable, but not actually and fully realisable. Education, considered as a process of forming our mental habits and our outlook on the world, is to be judged successful in proportion as its outcome approximates to this ideal; in proportion, that is to say, as it gives us a true view of our place in society, of the relation of the whole-human society to its non-human environment, and of the nature of the non-human world as it is in itself apart from our desires and interests. If this standard is admitted, we can return to the consideration of science, inquiring how far science contributes to such an aim, and whether it is in any respect superior to its rivals in educational practice. /204/

II

Two opposite and at first sight conflicting merits belong to science as against literature and art. The one, which is not inherently necessary, but is certainly true at the present day, is hopefulness as to the future of human achievement, and in particular as to the useful work that may be accomplished by any intelligent student. This merit and the cheerful outlook which it engenders prevent what might otherwise be the depressing effect of another aspect of science, to my mind also a merit, and perhaps its greatest merit—I mean the irrelevance of human passions and of the whole subjective apparatus where scientific truth is concerned. Each of these reasons for preferring the study of science requires some amplification. Let us begin with the first.

In the study of literature or art our attention is perpetually rivetted upon the past: the men of Greece or of the Renaissance did better than any men do now; the triumphs of former ages, so far from facilitating fresh triumphs in our own age, actually increase the difficulty of fresh triumphs by rendering originality harder of attainment; not only is artistic achievement not cumulative, but it seems even to depend upon a certain freshness and *naiveté* of impulse and vision which civilisation tends to destroy. Hence comes, to those who have been nourished on the literary and artistic productions of former ages, a certain peevishness and undue fastidiousness towards the present, from which there seems no escape except into the deliberate vandalism which ignores tradition and in the search after originality achieves only the eccentric. But in such vandalism there is none of the simplicity and spontaneity out of which great art springs: theory is still the canker in its /234/ core, and insincerity destroys the advantages of a merely pretended ignorance.

The despair thus arising from an education which suggests no pre-eminent mental activity except that of artistic creation is wholly absent from an education which gives the knowledge of scientific method. The discovery of scientific method, except in pure mathematics, is a thing of yesterday; speaking broadly, we may say that it dates from Galileo. Yet already it has transformed the world, and its success proceeds with ever-accelerating velocity. In science men have discovered an activity of the very highest value in which they are no longer, as in art, dependent for progress upon the appearance of continually greater genius, for in science the successors stand upon the shoulders of their predecessors; where one man of supreme genius has invented a method, a thousand lesser men can apply it. No transcendent ability is required in order to make useful discoveries in science; the edifice of science needs its masons, bricklayers, and common labourers as well as its foremen, master-builders, and architects. In art nothing worth doing can be done without genius; in science even a very moderate capacity can contribute to a supreme achievement.

In science the man of real genius is the man who invents a new method. The notable discoveries are often made by his successors, who can apply the method with fresh vigour, unimpaired by the previous labour of perfecting it; but the mental calibre of the thought required for their work, however brilliant, is not so great as that required by the first inventor of the method. There are in science immense numbers of different methods, appropriate to different classes of problems; but over and above them all, there is something not easily definable, which may be called *the* method of science. It was formerly customary to identify this with the inductive method, and to associate it with the name of Bacon. But the true inductive method was not discovered by Bacon, and the true method of science is something which includes deduction as much as induction, logic and mathematics as much as botany and geology. I shall not attempt the difficult task of stating what the scientific method is, but I will try to indicate the temper of mind out of which the scientific method grows, which is the second of the two merits that were mentioned above as belonging to a scientific education.

The kernel of the scientific outlook is a thing so simple, so obvious, so seemingly trivial, that the mention of it may almost excite derision. The kernel of the scientific outlook is the refusal to regard our own desires, tastes, and interests as affording a key to the understanding of the world. Stated thus baldly, this may seem no more than a trite truism. But to remember it consistently in matters arousing our passionate partisanship is by no means easy, especially where the available evidence is uncertain and inconclusive. A few illustrations will make this clear.

Aristotle, I understand, considered that the stars must move in circles because the circle is the most perfect curve. In the absence of evidence to the contrary, he allowed himself to decide a question of fact by an appeal to aesthetico moral considerations. In such a case it is at once obvious to us that this appeal was unjustifiable. We know now how to ascertain as a fact the way in which the heavenly bodies move, and we know that they do not move in circles, or even in accurate ellipses, or in any other kind of simply describable curve. This may be painful to a certain hankering after simplicity of pattern in the universe, but we know that in astronomy such feelings are irrelevant. Easy as this knowledge seems now, we owe it to the courage and insight of the first inventors of scientific method, and more especially of Galileo.

We may take as another illustration Malthus's doctrine of population. This illustration is all the better for the fact that his actual doctrine is now known to be largely erroneous. It is not his conclusions that are valuable, but the temper and method of his inquiry. As everyone knows, it was to him that

Darwin owed an essential part of his theory of natural selection, and this was only possible because Malthus's outlook was truly scientific. His great merit lies in considering man not as the object of praise or blame, but as a part of nature, a thing with a certain characteristic behaviour from which certain consequences must follow. If the behaviour is not quite what Malthus supposed, if the consequences are not quite what he inferred, that may falsify his conclusions, but does not impair the value of his method. The objections which were made when his doctrine was new — that it was horrible and depressing, that people ought not to act as he said they did, and so on — were all such as implied an unscientific attitude of mind; as against all of them, his calm determination to treat man as a natural phenomenon marks an important advance over the reformers of the eighteenth century and the Revolution.

Under the influence of Darwinism the scientific attitude towards man has now become fairly common, and is to some people quite natural, though to most it is still a difficult and artificial intellectual contortion. There is, however, one study which is as yet almost wholly untouched by the scientific spirit — I mean the study of philosophy. Philosophers and the public imagine that the scientific spirit must pervade pages that bristle with allusions to ions, germ-plasms and the eyes of shell-fish. But as the devil can quote Scripture, so the philosopher can quote science. The scientific spirit is not an affair of quotation, of externally acquired information, any more than manners are an affair of the etiquette-book. The scientific attitude of mind involves a sweeping away of all other desires in the interests of the desire to know — it involves suppression of hopes and fears, loves and hates, and the whole subjective emotional life, until we become subdued to the material, able to see it frankly, without preconceptions, without bias, without any wish except to see it as it is, and without any belief that what it is must be determined by some relation, positive or negative, to what we should like it to be, or to what we can easily imagine it to be.

Now in philosophy this attitude of mind has not as yet been achieved. A certain self-absorption, not personal, but human, has marked almost all attempts to conceive the universe as a whole. Mind, or some aspect of it — thought or will or sentience — has been regarded as the pattern after which the universe is to be conceived, for no better reason, at bottom, than that /235/ such a universe would not seem strange, and would give us the cosy feeling that every place is like home. To conceive the universe as essentially progressive or essentially deteriorating, for example, is to give to our hopes and fears a cosmic importance which *may*, of course, be justified, but which we have as yet no reason to suppose justified. Until we have learnt to think of it in ethically neutral terms, we have not arrived at a scientific attitude in philosophy; and until we have arrived at such an attitude, it is hardly to be hoped that philosophy will achieve any solid results.

Human beings cannot, of course, wholly transcend human nature; something subjective, if only the interest that determines the direction of our attention, must remain in all our thought. But science comes nearer to objectivity than any other human pursuit, and gives us, therefore, the closest contact and the most intimate relation with the outer world that it is possible to achieve. To the primitive mind everything is either friendly or hostile; but experience has shown that friendliness and hostility are not the conceptions by which the world is to be understood. Science thus represents, though as yet only in a nascent condition, a higher stage of evolution than any pre-scientific thought or imagination, and, like every approach to self-transcendence, it brings with it a rich reward in increase of scope and breadth and comprehension. I have spoken so far largely of the negative aspect of the scientific spirit, but it is from the positive aspect that its value is derived. The instinct of constructiveness, which is one of the chief incentives to artistic creation, can find in scientific systems a satisfaction more massive than any epic poem. Disinterested curiosity, which is the source of almost all intellectual effort, finds with astonished delight that science can unveil secrets which might well have seemed for ever undiscoverable. The desire for a larger life and wider interests, for an escape from private circumstances, and even from the whole recurring human cycle of birth and death, is fulfilled by the impersonal cosmic outlook of science as by nothing else. To all these must be added, as contributing to the happiness of the man of science, the admiration of splendid achievement, and the consciousness of inestimable utility to the human race. A life devoted to science is therefore a happy life, and its happiness is derived from the very best sources that are open to dwellers on this troubled and passionate planet. /236/

Archibald MacLeish

WHY DO WE TEACH POETRY?

Archibald MacLeish (1892 –   ) published his first volume of poetry in 1917. Since then he has received, among other awards, two Pulitzer Prizes and the Bollingen Prize for his poetry. In 1939 MacLeish was named Librarian of Congress, and subsequently he held high government offices during the administration of Franklin D. Roosevelt. He served as Assistant Secretary of State in 1944–1945. In 1949 he accepted a chair at Harvard University. Although MacLeish had written a number of highly successful verse plays for radio—especially The Fall of the City *(1937)—he was not generally thought of as a dramatist until the production, in 1958, of his verse-drama* JB, *which was awarded the Pulitzer Prize for Drama and received high acclaim both in the United States and in Europe.*

There is something about the art of poetry which induces a defensive posture. Even in the old days when the primacy of poetry was no more challenged than the primacy of Heaven, which is now also challenged, the posture was habitual. If you published your reflections on the art in those days you called them a *Defense.* Today, when the queen of sciences is Science, you do not perhaps employ that term but you mean it. It is not that the gentlemen at the long table in the Faculty Club whose brains have been officially cleared to serve as depositories of scientific secrets of the eighth and thirteenth classes are patronizing in their manner. They are still gentlemen and therefore still modest no matter how great their distinction or how greatly certified. But one knows one's place. One knows that whereas the teachers of science meet to hear of new triumphs which the newspapers will proudly report, the teachers of poetry meet to ask old questions—which no one will report: such questions as, why teach poetry anyway in a time like this?

It is a relief in this general atmosphere to come upon someone who feels no defensiveness whatever: who is perfectly certain that poetry ought to be taught now as at any other time and who is perfectly certain also that he knows why. The paragon I have in mind is a young friend of mine, a devoted teacher,

"Why Do We Teach Poetry?" *The Atlantic Monthly* (March 1956), pp. 48–53.

who was recently made headmaster of one of the leading American preparatory schools, and who has been taking stock, for some time past, of his curriculum and his faculty. Poetry, as he sees it, ought to be taught "as a most essential form of human expression as well as a carrier throughout the ages of some of the most important values in our heritage." What troubles him is that few teachers, at least in the schools he knows, seem to share his conviction. He is not too sure that teachers themselves have "an abiding and missionary faith in poetry" which would lead them to see it as a great clarifier—a "human language" capable of competing with the languages and mathematics and science.

But though teachers lack the necessary faith, the fault, as my young friend sees it, is not wholly theirs. The fault is the fault of modern criticism, which has turned poetry into something he calls "poetry itself"—meaning, I suppose, poetry for poetry's sake. "Poetry itself" turns out to be poetry with its meanings distilled away, and poetry with its meanings distilled away is difficult if not impossible to teach in a secondary school—at least *his* secondary school. The result is that secondary school teachers have gone back, as to the lesser of two evils, to those historical and anecdotal practices sanctified by American graduate schools in generations past. They teach "poets and not poetry." With the result that "students become acquainted with poets from Homer to MacLeish" (quite a distance no matter how you measure it!) "but the experience doesn't necessarily leave them with increased confidence in what poetry has to offer." I can well believe it.

The reason why modern criticism has this disastrous effect, the reason why it produces "an almost morbid apathy toward 'content' or 'statement of idea,' " is its excessive "preoccupation with aesthetic values." Modern criticism insists that poems are primarily works of art; and when you insist that poems are primarily works of art you cannot, in my friend's view, teach them as carriers "throughout the ages of some of the most important values in our heritage." What is important about Homer and Shakespeare and the authors of the Bible is that they were "realists with great vision . . . whose work contains immensely valuable constructions of /48/ the meaning of life"; and if you talk too much about them as artists, those constructions of the meaning of life get lost.

Now this, you will observe, is not merely another walloping of the old horse who was once called the New Criticism. It goes a great deal farther. It is a frontal attack upon a general position maintained by many who never accepted the New Criticism or even heard of it. It is an attack upon those who believe— as most poets, I think, have believed—that a poem *is* primarily a work of art and must be read as a work of art if it is to be read at all. It is a high-minded and disinterested attack delivered for the noblest of purposes, but an attack notwithstanding—and an effective one. What it contends is that an approach to poetry which insists that a poem is a work of art blocks off what the poem has to say, whereas what the poem has to say is the principal reason for teaching it. What the argument comes down to, in other words, is the proposition that it is a mistake, in teaching poetry, to insist that poetry is art, because, if you do so insist, you will not be able to bring your students to the meaning of the poem, the idea of the poem, what the poem has to tell them about man and world and life and death—and it is for these things the teaching of the poem is important.

Now, I can understand this argument and can respect the reasons for making it. Far too many of those who define poetry in exclusively artistic terms use their definition as a limiting and protective statement which relieves them of all obligation to drive the poem's meanings beyond the meanings of the poem:

beyond the mere translation of the symbols and metaphors and the classical or other references—the whole apparatus of *explication du texte*. Far too many, indeed, of those who have to do with literature generally in our time, and particularly with modern literature, consider that meanings in any but a literary (which includes a Freudian) sense are not only outside, but beneath, their proper concern—that the intrusion of questions of morality and religion into the world of art is a kind of trespass and that works of literary art not only should but *can* be studied in a moral vacuum. Literature in the hands of such teachers is well on the way to becoming again that "terrible queen" which the men of the nineties raised above life and which Yeats, when he outgrew the men of the nineties, rejected.

But although I can understand this argument, and although I can respect its reasons, and although I believe it raises a true issue and an important issue, I cannot accept it; for it rests, or seems to me to rest, on two quite dubious assumptions. The first is the assumption, familiar in one form or another to all of us, that the "idea" of a work of art is somehow separable from the work of art itself. The most recent—and most egregious—expression of this persistent notion comes from a distinguished Dean of Humanities in a great institution of learning who is reported by the New York *Times* to have argued in a scholarly gathering that "the idea which the reader derives from Ernest Hemingway's *The Old Man and The Sea* comes after the reader has absorbed some 60,000 words. This takes at least an hour. . . . A similar understanding could come after a few minutes study of a painting by a skillful artist." Precisely, one imagines, as the Doré illustrations gave one the "idea" of the *Inferno* in a few easy looks!

2

It is the second assumption, however, which divides me most emphatically from my young friend. For the second assumption seems to be that *unless* idea and work of art are distinguished from each other in the teaching of a poem, the idea—and so the effectiveness of the teaching—will be lost. At this point my friend and I part company. I am ready, and more than ready, to agree that it is for the meanings of life that one reads (and teaches) poetry. But I am unable to see how there can be a distinction between a poem as a conveyer of such meanings and a poem as a work of art. In brief, the distinction between art and knowledge which is made throughout my friend's argument seems to me wholly without foundation. That it is a distinction almost universally recognized in our epoch I know well enough. Science makes it. Poetry makes it. And the world agrees with both. "Whatever can be *known*," says Bertrand Russell, "can be known by means of science." Poetry, say its professors, has no "messages" to deliver. And no one dissents from either. The exclusive proprietary right of science to know and to communicate knowledge is not only commonly recognized in our civilization: in a very real sense it is our civilization. For the characteristic of our civilization—that which distinguishes it from the civilizations which have preceded it—is the characteristic which knowledge-by-science has conferred upon it: its abstractness.

But though the agreement is general, the proposition is not one I can accept. I argue that the apologists for science are not justified in claiming, nor the apologists for poetry in admitting, the sole right of science to know. I insist that poetry is also capable of knowledge; that poetry, indeed, is capable of a kind of knowledge of which science is not capable; that it is capable of that knowledge *as poetry;* and that the teaching of poetry as poetry, the teaching of poem as work of art, is not only not incompatible with the teaching of poetry as knowledge but is, indeed, the only possible way of teaching poetry as knowledge.

To most of us, brought up as we have been in the world of abstractions which science has prepared for us, and in the kind of school which that world produces—schools in which almost all teaching is /49/ teaching of abstractions—the notion of poetry as knowledge, the notion of art as knowledge, is a fanciful notion. Knowledge by abstraction we understand. Science can abstract ideas about apple from apple. It can organize those ideas into knowledge about apple. It can then, by some means, introduce that knowledge into our heads—possibly because our heads are abstractions also. But poetry, we know, does not abstract. Poetry presents. Poetry presents the thing as the thing. And that it should be possible to *know* the thing *as the thing it is*—to *know* apple *as* apple—this we do not understand; this, the true child of the time will assure you, cannot be done. To the true child of abstraction you can't know apple as apple. You can't know tree as tree. You can't know man as man. All you can *know* is a world dissolved by analyzing intellect into abstraction—not a world composed by imaginative intellect into itself. And the result, for the generations of abstraction, is that neither poetry nor art can be a means to knowledge. To inspiration, yes: poetry can undoubtedly lead to that—whatever it is. To revelation, perhaps: there may certainly be moments of revelation in poetry. But to knowledge, no. The only connection between poetry and knowledge we can see is the burden of used abstractions—adages and old saws—which poetry, some poetry, seems to like to carry—adages most of which we knew before and some of which aren't even true.

But if all this is so, what then is the "experience of art"—the "experience of poetry"—which all of us who think about these things at all have known? What is the experience of *realization* which comes over us with those apples on a dish of Cézanne's or those three pine trees? What is the experience of realization which comes over us with Debussy's *Nuages*? What is the experience of realization which comes over us when Coleridge's robin sits and sings

> Betwixt the tufts of snow on the bare branch
> Of mossy apple-tree, while the nigh thatch
> Smokes in the sun thaw; . . .

or when his eave-drops fall

> Heard only in the trances of the blast,
> Or if the secret ministry of frost
> Shall hang them up in silent icicles,
> Quietly shining to the quiet Moon.

And if all this is so, why does one of the most effective of modern definitions of poetry (Arnold's in his letter to Maurice de Guérin) assign to that art the peculiar "power of so dealing with *things* as to awaken in us a wonderfully full, new and intimate sense of them and of our relation with them"?

The answer is, of course, that the children of abstraction are wrong—and are impoverished by their error, as our entire time is impoverished by it. They are wrong on both heads. They are wrong when they think they *can* know the world through its abstractions: nothing can be known through an abstraction but the abstraction itself. They are wrong also when they think they *cannot* know the world as the world: the whole achievement of art is a demonstration to the contrary. And the reason they are wrong on both heads is the reason given, quite unintentionally, by Matthew Arnold. They are wrong because they do not realize that all true knowledge is a matter of relation: that we *really* know a thing only when we are filled with "a wonderfully full, new and intimate sense of it" and, above all, of "our relation with" it. This sense — this *knowledge* in the truest meaning of the word knowledge — art can give but abstraction cannot.

There are as many proofs as there are successful works of art. Take, for obvious example, that unseen mysterious phenomenon, the wind. Take any attempt, by the familiar processes of abstraction, to "know" the wind. Put beside it those two familiar lines of George Meredith: —

Mark where the pressing wind shoots javelin-like
Its skeleton shadow on the broad-backd wave!

What will be the essential difference between the two? Will it not be that the first, the analytical, statement is or attempts to be a wholly objective statement made without reference to an observer (true everywhere and always), whereas an observer — *one's self* as observer! — is involved in the second? And will not the consequential difference be that a relation involving one's self is created by the second but not by the first? And will not the end difference be that the second, but not the first, will enable us to know the thing itself — to know what the thing is *like?*

It would be quite possible, I suppose, to semanticize this difference between knowledge by poetry and knowledge by abstraction out of existence by demonstrating that the word, know, is being used in two different senses in the two instances, but the triumph would be merely verbal, for the difference is real. It is indeed the realest of all differences, for what it touches is the means by which we come at reality. How are we to find the knowledge of reality in the world without, or in the shifting, flowing, fluid world within? Is all this a task for the techniques of abstraction — for science as it may be or as it is? Is it through abstraction alone that we are to find what is real in our experience of our lives — and so, conceivably, what is real in ourselves? Or do we need another and a different way of knowing — a way of knowing which will make that world out there, this world in here, available to us, not by translating them into something else — into abstractions of quantity and measure — but by bringing us ourselves to confront them as they are — man and tree face to face in the shock of recognition, man and love face to face?

The question, I beg you to see, is not what we /50/ *ought* to do. There is no ought. A man can "live" on abstractions all his life if he has the stomach for them, and many of us have — not the scientists only, but great numbers of the rest of us in this contemporary world, men whose days are a web of statistics, and names, and business deals, held together by the parentheses of a pair of commuting trains with three Martinis at the close. The question is not what we ought to do. The question is what we have the choice of doing — what alternatives are open to us. And it is here and in these terms that the issue presents itself to the teacher of poetry.

3

Colleges and universities do not exist to impose duties but to reveal choices. In a civilization like ours in which one choice has all but overwhelmed the other, a civilization dominated by abstraction, in which men are less and less able to deal with their experience of the world or of themselves unless experience and self have first been translated into abstract terms—a civilization like a foreign language—in such a civilization the need for an understanding of the alternative is urgent. What must be put before the generation of the young is the possibility of a knowledge of experience *as* experience, of self *as* self, and that possibility only the work of art, only the poem, can reveal. That it is so rarely, or so timidly, presented in our schools is one of the greatest failures of our educational system. Young men and young women graduate from American schools and colleges by the hundreds of thousands every year to whom science is the only road to knowledge, and to whom poetry is little more than a subdivision of something called "literature"—a kind of writing printed in columns instead of straight across the page and primarily intended to be deciphered by girls, who don't read it either.

This sort of thing has consequences. Abstractions are wonderfully clever tools for taking things apart and for arranging things in patterns but they are very little use in putting things together and no use at all when it comes to determining what things are *for*. Furthermore, abstractions have a limiting, a dehumanizing, a dehydrating effect on the relation to things of the man who must live with them. The result is that we are more and more left, in our scientific society, without the means of knowledge of ourselves as we truly are or of our experience as it actually is. We have the tools, all the tools—we are suffocating in tools—but we cannot find the actual wood to work or even the actual hand to work it. We begin with one abstraction (something we think of as ourselves) and a mess of other abstractions (standing for the world) and we arrange and rearrange the counters, but who we are and what we are doing we simply do not know—above all what we are doing. With the inevitable consequence that we do not know either what our purpose is or our end. So that when the latest discoveries of the cyclotron are reported we hail them with the cry that we will now be able to control nature better than ever before—but we never go on to say for what purpose, to what end, we will control her. To destroy a city? To remake a world?

It was something of this kind, I imagine, that Adlai Stevenson had in mind when he startled a Smith Commencement last spring by warning his newly graduated audience of prospective wives that the "typical Western man—or typical Western husband—operates well in the realm of means, as the Roman did before him. But outside his specialty, in the realm of ends he is apt to operate poorly or not at all. . . . The neglect of the cultivation of more mature values," Mr. Stevenson went on, "can only mean that his life, and the life of the society he determines, will lack valid purpose, however busy and even profitable it may be."

As he has so often done before, Mr. Stevenson there found words for an uneasiness which has been endemic but inarticulate in the American mind for many years—the sense that we are getting nowhere far too fast and that, if something doesn't happen soon, we may arrive. But when he came to spell out the causes for "the neglect of the cultivation of more mature values" Mr. Stevenson failed, or so it seems to me, to identify the actual villain. The contemporary environment in America, he told his young listeners, is "an environment in which 'facts,' the data of the senses, are glorified and value judgments are assigned inferior status as 'mere matters of opinion.' It is an environment in which art is often regarded as an adornment of civilization rather than a vital element of it, while philosophy is not only neglected but deemed faintly disreputable because 'it never gets you anywhere.' " It is true that philosophy is neglected, and even truer that art is regarded in this country generally as it seems to be regarded by the automobile manufacturers of Detroit: as so much enamel paint and chromium to be applied for allegedly decorative purposes to the outside of a car which would run better without it. But the explanation is not, I think, that we set facts — even facts in quotation marks — above values, or that we glorify the data of the senses, unless one means by that latter phrase not what the senses tell us of the world we live in but what the statistics that can be compiled out of the data of the senses would tell us if we were ever in touch with our senses.

In few civilizations have the senses been less alive than they are with us. Look at the cities we build and occupy — but look at them! — the houses we live in, the way we hold ourselves and move; listen to the speaking voices of the greater part of our women. And in no civilization, at least in recorded time, have human beings been farther from the *facts* if we mean by that word, facets of reality. Our in- /51/ difference to ends is the result of our obsession with abstractions rather than facts: with the ideas of things rather than with things. For there can be no concern for ends without a hunger for reality. And there can be no hunger for reality without a sense of the real. And there can be no sense of the real in the world which abstraction creates, for abstraction is incapable of the real: it can neither lay hold of the real itself nor show us where to find it. It cannot, that is to say, create the *relation* between reality and ourselves which makes *knowledge* of reality possible, for neither reality nor ourselves exist in abstraction. Everything in the world of abstraction is object. And, as George Buttrick pointedly says, *we* are not objects: we are subjects.

4

But all this is a negative way of saying what a defender of poetry should not be afraid of saying positively. Let me say it. We have lost our concern with ends because we have lost our touch with reality and we have lost our touch with reality because we are estranged from the means to reality which is the poem — the work of art. To most members of our generation this would seem an extravagant statement but it is not extravagant in fact and would not have seemed so in another time. In ancient China the place of poetry in men's lives was assumed as matter of course; indeed, the polity was based on it. The three hundred and five odes or songs which make up the Song-word Scripture survived to the fourth century B.C., when Confucius is said to have collected them because they were part of the government records preserved in the Imperial Archive. For thousands of years the examinations for the Chinese civil service were examinations in poetry, and there is no record that the results were more disappointing to the throne than examinations of a different character might have been. Certainly there is no record that a Chinese civil servant ever attempted to deny an honor student in a military academy his commission in the imperial army *or* navy because he was friendly with his own mother! Idiocies which the study of science and of other abstractions in contemporary institutions of naval education in the United States seem to nourish were apparently cauterized from the mind by the reading of poems.

It was not for nothing that Confucius told his disciples that the three hundred and five songs of the Song-word Scripture could be boiled down to the commandment: "Have no twisty thoughts." You cannot have twisty thoughts if you are real and if you are thinking about real things. But if a mother is merely a biological event to you and if you yourself are merely a military event called an admiral, anything may happen: you may make your country ridiculous, humiliate a promising boy, and deprive the navy of a good officer, all in the twisted belief that you are being a wise man and a patriot.

One can see, not only in the three hundred and five songs, but in Chinese poetry of other periods, what Confucius meant. Consider two Chinese poems of the second century B.C. and the sixth of our era, both written by Emperors. The first is a poem of grief—of the sense of loss of someone loved: a poem therefore of that inward world of feeling, of emotion, which seems to us most nearly ourselves and which, because it is always in flux, always shifting and changing and flowing away, is, of all parts of our experience of our lives, most difficult to know. We cannot know it through science. We cannot know it by knowing things *about* it—even the shrewdest and most intelligent things, helpful though they may be to us in other ways. We cannot know it either by merely feeling it—by uttering its passing urgencies, crying out "I love" meaning "I think of myself as loving" or sobbing "I grieve" meaning "I think of myself as grieving." How then can we know it?

The Emperior Wu-ti wrote (this is Arthur Waley's beautiful translation):—

The sound of her silk skirt has stopped.
On the marble pavement dust grows.
Her empty room is cold and still.
Fallen leaves are piled against the doors.

    Longing for that lovely lady
How can I bring my aching heart to rest?

Four images, one of sound, two of sight, one of feeling, each like a note plucked on a stringed instrument. Then a question like the chord the four would make together. And all at once we *know*. We know this grief which no word could have described, which any abstraction the mind is capable of would have destroyed. But we know more than this grief: we know our own— or will when it shall visit us—and so know something of ourselves.

The second is a poem of that emotion, that feeling, which is even more difficult to know than grief itself. The second is a poem of delight: youth and delight—the morning of the world—the emotion, of all emotions, most difficult to stop, to hold, to see. "Joy whose hand is ever at his lips bidding adieu." How would you *know* delight in yourself and therefore yourself delighting? Will the psychiatrists tell you? Is there a definition somewhere in the folios of abstraction by which we attempt to live which will capture it for you? The Emperor Ch'ien Wen-ti (again Waley's translation) knew that there is only one mirror which will hold that vanishing smile: the mirror of art, the mirror of the poem:—

A beautiful place is the town of Lo-yang:
The big streets are full of spring light.
The lads go driving out with harps in their hands:
The mulberry girls go out to the fields with their baskets. /52/
Golden whips glint at the horses' flanks,
Gauze sleeves brush the green boughs.
Racing dawn the carriages come home—
And the girls with their high baskets full of fruit.

In this world within, you see, this world which is ourselves, there is no possibility of knowing by abstracting the meaning out—or what we hope will be the meaning. There we must know things *as* themselves and it must be *we* who know them. Only art, only poetry, can bring about that confrontation, because only art, only poetry, can show us what we are and ourselves confronting it. To be ignorant of poetry is to be ignorant therefore of the one means of reaching the world of our experience of the world. And to be ignorant of *that* world is to be ignorant of who and what we are. And to be ignorant of who and what we are is to be incapable of reality no matter what tools we have, or what intelligence, or what skills. It is this incapacity, this impotence, which is the tragedy of the time we live in. We are spiritually impotent because we have cut ourselves off from the poem. And the crowning irony is that it is only in the poem that we can know how impotent we have become.

Why do we teach poetry in this scientific age? To present the great alternative not to science but to that knowledge by abstraction which science has imposed. And what is this great alternative? Not the "messages" of poems, their interpreted "meanings," for these are abstractions also—abstractions far inferior to those of science. Not the explications of poetic texts, for the explication of a poetic text which goes no farther ends only in abstraction.

No, the great alternative is the poem as itself, the poem as a poem, the poem as a work of art—which is to say, the poem in the context in which alone the work of art exists: the context of the world, of the man and of the thing, of the infinite relationship which is our lives. To present the great alternative is to present the poem not as a message in a bottle, and not as an object in an uninhabited landscape, but as an action in the world, an action in which we ourselves are actors and our lives are known. /53/

Hopes and Fears

Any writer who sets out to extoll the benefits of scientific and technological progress has only to point around him — to tangible, material achievements, the benefits of which appear to be self-evident. The writer who takes an opposing view, on the other hand, has a more difficult task. He will necessarily be more concerned with intangibles, with questions of human value — moral, spiritual, or aesthetic. He is likely to maintain that certain attitudes and ways of life are more properly "human" than others, and that these are threatened as the methods and objectives of modern scientific technology come to dominate ever-increasing areas of human existence. The apologist for science may assert that these intangibles are, at best, of secondary significance measured against the material gains made possible by an increasing control over nature; or, more fruitfully, he may contend that the disciplines of science and technology nurture the inner life quite as effectively as do the humanities. He may further insist that for the greater part of mankind, improved material well-being is a precondition to fuller human development.

Writers on both sides of this issue have frequently indulged in prophecy, projecting their hopes or fears upon the wide screen of the future. We read daily accounts of the marvels that science and technology hold in store: the conquest of space, the elimination of hunger and disease, the blessings of leisure, comfort, and mobility. At the same time, such familiar works as Aldous Huxley's Brave New World *and George Orwell's* 1984 *image the future as a sinister anti-utopia in which man, under the ubiquitous control of scientific powers wielded by a totalitarian state, is dehumanized.*

The readings in this section represent both of these attitudes. The optimistic predictions of H. G. Wells and J. Bronowski and James T. Shotwell's exultant account of the empowering relationship between man and machine are poised against Erich Fromm's analysis of contemporary "alienation," D. H. Lawrence's brooding picture of what mechanism has made of modern man, and E. M. Forster's terrible vision of a mechanized world of the future.

H. G. Wells

IS LIFE BECOMING HAPPIER?

Herbert George Wells (1866–1946) possessed superabundant vitality and an optimistic faith in the benefits of scientific progress. His more than eighty published works include treatises on social, political, and religious matters, volumes of essays and short stories, and novels of fantasy and science, of character and humor, and of political and social propaganda. The essay reprinted here is one of the many journalistic articles that Wells wrote for popular magazines on both sides of the Atlantic and that he later collected and published in book form.

From "Is Life Becoming Happier?" *The Way the World Is Going* (Garden City, New York: Doubleday, Doran and Company, Inc., 1929), pp. 204–213.

Wells and C. P. Snow are comparable in achievement and outlook. Each emerged from a lower middle-class background, and each was trained in science. Both have laid stress on improving social conditions by enlarging and extending the benefits of scientific technology. Each has established a-reputation as a novelist and essayist, yet each has asserted the superiority of science over art.

It was pretended in that film "Metropolis," for example, that the development of a great mechanical civilization must reduce a large part of the population from some imaginary old-world happiness, sweet, golden, tender, and true, to machine-minding drudgery. That is a quite common assertion made without a shadow of justification in fact. And we are constantly being told that the human animal is "degenerating," body and mind, through the malign influence of big towns; that a miasma of "vulgarity" and monotony is spreading over a once refined and rich and beautifully varied world, that something exquisite called the human "soul," which was formerly quite all right, is now in a very bad way, and that plainly before us, unless we mend our ways and return to mediæval dirt and haphazard, the open road, the wind upon the heath, brother, simple piety, an unrestricted birth-rate, spade husbandry, handmade furniture, honest, homely surgery without anæsthetics, long skirts and hair for women, a ten-hour day for workmen, and more slapping and snubbing for the young, there is nothing before us but nervous wreckage and spiritual darkness. This sort of stuff is exuded in enormous volume, and it offers an immense resistance to systematic progress. It is sustained by multitudes of people who are in a position to be better informed. The Gummidge chorus is never silent; the thoughtful headshaker moping for /205/ a return to mediævalism casts his daily shadow on every patch of sunshine, on each new social enterprise and hopeful effort. Everything we have is cheapened by comparison with an entirely legendary past and with an entirely imaginary state of "natural" health and joyfulness.

Let us admit that life still displays much unhappiness and that it is overhung by the frightful dangers of modern war. Let us concede the black possibilities latent in nationalism, flag worship, educational slackening, and the class jealousy and class malignancy of the prosperous. Even so, there are the soundest reasons for maintaining that never, since life first appeared upon this planet, has there been so great a proportion of joy, happiness, and contentment as there is about us now, nor so bright an outlook. . . . /206/

The story of the common man since the beginning of social life has been anything but a record of innocent festivals and homely happiness. With the development of agriculture he began to escape from the hunger and fear, the tramp's life in the wilderness, of the wandering savage, but only by accepting an increasing burthen of regular toil. History and archæology preserve only the records of the successful few; we must guess how many myriads of drudges worked the mines, pulled the galleys, and hoed the fields for the greatness of the Pyramids or the pretty palaces of Cnossus. And pestilence and famine returned in /208/ every lifetime. Pestilence and famine have disappeared from the general routine of life in the last hundred years or less, and that only in the Atlantic civilizations. The social history of the Old Testament goes to the accompaniment of a prolonged groan from the common people. The Roman Empire was an administrative pyramid based on slaves, serfs, and distressed taxpayers. Its distinctive instrument of social discipline was the cross. There is no period in the past upon which a well-informed man can put his finger and say, "At this time commen men had more joyful lives than they have to-day."

There is only a very scanty account of the life of the common man through most of the historical period. It was not worth writing about. As M. Abel Chevalley points out in his admirable study of that father of the English novel, Thomas Deloney, it is suddenly in the Elizabethan period that literature stoops so low as to tell of tradespeople and their servants. Peasant life still remained in darkness. Even now we get only half-lit pictures of that earthly underworld. Mr. Liam O'Flaherty's glimpses of the Irish cultivator and Mr. Caradoc Evans's sketches of the primitive folk in Wales are more convincing than pleasant. Deloney shows us a squabbling, insecure, undignified life, much pervaded by envy and malice, ill-housed, ill-clothed, and irregularly fed, without medical attention, amusement, reading, change of scene. It is much the same squalor that we find as the background of the adventures in the Roman world of /209/ Petronius. And still it was a marked advance, as Chevalley notes, on mediæval life.

That squalid life remained the common life until the third or fourth decade of the nineteenth century. There seemed little hope of any improvement. There were great social changes, an increase of productivity and population in the eighteenth century, but they brought no perceptible amelioration of the common lot. The common man remained dirty and ignorant, needy, or incessantly laborious. The first clumsy machines brought trouble rather than relief; they threw multitudes out of employment; they needed drudges to prepare the way for them; they needed drudges to supplement their mechanical imperfections.

It was only after the middle of the nineteenth century that the real significance of mechanical invention and the practical applications of scientific knowledge and method became apparent. Then it began to dawn upon mankind that the age of the mere drudge was at an end. The outbreak of universal education in Western Europe was the practical recognition of this. Meanly and grudgingly planned, against the resistance of many privileged people, and much disturbed by their intense jealousy of their "social inferiors," the establishment of compulsory elementary education marks, nevertheless, a new phase in the history of our species. It is the beginning of at least a chance for everybody. Close upon it came a fall in the birth-rate, and an even greater fall in the infantile death-rate — clear intimations that /210/ the common people no longer consented to leave their increase to the unchecked urgency of bestial instincts nor the health of their offspring to chance. Concurrently, too, there began such a shortening of the hours of work as to extend leisure, which had once been the privilege of a minority, to nearly the whole population.

The present phase of these changes shows us the old once necessary drudge population becoming in part an unemployable and unwanted abyss of people who are either natural inferiors or exceptionally unlucky individuals, and in part a much larger and increasing new mass of comparatively versatile semi-skilled workers, whose efficiency and standards of life are rising, whose security, leisure, and opportunity increase. These latter are the new common people that the extension of knowledge and machine production has given the world, and their development will be the measure of civilization in the future. Even at its present level it is an unprecedented mass of happy and hopeful life in comparison with any common life that has ever existed before, and there are many reasons for hoping — if great wars can be avoided and if it does not swamp itself by unrestrained proliferation — that it will go on to much higher levels still.

This expanding mass of new common people bulks largest in the United

States of America, but it is as highly developed in the more complex British system even though proportionally it is not so great, and it /211/ exists with qualifications and differences in all industrialized Europe. It needs only a decade or so of peace and security to appear in China, and as the economic reconstruction of Russia brings that country into line and co-operation again with other European developments, we shall probably find that there also the conditions of machine production have evoked a new town population and a new agricultural worker, able to read, write, discuss, and think, with much the same amount of leisure and freedom as his Western comrade. The dictatorship of the proletariat may dictate what it likes, but the machine will insist, there as everywhere, that the people who will work it and for whom it will work must have minds quickened by education and refreshed by leisure, must be reasonably versatile, and must not be overworked or embittered.

Let me note one or two other points making for happiness in our days. For the first time in history over large parts of the earth the beating of inferiors has disappeared. For the first time in history the common worker has leisure assigned to him as his right. Never have common people been so well clad or so well housed. Never have they had so much freedom of movement. There is a horror of cruelty to men and animals more widely diffused than it has ever been before. There has been an extraordinary increase in social gentleness. There has never been so small a proportion of sickness and death in the community. All these things mean happiness—more universal than it has ever been. /212/

But this general march towards happiness is not fated and assured. There is no guarantee in progress. This much of release for the common man from disease, privation, and drudgery has come about very rapidly as a consequence of inventions and discoveries that were not made to that end, and the development of the new common people into a world of civilization of free and happy individuals is manifestly challenged by enormous antagonistic forces. It may be impeded, delayed, or defeated. Flags and the loyalties and passions of insensate nationalism are flatly opposed to the attainment of a general human welfare. Every man in military uniform is a threat of violence; every gun and military implement is a man-trap in the path to a universal order. The false legend of the glorious past of our race is in a perpetual struggle against the hope of its future. Obscurantism and fear lie in wait for every courageous innovation in social and economic life. Indolence is their ally and false thinking their friend. Continual progress can only be assured by an incessant acutely critical vigilance. None the less, the common man to-day is happier than he has ever been, and with a clearer hope of continuing betterment. The common man in quite a little space of years may be better off than are even the fortunate few to-day.

And now call me a pessimist if you can! /213/

D. H. Lawrence

THE INDUSTRIAL MAGNATE

David Herbert Lawrence (1885–1930), a prolific writer in various genres, is best known as a novelist. Among his novels are Sons and Lovers *(1913),* The Rainbow

From "The Industrial Magnate," *Women in Love* (New York: The Modern Library, 1937), pp. 240–265.

(1915), Women in Love *(first publication, private edition, 1920), and* Lady Chatterley's Lover *(1928). In these works, especially in* The Rainbow *and* Women in Love, *which are considered by many to be his two masterpieces, Lawrence deals with the problems of human relationships in modern industrial civilization. Lawrence felt that many modern men too greatly repressed the instinctual and emotional elements of their nature and overstressed the rational. For him spiritual health consists in a psychological wholeness integrating both of these sides of human nature. In the selection which follows, the story of Gerald Crich, a minor strain in the novel, dramatizes one of these modern men. By force of will and idea he reorganizes the coal mines into an efficient machine by substituting a mechanistic principle for the humanitarian ideal that had governed his father's operation of the mines. In doing so, however, he takes the joy out of the miners' lives and brings about a void in himself. At the end of the novel he meets a symbolic and physical death in a snow world high in the Tirolese Alps.*

Then there was need for a complete break. The mines were run on an old system, an obsolete idea. The initial idea had been to obtain as much money from the earth as would make the owners comfortably rich, would allow the workmen sufficient wages and good conditions, and would increase the wealth of the country altogether. Gerald's father, following in the second generation, having a sufficient fortune, had thought only of the men. The mines, for him, were primarily great fields to produce bread and plenty for all the hundreds of human beings gathered about them. He had lived and striven with his fellow owners to benefit the men every time. And the men had been benefited in their fashion. There were few poor, and few needy. All was plenty, because the mines were good and easy to work. And the miners, in those days, finding themselves richer than they might have expected, felt glad and triumphant. They thought themselves well-off, they congratulated themselves on their good-fortune, they remembered how their fathers had starved and /255/ suffered, and they felt that better times had come. They were grateful to those others, the pioneers, the new owners, who had opened out the pits, and let forth this stream of plenty.

But man is never satisfied, and so the miners, from gratitude to their owners, passed on to murmuring. Their sufficiency decreased with knowledge, they wanted more. Why should the master be so out of all proportion rich?

There was a crisis when Gerald was a boy, when the Masters' Federation closed down the mines because the men would not accept a reduction. This lock-out had forced home the new conditions to Thomas Crich. Belonging to the Federation, he had been compelled by his honour to close the pits against his men. He, the father, the Patriarch, was forced to deny the means of life to his sons, his people. He, the rich man who would hardly enter heaven because of his possessions, must now turn upon the poor, upon those who were nearer Christ than himself, those who were humble and despised and closer to perfection, those who were manly and noble in their labours, and must say to them: "Ye shall neither labour nor eat bread."

It was this recognition of the state of war which really broke his heart. He wanted his industry to be run on love. Oh, he wanted love to be the directing power even of the mines. And now, from under the cloak of love, the sword was cynically drawn, the sword of mechanical necessity. . . . /256/

When Gerald grew up in the ways of the world, he shifted the position. He did not care about the equality. The whole Christian attitude of love and self-sacrifice was old hat. He knew that position and authority were the right thing in the world, and it was useless to cant about it. They were the right thing, for the simple reason that they were functionally necessary. They were not the be-all and the end-all. It was like being part of a machine. He himself happened to be a con- /258/ trolling, central part, the masses of men were the parts variously controlled. This was merely as it happened. As well get excited because a central hub drives a hundred outer wheels—or because the whole universe wheels round the sun. After all, it would be mere silliness to say that the moon and the earth and Saturn and Jupiter and Venus have just as much right to be the centre of the universe, each of them separately, as the sun. Such an assertion is made merely in the desire of chaos.

Without bothering to *think* to a conclusion, Gerald jumped to a conclusion. He abandoned the whole democratic-equality problem as a problem of silliness. What mattered was the great social productive machine. Let that work perfectly, let it produce a sufficiency of everything, let every man be given a rational portion, greater or less according to his functional degree or magnitude, and then, provision made, let the devil supervene, let every man look after his own amusements and appetites, so long as he interfered with nobody.

So Gerald set himself to work, to put the great industry in order. In his travels, and in his accompanying readings, he had come to the conclusion that the essential secret of life was harmony. He did not define to himself at all clearly what harmony was. The word pleased him, he felt he had come to his own conclusions. And he proceeded to put his philosophy into practice by forcing order into the established world, translating the mystic word harmony into the practical word organisation.

Immediately he *saw* the firm, he realised what he could do. He had a fight to fight with Matter, with the earth and the coal it enclosed. This was the sole idea, to turn upon the inanimate matter of the underground, and reduce it to his will. And for this fight with matter, one must have perfect instruments in perfect organisation, a mechanism so subtle and harmonious in its workings that it represents the single mind of man, and by its relentless repetition of given movement will accomplish a purpose irresistibly, inhumanly. It was this inhuman principle in the mechanism he wanted to construct that inspired Gerald with an almost religious exalta- /259/ tion. He, the man, could interpose a perfect, changeless, godlike medium between himself and the Matter he had to subjugate. There were two opposites, his will and the resistant Matter of the earth. And between these he could establish the very expression of his will, the incarnation of his power, a great and perfect machine, a system, an activity of pure order, pure mechanical repetition, repetition ad infinitum, hence eternal and infinite. He found his eternal and his infinite in the pure machine-principle of perfect co-ordination into one pure, complex infinitely repeated motion, like the spinning of a wheel; but a productive spinning, as the revolving of the universe may be called a productive spinning, a productive repetition through eternity, to infinity. And this is the God-motion, this productive repetition ad infinitum. And Gerald was the God of the machine, Deus ex Machina. And the whole productive will of man was the Godhead.

He had his life-work now, to extend over the earth a great and perfect system in which the will of man ran smooth and unthwarted, timeless, a Godhead in process. He had to begin with the mines. The terms were given: first the resistant Matter of the underground; then the instruments of its subjugation, instruments human and metallic; and finally his own pure will, his own mind. It would need a marvellous adjustment of myriad instruments, human, animal, metallic, kinetic, dynamic, a marvellous casting of myriad tiny wholes into one great perfect entirety. And then, in this case there was perfection attained, the will of the highest was perfectly fulfilled, the will of mankind was perfectly enacted; for was not mankind mystically contra-distinguished against inanimate Matter, was not the history of mankind just the history of the conquest of the one by the other?

The miners were overreached. While they were still in the toils of divine equality of man, Gerald had passed on, granted essentially their case, and proceeded in his quality of human being to fulfil the will of mankind as a whole. He merely represented the miners in a higher sense when he perceived that the only way to fulfil perfectly the will of man was to establish the perfect, inhuman machine. But he represented /260/ them very essentially, they were far behind, out of date, squabbling for their material equality. The desire had already transmuted into this new and greater desire, for a perfect intervening mechanism between man and Matter, the desire to translate the Godhead into pure mechanism.

As soon as Gerald entered the firm, the convulsion of death ran through the old system. He had all his life been tortured by a furious and destructive demon, which possessed him sometimes like an insanity. This temper now entered like a virus into the firm, and there were cruel eruptions. Terrible and inhuman were his examinations into every detail; there was no privacy he would spare, no old sentiment but he would turn it over. The old grey managers, the old grey clerks, the doddering old pensioners, he looked at them, and removed them as so much lumber. The whole concern seemed like a hospital of invalid employees. He had no emotional qualms. He arranged what pensions were necessary, he looked for efficient substitutes, and when these were found, he substituted them for the old hands.

"I've a pitiful letter here from Letherington," his father would say, in a tone of deprecation and appeal. "Don't you think the poor fellow might keep on a little longer? I always fancied he did very well."

"I've got a man in his place now, father. He'll be happier out of it, believe me. You think his allowance is plenty, don't you?"

"It's not the allowance that he wants, poor man. He feels it very much, that he is superannuated. Says he thought he had twenty more years of work in him yet."

"Not of this kind of work I want. He doesn't understand."

The father sighed. He wanted not to know any more. He believed the pits would have to be overhauled if they were to go on working. And after all, it would be worse in the long run for everybody, if they must close down. So he could make no answer to the appeals of his old and trusty servants, he could only repeat "Gerald says."

So the father drew more and more out of the light. The whole frame of the real life was broken for him. He had /261/ been right according to his lights. And his lights had been those of the great religion. Yet they seemed to have become obsolete, to be superseded in the world. He could not understand. He only withdrew with his lights into an inner room, into the silence. The beautiful candles of belief, that would not do to light the world any more, they would still burn sweetly and sufficiently in the inner room of his soul, and in the silence of his retirement.

Gerald rushed into the reform of the firm, beginning with the office. It was needful to economise severely, to make possible the great alterations he must introduce.

"What are these widows' coals?" he asked.

"We have always allowed all widows of men who worked for the firm a load of coal every three months."

"They must pay cost price henceforward. The firm is not a charity institution, as everybody seems to think."

Widows, these stock figures of sentimental humanitarianism, he felt a dislike at the thought of them. They were almost repulsive. Why were they not immolated on the pyre of the husband, like the sati in India? At any rate, let them pay the cost of their coals.

In a thousand ways he cut down the expenditure, in ways so fine as to be hardly noticeable to the men. The miners must pay for the cartage of their coals, heavy cartage too; they must pay for their tools, for the sharpening, for the care of lamps, for the many trifling things that made the bill of charges against every man mount up to a shilling or so in the week. It was not grasped very definitely by the miners, though they were sore enough. But it saved hundreds of pounds every week for the firm.

Gradually Gerald got hold of everything. And then began the great reform. Expert engineers were introduced in every department. An enormous electric plant was installed, both for lighting and for haulage underground, and for power. The electricity was carried into every mine. New machinery was brought from America, such as the miners had never seen before, great iron men, as the cutting machines were called, and unusual appliances. The working of the pits was thor- /262/ oughly changed, all the control was taken out of the hands of the miners, the butty system was abolished. Everything was run on the most accurate and delicate scientific method, educated and expert men were in control everywhere, the miners were reduced to mere mechanical instruments. They had to work hard, much harder than before, the work was terrible and heart-breaking in its mechanicalness.

But they submitted to it all. The joy went out of their lives, the hope seemed to perish as they became more and more mechanised. And yet they accepted the new conditions. They even got a further satisfaction out of them. At first they hated Gerald Crich, they swore to do something to him, to murder him. But as time went on, they accepted everything with some fatal satisfaction. Gerald was their high priest, he represented the religion they really felt. His father was forgotten already. There was a new world, a new order, strict, terrible, inhuman, but satisfying in its very destructiveness. The men were satisfied to belong to the great and wonderful machine, even whilst it destroyed them. It was what they wanted. It was the highest that man had produced, the most wonderful and superhuman. They were exalted by belonging to this great and superhuman system which was beyond feeling or reason, something really godlike. Their hearts died within them, but their souls were satisfied. It was what they wanted. Otherwise Gerald could never have done what he did. He was just ahead of them in giving them what they wanted, this participation in a great and perfect system that subjected life to pure mathematical principles. This was a sort of freedom, the sort they really wanted. It was the first great step in undoing, the first great phase of chaos, the substitution of the mechanical principle for the organic, the destruction of the organic purpose, the organic unity, and the subordination of every organic unit to the great mechanical purpose. It was pure organic disintegration and pure mechanical organisation. This is the first and finest state of chaos.

Gerald was satisfied. He knew the colliers said they hated him. But he had long ceased to hate them. When they streamed past him at evening, their heavy boots slurring on the /263/ pavement wearily, their shoulders slightly distorted, they took no notice of him, they gave him no greeting whatever, they passed in a grey-black stream of unemotional acceptance. They were not important to him, save as instruments, nor he to them, save as a supreme instrument of control. As miners they had their being, he had his being as director. He admired their qualities. But as men, personalities, they were just accidents, sporadic little unimportant phenomena. And tacitly, the men agreed to this. For Gerald agreed to it in himself.

He had succeeded. He had converted the industry into a new and terrible purity. There was a greater output of coal than ever, the wonderful and delicate system ran almost perfectly. He had a set of really clever engineers, both mining and electrical, and they did not cost much. A highly educated man cost very little more than a workman. His managers, who were all rare men, were no more expensive than the old bungling fools of his father's days, who were merely colliers promoted. His chief manager, who had twelve hundred a year, saved the firm at least five thousand. The whole system was now so perfect that Gerald was hardly necessary any more.

It was so perfect that sometimes a strange fear came over him, and he did not know what to do. He went on for some years in a sort of trance of activity. What he was doing seemed supreme, he was almost like a divinity. He was a pure and exalted activity.

But now he had succeeded—he had finally succeeded. And once or twice lately, when he was alone in the evening and had nothing to do, he had suddenly stood up in terror, not knowing what he was. And he went to the mirror and looked long and closely at his own face, at his own eyes, seeking for something. He was afraid, in mortal dry fear, but he knew not what of. He looked at his own face. There it was, shapely and healthy and the same as ever, yet somehow, it was not real, it was a mask. He dared not touch it, for fear it should prove to be only a composition mask. His eyes were blue and keen as ever, and as firm in their look. Yet he was not sure that they were not blue false bubbles that would burst in a moment and leave clear annihilation. He could see the dark- /264/ ness in them, as if they were only bubbles of darkness. He was afraid that one day he would break down and be a purely meaningless bubble lapping round a darkness.

But his will yet held good, he was able to go away and read, and think about things. He liked to read books about the primitive man, books of anthropology, and also works of speculative philosophy. His mind was very active. But it was like a bubble floating in the darkness. At any moment it might burst and leave him in chaos. He would not die. He knew that. He would go on living, but the meaning would have collapsed out of him, his divine reason would be gone. In a strangely indifferent, sterile way, he was frightened. But he could not react even to the fear. It was as if his centres of feeling were drying up. He remained calm, calculative and healthy, and quite freely deliberate, even whilst he felt, with faint, small but final sterile horror, that his mystic reason was breaking, giving way now, at this crisis.

And it was a strain. He knew there was no equilibrium. He would have to go in some direction, shortly, to find relief. Only Birkin kept the fear definitely off him, saved him his quick sufficiency in life, by the odd mobility and changeableness which seemed to contain the quintessence of faith. But then Gerald must always come away from Birkin, as from a Church service, back to the outside real world of work and life. There it was, it did not alter, and words were futilities. He had to keep himself in reckoning with the world of work and material life. And it became more and more difficult, such a strange pressure was upon him, as if the very middle of him were a vacuum, and outside were an awful tension.

He had found his most satisfactory relief in women. After a debauch with some desperate woman, he went on quite easy and forgetful. The devil of it was, it was so hard to keep up his interest in women nowadays. He didn't care about them any more. . . . /265/

James T. Shotwell

MECHANISM AND CULTURE

James T. Shotwell (1874–   ), professor of history at Columbia University from 1908 to 1942, is the author of many works in the fields of history and international relations and has played a part in the editing of some two hundred volumes of historical materials. He has gained international recognition for his efforts in the cause of world peace.

Socrates, according to Plato, lamented the passing of that time in Greece when the only known facts about the past were those treasured in the memory of the tribal bard, and the coming of that degenerate age when people no longer would bother remembering things they could read in books. He deprecated the invention of writing. Yet it was by the written page of his pupil Plato that the conversations in the cool gardens on the outskirts of Athens have survived, to secure his own immortality.

This objection of Socrates to the invention of an alphabet was something more than the proposition of a philosopher in need of an argument. It was a protest against mechanism. Making black marks on Egyptian papyri or skins from Asia—those skins the merchants of Pergamum later made into parchments (pergamenta)—compares with reciting an epic as the use of machinery compares with hand labor. Socrates, we suppose, would have preferred telling the time by a guess at the lengthening shadow on the square rather than by the use of such an instrument as a watch. By ignoring inventions one kept "close to nature."

This is an attitude to be found throughout the whole history of culture. Its most earnest advocates have been the artists, impatient of anything interposed between nature and the individual. But idealists generally have joined in the denunciation or shared the contempt for mechanism, no matter what their field. Literature has held aloof, except in patronizing, romantic moods, until the present. History has ignored the very implements of progress—the tools of work, the mechanism of effort—even while recording the results. There has, therefore, devel- /151/ oped a gulf between "culture" and achievement which has widened with each new invention.

There have been, in recent years, some signs of a revolt against the conspiracy of the poetically-minded to ignore the creations of the practically-minded, but unless the revolt becomes a revolution we shall never square ourselves with reality. If we are to make anything intelligent out of the world we live in, we must free ourselves from this romantic sentimentality, which goes back to Socrates and beyond. Idealism, left to itself, is futility. There is no sadder fact in the tragic circumstances of the present than that idealism failed to avert the desolation of Europe. It will always fail, so long as it holds itself aloof from the grimy facts of daily life.

"Mechanism and Culture," *Science and Man,* ed. Ruth Nanda Anshen (New York: Harcourt, Brace and World, Inc., 1942), pp. 151–162.

Like the forces of nature, ideas must be harnessed and set to work, or things will remain exactly as they were before. One cannot weave cloth with an idea, but embody the idea in wood and iron and it will replace all the hand-loom workers in the world. Wherever a locomotive sends its puff of steam through the smoke-stack, the idea of George Stephenson is at work—an idea that a forced draught on the fire would give the engine enough power to pull its load. There are spindle whorls in the Grimaldi caves along the slopes of Menton, used by the fingers of spinning women of the late stone age, over 10,000 years ago. How often in all that stretch of years have spinners dreamed of something to carry on the motion of the whorl besides the arm and hand! Out of such longings came—no one knows from where—the simple spinning wheels of the late Middle Ages. Yet it was only in the 18th Century that a tinkering watch-maker helped Arkwright to get his roller-frame to work, and the work of spinning passed forever from the fireside to the mill. New cities arose by the marshy waste of Lancashire, and the shipping of Britain carrying its goods overseas, made possible a world-empire—not created in a fit of absent-mindedness, as an idealist historian declared, but through the might of the Industrial Revolution.

Few students of literature stop to think that its existence depends upon paper and ink as well as thought! The records of history depend upon the cutting of the chisel in the stone, the /152/ sharp impress of the scratching stick, on clay or on wax tablet, the scrawl of charcoal or ink on leaves of trees, papyri wrappings or leather. Before these devices were used lie the unnumbered centuries of that period we call the prehistoric; this side of it, is the world of history. History begins with writing; the prehistoric, as we use the term, is a synonym for the preliterate. History depends upon that mechanism which transfers thought from brains to material substances, and so enables thought to endure while the thinkers come and go.

It is strange that the extent to which thought depends upon mechanism for its preservation seldom occurs to us except when the mechanism fails. We know that the burning of the library at Alexandria blotted out for all time much of the culture of the distant antiquity which it had gathered in the papyri on its shelves. We know as well that the last classics of Greece and Rome perished in the moldy rolls of papyri which could not last in the climate of the northern Mediterranean as it does in Egypt. The book trade of the ancients was careless of the future—as ours is today. But had it not been for papyri rolls dealt in by those astute traders who brought their goods to the wharves of Athens and Ostia, it is doubtful if the literature of classic Greece and Rome would have been produced at all. Had there been nothing better than clay tablets to scratch, how would the Augustan Age have achieved what it did? Imagine Dante in his exile, accumulating the mud cylinders necessary for the *Divine Comedy*. Or, to bring the matter down to our own time, what would our modern literature and journalism amount to if the Arabs had not invented paper? A printing press without paper is unthinkable; and literature cannot exist without them both. We need a *Sartor Resartus* in the history of literature to show us how naked and helplessly limited is thought except when provided with mechanism.

There have been two great creative epochs in the history of our civilization; that of ancient Greece and that of today. The one produced critical thought; the other applied it to produce machines. Beside these two contributions to secular society, all others rank as minor. The one stirred into activity that critical intelligence, upon which rests our whole apparatus of knowl- /153/ edge; the other made nature our ally not merely by applying its power to do our work, but also by supplying the means for extending knowledge itself, almost to the infinite. Seen in this light the protest of our modern humanists against mechanism has little of that insight into reality which was the characteristic note of Socrates.

What is needed in both humanists and scientists is the Hellenic sense of just proportion, so that neither thought nor machines shall become master of life. For thought turned upon itself, divorced from the setting in a real world, becomes as idle as the speculations of the schoolmen; and machines become, not instruments for human liberation, but the dominant element in society. Education in a modern world must respond to both these demands. It cannot be purely literary or idealistic without losing touch with the spirit of the age in which we live; it cannot be purely technical and remain education.

How many of us realize that a steam engine is as genuinely a historic product, as fittingly the symbol of an age as the feudal castle or the medieval cathedral; that a modern factory is as much the center of historical forces as the ancient city?

We shall never see the true perspective of history so long as we accept unquestioned the mediocre outlook of what we call common-sense people. We need imagination and insight even more than judgment for, otherwise, our judgments simply circumscribe and limit our activities. If there were only one factory in the world, if the power that Watt released from the coal mines were so concentrated that instead of invading every hamlet of the civilized world it was confined to the single valley of the Clyde and drew to it there the work of the world, we should have some feeling for the importance in history of one of the great inventions. But instead, its effects penetrate the environment of common life everywhere; and so we miss its meaning.

Invention is an art. It is the projection into matter itself of the conscious will. It makes matter a part of the agency of control, and also a part of intelligence. Loose grains of muddy ore, lying in the bosom of the hills, become iron axes. They have nothing in themselves to indicate axes. They might, if /154/ placed too close to a fire, under certain circumstances become hardened into a mass. But while the ore is merely matter, the ax is matter plus mind. It bears the impress of intelligence, and that to so great a degree that the anthropologists passing before the rows of axes in the cases at a museum can reconstruct from their form and composition the state of culture of the makers, like a pianist whose symphonies arise from the keys of his piano. The ax implies both consciousness and purpose; it means cutting. The same is even true of a forked stick which the savage uses as a spade, though here the injection of the human element into the material is less obvious, because the object has not been refashioned. The fork was a result of its nature as a branch; that is, a part of a vegetable mechanism for catching air in leaves and conveying nitrogen to the trunk. It was not produced by nature to dig potatoes. Nature leaves the branch in the air and the potato in the ground. But in the hands of man the fibers of wood, like the particles of iron are turned into something else, they become part of conscious action, a continuation of muscle and an agency of mind. The potentialities of the tool are those of the brain that conceived it and controlled the fashioning hand, as much as they are those of matter. Invention is a projection of consciousness into the unconscious; a creation.

If this can be said at the dawn of invention, and of a tool like a digging stick, which itself embodies no thought, which is not a tool except when so regarded or used, the utility of which is accidental, it is abundantly evident when invention produces not a tool but a machine. The difference between a tool and a machine is that the tool helps a man to do his work, but the machine does the work itself. The man changes his position entirely with reference to it. His business with the machine is simply to make it work. The factory operative does no spinning; he mends threads and makes the spindles spin, forces the steam to move the iron and the iron to transmit its energy to the whirling spools, and they in turn to gather up that energy and imprison it in the spirals of thread or yarn, where our fingers later may find it stored up—a source of strength against strains and pulls. The factory spinner merely assists /155/ at this transformation like the impresario at a theater. Steam and iron and fiber dance before him into new combinations, like a dream from the *Arabian Nights.*

The machines that do these things are the perpetuation of the initial energy of their inventors. In the steam engine, for instance, Papin, Newcomen and Watt have found an immortality larger than we have yet realized. In its gliding rods and noiseless wheels the brain of the inventor lives as that of Virgil in the *Aeneid.* But while the art of the one is cast cathedral-like, in static mold, to resist the forces of time by its perfection and its strength, that of the other— the invention—is thrown, as it were into the crucible of change, and creates itself the forces that reveal its imperfections and weakness. The engine develops the speed that breaks it down. Yet the immortality of the invention is perhaps the surer of the two, for it enlists its destroyer as its ally. It becomes part of change itself, and so gains some control over it. It sets going the irrecoverable march of events, which make up what we call time, and becomes an integral part of the ever-fleeting present. For its immortality lies in its use. By the work it does it disturbs the poise of phenomena so that once started it creates the demand for its own continuance. It contains its own stimulation, for its imperfections call as much for further invention as its successes encourage new ones. So it is a social phenomenon of the most complex nature. If it immortalizes the Watts and Arkwrights, it is only by merging their creations into that of a vast composite whole. The original engine of Watts and spinning frame of Arkwright are in museums; but both machines are also preserved wherever engines are at work or cotton is being spun. The original inventors have become contributors to a more august creation than they guessed. The brain of the individual scientist or mechanic fuses its creation (steam valve or automatic brake) into those of all society and all future time. It will live only so long as it can be adjusted to the changing machine. Each bolt and bar, each wheel or crank is the crystallized thought of some nameless engineer. When they fit and go, the structure lives, and each part is instinct with life. Apart or unfitted they die. The cylinder that might hold the power /156/ to drive ocean-liners is good only for the scrapheap unless the pistons fit and the gearings work. And so, if one could imagine the whole dynamic force of the Industrial Revolution gathered together and concentrated in a single cylinder, with a power compared to which that of Niagara would be like that of a rivulet, it would be as useless as the energy of ocean tides today, unless there were the nicest adjustment in the parts of the machine. Machinery is a social creation and is itself a sort of society!

Thus, in the social preservation of inventive thought, by a strange paradox, this individualistic age is the annihilation of the individual. Its greatest art-creation, machinery, it maintains and treasures only so long as the individual contributions are in tune with the whole.

There are two kinds of immortality: the immortality of monuments,—of things to look at and recall; and the immortality of use,—of things which surrender their identity but continue to live, things forgotten but treasured, and incorporated in the vital forces of society. Thought can achieve both kinds. It embodies itself in forms, — like epics, cathedrals and even engines, — where the endurance depends upon the nature of the stuff used, the perfection of the workmanship and the fortunes of time. But it also embodies itself in use; that is, it can continue to work, enter into other thought and continue to emit its energy even when its original mold is broken up.

It is the first kind of immortality — the monumental kind — which has mainly drawn our attention, for it is clearer, if not larger, in our consciousness. Use, on the other hand, obliterates outlines so that the things used most are often least seen. So in keeping with our natural tendency to visualize our thought even in the things of use, as if to make up for this indistinctness, we encourage the perpetuation of form, — in institutions and traditions, — and enshrine it in art.

Let us be clear about this monumental side. Poems live in themselves and not simply as stimulations to deeds or other thoughts. Form imposes itself on thought and preserves by means of its external beauty, even though it is often only a successful distortion of the thought with which it started. /157/ Cathedrals stand before us out of the Middle Ages which created them, defying time in their own right, by the double strength of poise and beauty in stately columns and towering walls. These formal perpetuations of thought in its own expression are the most appreciated, as they are the most obvious. They require no penetrating analysis to detect; they are matters of pure observation. Thought grips materials without effort, but hesitates to tackle thought; so the concrete world lodges in the memory while the abstractions slip by unnoticed.

So important is this formal apprehension of things, that it has been taken at its face value by society, — as society takes things at their face value (which includes of course the value of the face not simply its looks), — and made synonymous with art; as if there were not a greater art in the mastery of those intangible, elusive forces which have escaped from their mold and penetrate wherever thought can go, — the art of mathematics, science, and invention. Indeed the same tendency which makes us see the obvious first and prize it most, carries us still farther. It tends to become a sort of sacramental attitude, consecrating not only the form in which the thought is cast, but the material embodied in it and the environment which molded it. The tongue of Dante, of Luther and of the King James' Bible, are monuments of such consecration. We even carry this sacramentalism to its primitive conclusion. Although we know better, a strain of fetish worship runs through us all. The bones of men receive our reverence, as if in them resided — or resides — the efficacy of their thought and action. Placards are posted where thinkers have lived and died, as if their thought belonged like some haunting spirit to walls and garden walks.

Now all of this is legitimate enough so long as much of our thought *is* sacramental and our feelings stir with fetishistic suggestions at historic sites or relics. But it obscures the larger life and the truer immortality of thought, — the immortality of use. Dante's vision has entered into many a scheme of the world besides that into which he wove the picture of the Florence of his day. In fact for centuries it molded the cosmology of all Christendom and it still colors the common dream of /158/ immortality. It is this larger vision, built of the universal hope and fear, that is the real *Divina Commedia*, not the epic locked in its stubborn Tuscan rhymes. No form of art, however perfect, can imprison or contain all of a living thought. If thought is alive it is more than its form. It will escape and live. Often it carries with it in its new use broken fragments of

its form, and so may still be recognized at sight, as the architecture which produced the medieval cathedral breaks up into the buttressed piles of a modern city, — a dome here, a flying arch there, walls soaring for the light, towers
that carry forever the memories of Italy, — but all disparate and merged into a
new creation. This new creation, however, is no massive, self-contained whole,
it is instinct with life and change. It is not static like the old, but eternally re-
creating itself, replacing arches and domes by girders, and leaving the old
architecture behind with the problems it faced and the material it faced them
with. The one imperishable thing is the science of which these are the fleeting
traces.

It is the same with history as with art. At first glance what one sees in it is
the formal event, the embodied institution, the externals of things. But when
we look deeper we find that what happens in a given time and place is only a
part of the real event. The cause and results are also parts of it. The result is
merely the prolongation of the event in other circumstances, the releasing or
the destruction of its potentialities. Battles are more than charging cavalry
and riddled squares; they are not over when the firing ceases. They still continue in the hatreds and enthusiasms they arouse, in policies of state, in armaments, in nations themselves. The German Empire was Sedan crystallized —
Sedan and other things. The battle itself is only the most concentrated form of
an event, just as a poem is the most perfect expression of an idea. But the real
significance, the essence of both is something larger than the form, however
concentrated or complete it seems.

Now, it is in the same way that the cylinder syringe and separate condensers
of Watt's first engine are curiosities for the historian, but the idea, the creative
power, of that invention is moving on with all the forces of the Industrial
Revolution. It /159/ was born of an application of Scottish ingenuity to Scottish
thrift for all that Watt had in mind when he set to work was to save coal by
making an engine that did not have to heat a cool cylinder at every stroke.
But the engine that was invented to save coal, in its generation of power has
eaten into the heart of every coal deposit of Britain, while the power it releases
has not merely changed the material environment of civilization, but actually
brought millions of human beings into existence — each with his and her own
world of thought and work — in the stimulation of population through the
production of wealth.

Indeed in a sense one may say that machines — the product and embodiment
of invention — attain a sort of life of their own. They enter the field of industry
to play their own role, always incalculable, often achieving what their creators
never dreamed of and the opposite of what they intended. They are not simply
aids to labor, doing more things than the hand-worker, producing more and
more things of the same kind, in an endless addition to the stock of goods.
They are changing the mental and moral outlook of society as well as its physical basis. To what extent they do this must be left to a consideration of the
economic interpretation of history. But when even philosophy (in the meta-
physics of Bergson) recognizes that the machine steps, as it were, into the main
problem of life, adjustment and adaptation — and so becomes an element, and
the largest element — in this present phase of our biological evolution, it is
time for history to wake up to this tremendous fact. It is not a fact for econo-
mists or philosophers alone. Not only is it, in itself, an *event* of keen human
interest, clear definition and notable prominence, but it underlies every other
event of large importance in the political history of the last half-century. The
Industrial Revolution and the machine will inevitably furnish the central text

of those histories of the future which deal with our era, as Bergson says. It is our privilege even now to see how magnificent the text will be.

Compare the transport of the 18th Century with that under the control of the engineers of the 20th. The overland trade in the goods of the world was carried or drawn by horse. Now there is more horsepower dragging the freight trains of this /160/ country than all the horsepower of all the ages put together. Go down to the great power-house where the force is generated to drive these trains and see what degree of control over nature has been reached with reference to the needs of civilization. There the power is generated from the coals. The heat stored in from suns of geologic ages is released once more under the exacting control of an engineer and adjusted by automatic devices to correspond with the weight upon the floors of the cars, so that it is hardly a figure of speech to say that as you step upon the train a few more leaves of prehistoric forests crackle away in the energy of heat, and that energy becomes a substitute for the human energy of the traveler. Talk of miracles, with such an annihilation of time and control of power!

No writer that I know has ever expressed so well the full significance of the inventive art as the man who protested most against the changes which it wrought in the society of the 19th Century. Let me close by quoting this extract tucked away in a hidden corner of the works of John Ruskin:

"What may be the real dignity of the mechanical art itself? I cannot express the amazed awe, the crushed humility, with which I sometimes watch a locomotive take its breath at a railway station, and think what work there is in its bars and wheels, and what manner of men they must be who dig brown ironstone out of the ground and forge it into that. What assemblage of accurate and mighty faculties in them, more than fleshly power over melting crag and coiling fire, fettered and finessed at last into the precision of watchmaking; Titanian hammer-strokes beating out of lava these glittering cylinders and timely respondent valves, and fine ribbed rods, which touch each other as a serpent writhes in noiseless gliding, and omnipotence of grasp, infinite complex anatomy of active steel, compared with which the skeleton of a living creature would seem, to the careless observer, clumsy and vile. What would be the men who thought out this, who beat it out, who touched it with its polished calm of power, and who set it to its appointed task, and triumphantly saw it fulfill the task to the utmost of their will, feel or think about this weak hand of mine, timidly leading a /161/ little stain of water color which I cannot manage, into the imperfect shadow of something else . . . mere failure in every motion and endless disappointment; what I repeat would these iron-dominant genii think of me? and what ought I to think of them?" /162/

J. Bronowski

"1984" CAN BE A GOOD YEAR

Jacob Bronowski (1908–   ) is a British scientist and mathematician who has held important posts in Government Service. He has written on a wide variety of subjects, his works including books and essays on science and intellectual history, radio plays, a study of the poet William Blake, and numerous papers in mathematics. The essay

"'1984' Can Be a Good Year," *The New York Times Magazine* (July 15, 1962), pp. 11–12, 41–43, 45.

*reprinted here was adapted from a speech delivered before a recent congress of the
Royal Society of Health.*

A writer who offers to forecast the future ought to begin by showing his
credentials. My credentials are that I am an optimist and a scientist. I know that
it is not usual for a prophet to be an optimist; most prophets prefer to play the
part of Jeremiah and Cassandra. But then, that is because most prophets have
not been scientists either; they have not really been in favor of progress.

We can see this in the most popular prophets of our own lifetime: in Aldous
Huxley and George Orwell. Every reader must be struck by the revulsion
against science and, joined with that, by the deep-seated fear of the future,
which Huxley and Orwell share. "Brave New World" and "1984" are surely
the most depressing societies that have ever been imagined, because their authors are so full of self-righteousness. They seem to me to be, not works of
prophecy, but Puritan works of morality, preaching on every page a fire-and-
brimstone sermon of foreboding. From the first page, the authors are sure that
progress must be wrong—that everything that is good is already known to
them.

I do not intend to follow the social and political preoccupations of Huxley
and Orwell. Certainly the political world will be very different fifty years from
now, when Asia and Africa will be immensely more developed and more vigorous in world affairs. But I shall not discuss politics, and I shall not even discuss
social life in the future, except in one way—the way in which they will be
shaped by the scientific discoveries and the inventions which can be foreseen
now. I shall stick to predictions which are rooted in technical grounds.

There are three outstanding scientific changes which, I believe, will dominate the next fifty years. One is a change in the use of energy: this change has
been set in motion by the discovery that men can tap the energy in the atomic
nucleus. The second is a change in the control of energy: this change has been
set in motion by the development of those electronic devices which go under
the general name of automation. And the third is what I call the biological
revolution: the discovery, which is still unfamiliar to us, that men can remake
their biological environment, including parts of the human body and mind.

Nuclear Energy

One result of the addition of nuclear power to our other resources of power
is, of course, to increase the amount of energy at the command of men the
world over. What I have to say on this subject is best said in strictly numerical
terms; and since I have already made these calculations once before, I should
like to quote them as I made them:

"Today the inhabitants of the United States command, every man, woman
and child, the amount of mechanical energy each year that would be genera
ted, roughly, by ten tons of coal. This is the backing that civilization provides
now, and it is equal, again at a rough estimate, to the work that would be done
by a hundred slaves. If we are no longer a slave civilization, it is because even a
child in the United States has as much work done for it as would require the
muscle of a hundred slaves. By contrast, Athens at her richest provided for the
average member of a citizen's family—man, woman or child—no more than
five slaves.

"In most parts of the world, people today still command only a fraction of the
American standard. In India, for example, the average use of energy amounts

to the equivalent of about half a ton of coal a year, or five slaves – the standard of Athens over 2,000 years ago. This is the figure that will rise most steeply in the next fifty years. It cannot rise to the standard of the United States in that time, but it can reach a fifth of that standard. We can expect that in the next fifty years the energy used in the poorest countries will reach at least the equivalent of twenty slaves a head each year.

"It may seem very cold to measure the lives of people by the mechanical equivalent of two tons of coal a year, or twenty slaves. But the figure is not at all cold. In the first place, it could not be achieved had nuclear energy not been discovered. All the resources of the traditional fuels in the world would not yield this figure; and the dreams of liberal minds, to raise the dark races to the standard of the white, were an illusion until nuclear energy was discovered. The standards of the West will become at least tangible to the backward countries in the next fifty years because nuclear energy can provide the power."

This is one important effect of the coming of nuclear energy; and yet, to my mind, it is not the most important. To my mind /12/ what is most important is that energy will be more evenly distributed in the future. It will no longer be necessary to concentrate industry where either coal or oil is plentiful. We shall not need to take the industry to the fuel, but the other way about – the fuel, the nuclear fuel, to the industry. For a nuclear fuel is more than a million times as concentrated as a chemical fuel; and where we could not take a million tons of coal or oil, to South America, to the copperbelt, to the Australian desert, we shall be able to take a ton of uranium or of heavy hydrogen.

True, it will, for example, still be proportionately cheaper to build a large nuclear power station than a small one. But there is now no longer an inherent difficulty in siting any power station far from the line of supply of its fuel. In the past, the logic of concentrating the generation of electric power in a few large stations was that it was easier to carry the current from the station in a wire than to carry the coal to the station in a truck. But if the fuel is nuclear fuel, this is no longer so; a small nuclear station can become the center of a remote township as effectively as it already drives a submarine or keeps an army camp alive under the polar ice.

Over the next fifty years, nuclear energy is also essential to the growing of food on a world scale. It is, of course, clear that if energy is cheap, then it is possible to make a substitute for any material that we need, all the way from industrial diamonds to vitamins. In this sense, then, we can count on finding a decent standard of living, in food as well as in energy, for all the six billion people who will be alive fifty years from now. And in agriculture, we shall need nuclear energy above all for the irrigation and exploitation of marginal lands, including the brackish lands now poisoned by salt water.

If energy is cheap and transportable anywhere, then irrigation is possible anywhere. In agriculture, what energy will buy fifty years from now is water; and water will be the key to growing food for the world's population, which will be twice as large as today.

Automation

Second, I want to discuss the future influence of automation. In one sense, an automatic machine is still a machine, and automation is no more than the logical use of machines. But, in fact, automation implies such a difference in outlook, such a change in the conception of the place of the machine itself, that I ought to discuss it quite fundamentally.

Two hundred years ago, the West discovered that a man's or a woman's output of work can be multiplied many times if the repetitive tasks which a hand worker must do are done by a machine. Machines were invented, all the way from the power loom to the mechanical digger, that could mimic those actions of the human muscle which a man must carry out laboriously and monotonously, time and time again, in order to get a piece of work finished. The wealth of the West, and its high standard of living, derive directly from the revolution in manufacture – the Industrial Revolution – which these machines created.

Until recently, the machines of industry confined themselves to those mechanical tasks which need muscle and no more. Only in the last years have we come to see, what now seems obvious enough, that any repetitive task is really best handled by a machine. This is true, whether the repetitive task is muscular, like rolling steel sheets, or whether it demands more delicate skills of calculation and judgment, such as controlling the thickness of the steel and computing its price.

This is the real nature of automation: the discovery that repetition is a machine task, even if the repetition is in adding up a ledger or controlling the distillation of a chemical. Men and women thrive on variety, but machines thrive on monotony. Machines do not get bored (and they seldom get tired), their attention does not wander, they do not feel that their gifts are being wasted. They /41/ like nothing better than to repeat themselves.

Fifty years from now, the machine operator of any kind will be as much a fossil as the hand-weaver has been since 1830. Today we still distinguish between skilled and unskilled jobs of repetition, between office worker and factory worker, between white collar and no collar. In fifty years from now, all repetitive jobs will be unskilled.

The social implications of this change are profound, and I believe that they, more than anything else that I have forecast, will shape the community of the future. For their effect will be to change the social status of the different jobs in the community. The ability to handle a column of figures will become no more desirable than the ability to drive a rivet; and even the ability to write business letters may become less sought after than the ability to repair the machine that writes them by rote. As a result, the clerk will sink in social status, and the electrical technician will rise; and that in itself is a change as far-reaching as was once brought about by the dissolution of the monasteries.

A Social Revolution

Here I want to turn boldly to make a social prophecy. I believe that the combined effect of nuclear energy and of automation will be to revolutionize the way in which men run their industries. Today industries are concentrated in large cities. The reasons for this are twofold: we find it convenient to generate energy on a large scale, and at the same time we have to have large labor forces.

I have already shown that nuclear energy will make it possible to generate electric power in quite small units, where it is wanted. One reason for working in large cities will therefore disappear. But industry has moved to (and has created) large cities for another reason also: in the search, above all, for people. A product, whether it is a car or a can of polish, goes through many stages, so that many hands are needed to process and pass it on step by step. Is there any reason to think that industry will be able to break away from the huge arrays of semi-skilled workers which have served it hitherto?

I think that industry *is* breaking away, and that the traditional mass of factory hands *is* shrinking. The new wind in industry is automation, and I believe that it can transform industrial life in the next fifty years. There has been a great deal of technical talk about automation in recent years, but once again its more remote but important social consequences seem to me to have been missed. Yet automation is likely to revolution- /42/ ize the balance between work and leisure, and the size and structure of community life, in the next fifty years.

Our industrial civilization has gone on herding people together in huge complexes of cities. Now there is a hope that the next fifty years may reverse this trend, and may begin to dissolve the ugly concentrations of the Ruhr and the Clyde, of Pittsburgh and Tokyo. In automation, joined to nuclear energy, we have the means to run industries on the scale of a small country town—a scale which does not dwarf the human sense of community.

This shift in the pattern of working life is the most far-reaching change that I foresee. The fifty years ahead of us will provide the means to create a social revolution: to create lively and efficient small communities which can hold their own in the industrial world.

There are many things to be gained by leaving the large cities. For example, we shall gain the hours (about one eighth of our waking hours) which most workers now spend in the tedium and discomfort of travel. This is a great gain in leisure, and some people will think that it will create new problems of leisure. I do not think so; I think that leisure is only a problem today in those places where tedium and discomfort have reduced everyone to a dull indifference.

I am not the first prophet, or the first dreamer, to hope that the monstrous cities of today, like glaciers of an industrial ice age, will begin to melt away. But when social reformers in the past have longed for small communities which could be self-sufficient, they have usually wanted to found them on agriculture. They have wanted to go back to the land literally—to work on the land. This is quite unrealistic, now and in the future.

In short, it is not necessary to retreat from the disaster of the metropolis into the inertia of the village. The small town of the future can be as well-equipped, physically and intellectually, as the largest modern city. It will be served physically by the new forms of travel, and intellectually by the new links of communication which we can already foresee. My guess is that it will then need to be large enough only to support those unpractical but delightful luxuries which give life to a community—a baseball club and a theatre and places where people play chess or go bowling. I think that you can do all these things in a town of about thirty thousand strong, and this is my forecast of the size of the new industrial communities in the future.

But the small community that I have sketched has no room for dullness and indifference. If thirty thousand people make an industrial town which is physically and intellectually self-sufficient, they must all be skilled. The one unpractical luxury that they cannot afford is a man with no skill.

The Biological Revolution

The third fundamental change which will, I think, shape the future is what I have called the biological revolution. We are just beginning to learn that we can mold our biological environment as well as our physical one. During the next fifty years, this will be the most exciting and, I believe, the most influential work in science.

Let me single out a few lines of work which seem to me especially interesting and promising.

There is, to begin with, the practical progress in the attack on organisms which damage us. They may be pests which damage our food supply, at one extreme, or microbes which invade our bodies at the other. Fine work has already been done in developing specific chemicals to tackle each specific enemy. I think this method of combat, the development of exact and specific chemicals, will play a growing part in making men healthier and richer.

Let me give one example. We used to think that a man could produce the antibodies which resist a virus infection (for example, smallpox) only if he were given a mild dose of the infection. Now we know that this is not necessary. We know that a virus consists of two parts—a living center of nucleic acid, and an outside covering of protein. And we know that the protein covering alone will suffice to stimulate the cells to produce the antibodies which fight the whole virus. This is how, for example, the protein in the killed polio vaccine works.

I believe in the future we shall go even further: we shall protect against a virus disease by making, in the chemical laboratory, the protein covering of that virus.

This leads me to the next outstanding field of study. We know that there are drugs which greatly sharpen a man's faculties, and others which /43/ help him to be at peace with himself. Each kind of drug helps a man to make better use of his natural (but often hidden) gifts. I am sure that there is a bright prospect here for the future and that, as a result, men and women will lead livelier and happier lives, in work and in leisure right into their old age.

Finally, I should pay tribute to the searching work that is being done in the study of biological processes on the smallest, molecular scale. This has already given us a new understanding of the nature and of the dynamics of life, and at this very moment it has opened a deep insight into the basis of all heredity. I believe that in the long run this fundamental knowledge, which still seems abstract and remote, will have the greatest effect of all in the practice of medicine.

Science for Peace

I began by saying that I am an optimist and a scientist, and you now see that the two go together. There is plenty of ground for pessimism in world affairs, and perhaps we shall not avoid the suicide of mankind. But can we not? Can we not prevent the leaders of nations from being proudest of those scientific inventions which make the loudest bang?

We *must,* exactly because science has so much better uses to offer for its fundamental discoveries. I have shown you the rich future that should grow out of the very discoveries that people dread most—out of nuclear energy, automation, and biological advance.

What people fear is the reach, the power of these discoveries. And these people are not foolish: they recognize that nuclear energy, automation, and biological advance are the most powerful social forces of this century. But that power can be as great in peace as in war; we can use it to create the future and not to murder it. Science promises a future in which men can lead intelligent and healthy lives in cities of a human size, and I think it is a future truly worth living for. /45/

Erich Fromm

THE SANE SOCIETY

Erich Fromm (1900 –   ) is a German-born psychoanalyst, social philosopher, and author who came to the United States during the thirties. He has specialized in applying psychoanalytic theory to social and cultural problems. Among his works are Escape from Freedom *(1941),* Man for Himself *(1947),* The Forgotten Language *(1951), and* The Sane Society *(1955).*

We have a literacy above 90 per cent of the population. We have radio, television, movies, a newspaper a day for everybody. But instead of giving us the best of past and present literature and music, these media of communication, supplemented by advertising, fill the minds of men with the cheapest trash, lacking in any sense of reality, with sadistic phantasies which a halfway cultured person would be embarrassed to entertain even once in a while. But while the mind of everybody, young and old, is thus poisoned, we go on blissfully to see to it that no "immorality" occurs on the screen. Any suggestion that the government should finance the production of movies and radio programs which would enlighten and improve the minds of our people would be met again with indignation and accusations in the name of freedom and idealism.

We have reduced the average working hours to about half what they were one hundred years ago. We today have more free time available than our forefathers dared to dream of. But what has happened? We do not know how to use the newly gained free /5/ time; we try to kill the time we have saved, and are glad when another day is over.

Why should I continue with a picture which is known to everybody? Certainly, if an individual acted in this fashion, serious doubts would be raised as to his sanity; should he, however, claim that there is nothing wrong, and that he is acting perfectly reasonably, then the diagnosis would not even be doubtful any more.

Yet many psychiatrists and psychologists refuse to entertain the idea that society as a whole may be lacking in sanity. They hold that the problem of mental health in a society is only that of the number of "unadjusted" individuals, and not that of a possible unadjustment of the culture itself. This book deals with the latter problem; not with individual pathology, but with the *pathology of normalcy,* particularly with the pathology of contemporary Western society. But before entering into the intricate discussion of the concept of social pathology, let us look at some data, revealing and suggestive in themselves, which make reference to the incidence of *individual* pathology in Western culture.

What is the incidence of mental illness in the various countries of the Western world? It is a most amazing fact that there are no data which answer this question. While there are exact comparative statistical data on material resources, employment, birth and death rates, there is no adequate information about mental illness. At the most we have some exact data for a number of countries, like the United States and Sweden, but they only refer to admissions of patients to mental institutions, and they are not helpful in making estimates of comparative frequency of mental illness. These figures tell us just as much

From *The Sane Society* (New York: Rinehart & Company, Inc., 1955).

about improved psychiatric care and institutional facilities as they tell us about increase /6/ in incidence of mental illness.[1] The fact that more than half of all hospital beds in the United States are used for mental patients on whom we spend an annual sum of over a billion dollars may not be an indication of any increase in mental illness, but only of an increasing care. Some other figures, however, are more indicative of the occurrence of the more severe mental disturbances. If 17.7 per cent of all rejections of draftees in the last war were for reasons of mental illness, this fact certainly bespeaks a high degree of mental disturbance, even if we have no comparative figures referring to the past, or to other countries.

The only comparative data which can give us a rough indication of mental health, are those for suicide, homicide and alcoholism. No doubt the problem of suicide is a most complex one, and no single factor can be assumed to be *the* cause. But even without entering at this point into a discussion of suicide, I consider it a safe assumption that a high suicide rate in a given population is expressive of a lack of mental stability and mental health. That it is not a consequence of material poverty is clearly evidenced by all figures. The poorest countries have the lowest incidence of suicide, and the increasing material prosperity in Europe was accompanied by an increasing number of suicides.[2] As to alcoholism, there is no doubt that it, too, is a symptom of mental and emotional instability.

The motives for homicide are probably less indicative of pathology than those for suicide. However, though countries with a high homicide rate show a low suicide rate, their combined rates bring us to an interesting conclusion. If we classify both homicide and suicide as "destructive acts," our tables demonstrate that /7/ their combined rate is not constant, but fluctuating between the extremes of 35.76 and 4.24. This contradicts Freud's assumption of the comparative constancy of destructiveness which underlies his theory of death instinct. It disproves the implication that destructiveness maintains an invariable rate, differing only in directions toward the self or the outside world.

The [tables on the following pages] show the incidence of suicide, homicide and alcoholism for some of the most important European and North American countries. /8/

A quick glance at these tables shows a remarkable phenomenon: Denmark, Switzerland, Finland, Sweden and the United States are the countries with the highest suicide rate, and the highest combined suicide and homicide rate, while Spain, Italy, Northern Ireland and the Republic of Ireland are those with the lowest suicide and homicide rate. The figures for alcoholism show that the same countries – the United States, Switzerland, Sweden and Denmark – which have the highest suicide rate, have also the highest alcoholism rate, with the main difference that the United States are leading in this group, and that France has the second place, instead of the sixth place it has with regard to suicide.

These figures are startling and challenging indeed. Even if we should doubt whether the high frequency of suicide alone indicates a lack of mental health in a population, the fact that suicide and alcoholism figures largely coincide, seems to make it plain that we deal here with symptoms of mental unbalance.

We find then that the countries in Europe which are among the most democratic, peaceful and prosperous ones, and the United States, the most prosperous country in the world, show the most severe symptoms of mental disturb-

1. cf. H. Goldhamer and A. Marshall, *Psychosis and Civilization*, Free Press, Glencoe, 1953. /7/
2. cf. Maurice Halbwachs, *Les Causes du Suicide*, Félix Alcan, Paris, 1930, pp. 109 and 112. /7/

ance. The aim of the whole socio-economic development of the Western world is that of the materially comfortable life, relatively equal distribution of wealth, stable democracy and peace, and the very countries which have come closest to this aim show the most severe signs of mental unbalance! It is true that these figures in themselves do not *prove* anything, but at least they are startling. Even before we enter into a more thorough discussion of the whole problem, these data raise a question as to whether there is not something fundamentally wrong with our way of life and with the aims toward which we are striving.

Could it be that the middle-class life of prosperity, while satisfying our material needs leaves us with a feeling of intense /10/ boredom, and that suicide and alcoholism are pathological ways of escape from this boredom? Could it be that these figures are a drastic illustration for the truth of the statement that "man lives not by bread alone," and that they show that modern civilization fails to satisfy profound needs in man? If so, what are these needs?

[The following remarks] are an attempt to answer this question, and to arrive at a critical evaluation of the effect contemporary Western culture has on the mental health and sanity of the people living under our system. However, before we enter into the specific discussion of these questions, it seems that we should take up the general problem of the pathology of normalcy, which is the premise underlying the whole trend of thought expressed in this book. . . . /11/

By alienation is meant a mode of experience in which the person experiences himself as an alien. He has become, one might say, estranged from himself. He does not experience himself as the center of his world, as the creator of

TABLE I.[1]*

COUNTRY	(Per 100,000 of adult population)	
	SUICIDE	HOMICIDE
Denmark	35.09	0.67
Switzerland	33.72	1.42
Finland	23.35	6.45
Sweden	19.74	1.01
United States	15.52	8.50
France	14.83	1.53
Portugal	14.24	2.79
England and Wales	13.43	0.63
Australia	13.03	1.57
Canada	11.40	1.67
Scotland	8.06	0.52
Norway	7.84	0.38
Spain	7.71	2.88
Italy	7.67	7.38
Northern Ireland	4.82	0.13
Ireland (Republic)	3.70	0.54

1. The information in the first and second tables is derived from 1. World Health Organization (1951) *Annual epidemiological and vital statistics, 1939–46. Part I. Vital statistics and causes of death,* Geneva, pp. 38–71, (the figures from this source have been converted for greater accuracy from total to adult population), and 2. World Health Organization, (1952) *Epidem. vital Statist. Rep. 5,* 377. That of the third table, from the Report on the First Session of the Alcoholism Subcommittee, of the Expert Committee on Mental Health, World Health Organization, Geneva, 1951. /8/
*Table I appeared on page 8 in the original—*Editors' note.*

his own acts—but his acts and their consequences have become his masters, whom he obeys, or whom he may even worship. The alienated person is out of touch with himself as he is out of touch with any other person. He, like the others, are experienced as things are experienced; with the senses and with common sense, but at the same time /120/ without being related to oneself and to the world outside productively. . . . /121/

Alienation as we find it in modern society is almost total; it pervades the relationship of man to his work, to the things he consumes, to the state, to his fellow man, and to himself. Man has /124/ created a world of man-made things as it never existed before. He has constructed a complicated social machine to administer the technical machine he built. Yet this whole creation of his stands over and above him. He does not feel himself as a creator and center, but as the servant of a Golem, which his hands have built. The more powerful and gigantic the forces are which he unleashes, the more powerless he feels himself as a human being. He confronts himself with his own forces embodied in things he has created, alienated from himself. He is owned by his own creation, and has lost ownership of himself. He has built a golden calf, and says "these are your gods who have brought you out of Egypt."

What happens to the *worker*? To put it in the words of a thoughtful and thorough observer of the industrial scene: "In industry the person becomes an economic atom that dances to the tune of atomistic management. Your place is just here, you will sit in this fashion, your arms will move x inches in a course of y radius and the time of movement will be .000 minutes.

"Work is becoming more repetitive and thoughtless as the planners, the micromotionists, and the scientific managers further strip the worker of his right to think and move freely. Life is being denied; need to control, creativeness, curiosity, and independent thought are being baulked, and the result,

TABLE II.*

COUNTRY	DESTRUCTIVE ACTS
	Homicide and Suicide combined
Denmark	35.76
Switzerland	35.14
Finland	29.80
United States	24.02
Sweden	20.75
Portugal	17.03
France	16.36
Italy	15.05
Australia	14.60
England and Wales	14.06
Canada	13.07
Spain	10.59
Scotland	8.58
Norway	8.22
Northern Ireland	4.95
Ireland (Republic)	4.24

(Both the above tables show the figures for 1946)

*Table II appeared on page 9 in the original—*Editors' note.*

the inevitable result, is flight or fight on the part of the worker, apathy or destructiveness, psychic regression."[1] . . . /125/

There is another aspect of alienation from the things we consume which needs to be mentioned. We are surrounded by things of whose nature and origin we know nothing. The .telephone, radio, phonograph, and all other complicated machines are almost as mysterious to us as they would be to a man from a primitive culture; we know how to use them, that is, we know which button to turn, but we do not know on what principle they function, except in the vaguest terms of something we once learned at school. And things which do not rest upon difficult scientific principles are almost equally alien to us. We do not know how bread is made, how cloth is woven, how a table is manufactured, how glass is made. We consume, as we produce, without any concrete relatedness to the objects with which we deal; we live in a world of things, and our only connection with them is that we know how to manipulate or to consume them.

Our way of consumption necessarily results in the fact that we are never satisfied, since it is not our real concrete person which consumes a real and concrete thing. We thus develop an ever-increasing need for more things, for more consumption. It is true that as long as the living standard of the population is below a dignified level of subsistence, there is a natural need for more consumption. It is also true that there is a legitimate need for more consumption as man develops culturally and has more refined needs for better food, objects of artistic pleasure, books, etc. But our craving for consumption has lost all connection with the real needs of man. Originally, the idea of consuming more and better things was meant to give man a happier, more satisfied life. Consumption was a means to an end, that of happiness. It now has become an aim in itself. The constant increase of needs forces /134/ us to an ever-increasing effort, it makes us dependent on these needs and on the people and institutions by whose help we attain them. "Each person speculates to create a new need in the other person, in order to force him into a new dependency, to a new form of pleasure, hence to his economic ruin. . . . With

TABLE III.*

COUNTRY	ESTIMATED NUMBER OF ALCOHOLICS *With or without complications* (Per 100,000 of adult population)	
United States	3,952	(1948)
France	2,850	(1945)
Sweden	2,580	(1946)
Switzerland	2,385	(1947)
Denmark	1,950	(1948)
Norway	1,560	(1947)
Finland	1,430	(1947)
Australia	1,340	(1947)
England and Wales	1,100	(1948)
Italy	500	(1942)

1. J. J. Gillespie, *Free Expression in Industry,* The Pilot Press Ltd., London, 1948. /125/
*Table III appeared on page 9 in the original—*Editors' note.*

a multitude of commodities grows the realm of alien things which enslave man."[1]

Man today is fascinated by the possibility of buying more, better, and especially, new things. He is consumption-hungry. The act of buying and consuming has become a compulsive, irrational aim, because it is an end in itself, with little relation to the use of, or pleasure in the things bought and consumed. To buy the latest gadget, the latest model of anything that is on the market, is the dream of everybody, in comparison to which the real pleasure in use is quite secondary. Modern man, if he dared to be articulate about his concept of heaven, would describe a vision which would look like the biggest department store in the world, showing new things and gadgets, and himself having plenty of money with which to buy them. He would wander around open-mouthed in this heaven of gadgets and commodities, provided only that there were ever more and newer things to buy, and perhaps that his neighbors were just a little less privileged than he.

Significantly enough, one of the older traits of middle-class society, the attachment to possessions and property, has undergone a profound change. In the older attitude, a certain sense of loving possession existed between a man and his property. It grew on him. He was proud of it. He took good care of it, and it was painful when eventually he had to part from it because it could not be used any more. There is very little left of this sense of property today. One loves the newness of the thing bought, and is ready to betray it when something newer has appeared. /135/

Expressing the same change in characterological terms, I can refer to what has been stated above with regard to the *hoarding* orientation as dominant in the picture of the nineteenth century. In the middle of the twentieth century the hoarding orientation has given way to the *receptive* orientation, in which the aim is to receive, to "drink in," to have something new all the time, to live with a continuously open mouth, as it were. This receptive orientation is blended with the marketing orientation, while in the nineteenth century the hoarding was blended with the exploitative orientation.

The alienated attitude toward consumption not only exists in our acquisition and consumption of commodities, but it determines far beyond this the employment of leisure time. What are we to expect? If a man works without genuine relatedness to what he is doing, if he buys and consumes commodities in an abstractified and alienated way, how can he make use of his leisure time in an active and meaningful way? He always remains the passive and alienated consumer. He "consumes" ball games, moving pictures, newspapers and magazines, books, lectures, natural scenery, social gatherings, in the same alienated and abstractified way in which he consumes the commodities he has bought. He does not participate actively, he wants to "take in" all there is to be had, and to have as much as possible of pleasure, culture and what not. Actually, he is not free to enjoy "his" leisure; his leisure-time consumption is determined by industry, as are the commodities he buys; his taste is manipulated, he wants to see and to hear what he is conditioned to want to see and to hear; entertainment is an industry like any other, the customer is made to buy fun as he is made to buy dresses and shoes. The value of the fun is determined by its success on the market, not by anything which could be measured in human terms. /136/

1. [Nationalökonomie und Philosophie, 1844, published in Karl Marx' *Die Frühschriften*, Alfred Kröner Verlag, Stuttgart, 1953], p. 254. /135/

E. M. Forster

THE MACHINE STOPS

Edward Morgan Forster (1879 –   ) has produced short stories and novels of distinction since the early years of the century. He first reached a wide audience with the publication, in 1924, of his most famous novel, A Passage to India. *A pervasive theme in Forster's writing is the conflict between a sensitive and perceptive individual and a convention-dominated and emotionally sterile society. Certain elements in his work anticipate themes that were to be developed more forcefully by D. H. Lawrence. The surface manner of Forster's novels is realistic, but in many of his short stories he adopted the devices of fantasy.*

PART I.   THE AIR-SHIP

Imagine, if you can, a small room, hexagonal in shape, like the cell of a bee. It is lighted neither by window nor by lamp, yet it is filled with a soft radiance. There are no apertures for ventilation, yet the air is fresh. There are no musical instruments, and yet, at the moment that my meditation opens, this room is throbbing with melodious sounds. An arm-chair is in the centre, by its side a reading-desk — that is all the furniture. And in the arm-chair there sits a swaddled lump of flesh — a woman, about five feet high, with a face as white as a fungus. It is to her that the little room belongs.

An electric bell rang.

The woman touched a switch and the music was silent. /13/

"I suppose I must see who it is," she thought, and set her chair in motion. The chair, like the music, was worked by machinery, and it rolled her to the other side of the room, where the bell still rang importunately.

"Who is it?" she called. Her voice was irritable, for she had been interrupted often since the music began. She knew several thousand people; in certain directions human intercourse had advanced enormously.

But when she listened into the receiver, her white face wrinkled into smiles, and she said:

"Very well. Let us talk, I will isolate myself. I do not expect anything important will happen for the next five minutes — for I can give you fully five minutes, Kuno. Then I must deliver my lecture on 'Music during the Australian Period.'"

She touched the isolation knob, so that no one else could speak to her. Then she touched the lighting apparatus, and the little room was plunged into darkness. /14/

"Be quick!" she called, her irritation returning. "Be quick, Kuno; here I am in the dark wasting my time."

But it was fully fifteen seconds before the round plate that she held in her hands began to glow. A faint blue light shot across it, darkening to purple, and presently she could see the image of her son, who lived on the other side of the earth, and he could see her.

"Kuno, how slow you are."

He smiled gravely.

"The Machine Stops," *The Eternal Moment and Other Stories* (New York: Harcourt, Brace and World, Inc., 1928), pp. 13–85.

"I really believe you enjoy dawdling."

"I have called you before, mother, but you were always busy or isolated. I have something particular to say."

"What is it, dearest boy? Be quick. Why could you not send it by pneumatic post?"

"Because I prefer saying such a thing. I want—— "

"Well?"

"I want you to come and see me."

Vashti watched his face in the blue plate. /15/

"But I can see you!" she exclaimed. "What more do you want?"

"I want to see you not through the Machine," said Kuno. "I want to speak to you not through the wearisome Machine."

"Oh, hush!" said his mother, vaguely shocked. "You mustn't say anything against the Machine."

"Why not?"

"One mustn't."

"You talk as if a god had made the Machine," cried the other. "I believe that you pray to it when you are unhappy. Men made it, do not forget that. Great men, but men. The Machine is much, but it is not everything. I see something like you in this plate, but I do not see you. I hear something like you through this telephone, but I do not hear you. That is why I want you to come. Come and stop with me. Pay me a visit, so that we can meet face to face, and talk about the hopes that are in my mind."

She replied that she could scarcely spare the time for a visit. /16/

"The air-ship barely takes two days to fly between me and you."

"I dislike air-ships."

"Why?"

"I dislike seeing the horrible brown earth, and the sea, and the stars when it is dark. I get no ideas in an air-ship."

"I do not get them anywhere else."

"What kind of ideas can the air give you?"

He paused for an instant.

"Do you not know four big stars that form an oblong, and three stars close together in the middle of the oblong, and hanging from these stars, three other stars?"

"No, I do not. I dislike the stars. But did they give you an idea? How interesting; tell me."

"I had an idea that they were like a man."

"I do not understand."

"The four big stars are the man's shoulders and his knees. The three stars in the middle are like the belts that men wore once, and the three stars hanging are like a sword." /17/

"A sword?"

"Men carried swords about with them, to kill animals and other men."

"It does not strike me as a very good idea, but it is certainly original. When did it come to you first?"

"In the air-ship—— " He broke off, and she fancied that he looked sad. She could not be sure, for the Machine did not transmit *nuances* of expression. It only gave a general idea of people—an idea that was good enough for all practical purposes, Vashti thought. The imponderable bloom, declared by a discredited philosophy to be the actual essence of intercourse, was rightly ignored by the Machine, just as the imponderable bloom of the grape was ignored by the manufacturers of artificial fruit. Something "good enough" had long since been accepted by our race.

"The truth is," he continued, "that I want to see these stars again. They are curious stars. I want to see them not from the air-ship, but from the surface of the earth, as our ancestors did, thou- /18/ sands of years ago. I want to visit the surface of the earth."

She was shocked again.

"Mother, you must come, if only to explain to me what is the harm of visiting the surface of the earth."

"No harm," she replied, controlling herself. "But no advantage. The surface of the earth is only dust and mud, no life remains on it, and you would need a respirator, or the cold of the outer air would kill you. One dies immediately in the outer air."

"I know; of course I shall take all precautions."

"And besides——"

"Well?"

She considered, and chose her words with care. Her son had a queer temper, and she wished to dissuade him from the expedition.

"It is contrary to the spirit of the age," she asserted.

"Do you mean by that, contrary to the Machine?" /19/

"In a sense, but——"

His image in the blue plate faded.

"Kuno!"

He had isolated himself.

For a moment Vashti felt lonely.

Then she generated the light, and the sight of her room, flooded with radiance and studded with electric buttons, revived her. There were buttons and switches everywhere—buttons to call for food, for music, for clothing. There was the hot-bath button, by pressure of which a basin of (imitation) marble rose out of the floor, filled to the brim with a warm deodorised liquid. There was the cold-bath button. There was the button that produced literature. And there were of course the buttons by which she communicated with her friends. The room, though it contained nothing, was in touch with all that she cared for in the world.

Vashti's next move was to turn off the isolation-switch, and all the accumulations of the last three minutes burst upon her. The room was filled with /20/ the noise of bells, and speaking-tubes. What was the new food like? Could she recommend it? Had she had any ideas lately? Might one tell her one's own ideas? Would she make an engagement to visit the public nurseries at an early date?—say this day month.

To most of these questions she replied with irritation—a growing quality in that accelerated age. She said that the new food was horrible. That she could not visit the public nurseries through press of engagements. That she had no ideas of her own but had just been told one—that four stars and three in the middle were like a man: she doubted there was much in it. Then she switched off her correspondents, for it was time to deliver her lecture on Australian music.

The clumsy system of public gatherings had been long since abandoned: neither Vashti nor her audience stirred from their rooms. Seated in her arm-chair she spoke, while they in their arm-chairs heard her, fairly well, and saw her, fairly well, She opened with a humorous account of /21/ music in the pre-Mongolian epoch, and went on to describe the great outburst of song that followed the Chinese conquest. Remote and primæval as were the methods of I-San-So and the Brisbane school, she yet felt (she said) that study of them might repay the musician of today: they had freshness; they had, above all, ideas.

Her lecture, which lasted ten minutes, was well received, and at its conclusion she and many of her audience listened to a lecture on the sea; there were ideas to be got from the sea; the speaker had donned a respirator and visited it lately. Then she fed, talked to many friends, had a bath, talked again, and summoned her bed.

The bed was not to her liking. It was too large, and she had a feeling for a small bed. Complaint was useless, for beds were of the same dimension all over the world, and to have had an alternative size would have involved vast alterations in the Machine. Vashti isolated herself—it was necessary, for neither day nor night existed under the ground—and reviewed all that had happened /22/ since she had summoned the bed last. Ideas? Scarcely any. Events—was Kuno's invitation an event?

By her side, on the little reading-desk, was a survival from the ages of litter —one book. This was the Book of the Machine. In it were instructions against every possible contingency. If she was hot or cold or dyspeptic or at loss for a word, she went to the book, and it told her which button to press. The Central Committee published it. In accordance with a growing habit, it was richly bound.

Sitting up in the bed, she took it reverently in her hands. She glanced round the glowing room as if some one might be watching her. Then, half ashamed, half joyful, she murmured "O Machine! O Machine!" and raised the volume to her lips. Thrice she kissed it, thrice inclined her head, thrice she felt the delirium of acquiescence. Her ritual performed, she turned to page 1367, which gave the times of the departure of the air-ships from the island in the southern hemisphere, under /23/ whose soil she lived, to the island in the northern hemisphere, whereunder lived her son.

She thought, "I have not the time."

She made the room dark and slept; she awoke and made the room light; she ate and exchanged ideas with her friends, and listened to music and attended lectures; she made the room dark and slept. Above her, beneath her, and around her, the Machine hummed eternally; she did not notice the noise, for she had been born with it in her ears. The earth, carrying her, hummed as it sped through silence, turning her now to the invisible sun, now to the invisible stars. She awoke and made the room light.

"Kuno!"

"I will not talk to you," he answered, "until you come."

"Have you been on the surface of the earth since we spoke last?"

His image faded.

Again she consulted the book. She became very nervous and lay back in her chair palpitating. /24/ Think of her as without teeth or hair. Presently she directed the chair to the wall, and pressed an unfamiliar button. The wall swung apart slowly. Through the opening she saw a tunnel that curved slightly, so that its goal was not visible. Should she go to see her son, here was the beginning of the journey.

Of course she knew all about the communication-system. There was nothing mysterious in it. She would summon a car and it would fly with her down the tunnel until it reached the lift that communicated with the air-ship station: the system had been in use for many, many years, long before the universal establishment of the Machine. And of course she had studied the civilisation that had immediately preceded her own — the civilisation that had mistaken the functions of the system, and had used it for bringing people to things, instead of for bringing things to people. Those funny old days, when men went for change of air instead of changing the air in their rooms! And yet — she was frightened of the tunnel: she /25/ had not seen it since her last child was born. It curved — but not quite as she remembered; it was brilliant — but not quite as brilliant as a lecturer had suggested. Vashti was seized with the terrors of direct experience. She shrank back into the room, and the wall closed up again.

"Kuno," she said, "I cannot come to see you. I am not well."

Immediately an enormous apparatus fell on to her out of the ceiling, a thermometer was automatically inserted between her lips, a stethoscope was automatically laid upon her heart. She lay powerless. Cool pads soothed her forehead. Kuno had telegraphed to her doctor.

So the human passions still blundered up and down in the Machine. Vashti drank the medicine that the doctor projected into her mouth, and the machinery retired into the ceiling. The voice of Kuno was heard asking how she felt.

"Better." Then with irritation: "But why do you not come to me instead?" /26/

"Because I cannot leave this place."

"Why?"

"Because, any moment, something tremendous may happen."

"Have you been on the surface of the earth yet?"

"Not yet."

"Then what is it?"

"I will not tell you through the Machine."

She resumed her life.

But she thought of Kuno as a baby, his birth, his removal to the public nurseries, her one visit to him there, his visits to her — visits which stopped when the Machine had assigned him a room on the other side of the earth. "Parents, duties of," said the book of the Machine, "cease at the moment of birth. P. 422327483." True, but there was something special about Kuno — indeed there had been something special about all her children — and, after all, she must brave the journey if he desired it. And "something tremendous might /27/ happen." What did that mean? The nonsense of a youthful man, no doubt, but she must go. Again she pressed the unfamiliar button, again the wall swung back, and she saw the tunnel that curved out of sight. Clasping the Book, she rose, tottered on to the platform, and summoned the car. Her room closed behind her: the journey to the northern hemisphere had begun.

Of course it was perfectly easy. The car approached and in it she found armchairs exactly like her own. When she signalled, it stopped, and she tottered into the lift. One other passenger was in the lift, the first fellow creature she had seen face to face for months. Few travelled in these days, for, thanks to the advance of science, the earth was exactly alike all over. Rapid intercourse, from which the previous civilisation had hoped so much, had ended by defeating itself. What was the good of going to Pekin when it was just like Shrewsbury? Why return to Shrewsbury when it would be just like Pekin? Men seldom moved their bodies; all unrest was concentrated in the soul. /28/

The air-ship service was a relic from the former age. It was kept up, because it was easier to keep it up than to stop it or to diminish it, but it now far exceeded the wants of the population. Vessel after vessel would rise from the vomitories of Rye or of Christchurch (I use the antique names), would sail into the crowded sky, and would draw up at the wharves of the south—empty. So nicely adjusted was the system, so independent of meteorology, that the sky, whether calm or cloudy, resembled a vast kaleidoscope whereon the same patterns periodically recurred. The ship on which Vashti sailed started now at sunset, now at dawn. But always, as it passed above Rheims, it would neighbour the ship that served between Helsingfors and the Brazils, and, every third time it surmounted the Alps, the fleet of Palermo would cross its track behind. Night and day, wind and storm, tide and earthquake, impeded man no longer. He had harnessed Leviathan. All the old literature, with its praise of Nature, and its fear of Nature, rang false as the prattle of a child. /29/

Yet as Vashti saw the vast flank of the ship, stained with exposure to the outer air, her horror of direct experience returned. It was not quite like the air-ship in the cinematophote. For one thing it smelt—not strongly or unpleasantly, but it did smell, and with her eyes shut she should have known that a new thing was close to her. Then she had to walk to it from the lift, had to submit to glances from the other passengers. The man in front dropped his Book—no great matter, but it disquieted them all. In the rooms, if the Book was dropped, the floor raised it mechanically, but the gangway to the air-ship was not so prepared, and the sacred volume lay motionless. They stopped—the thing was unforeseen—and the man, instead of picking up his property, felt the muscles of his arm to see how they had failed him. Then some one actually said with direct utterance: "We shall be late"—and they trooped on board, Vashti treading on the pages as she did so.

Inside, her anxiety increased. The arrangements /30/ were old-fashioned and rough. There was even a female attendant, to whom she would have to announce her wants during the voyage. Of course a revolving platform ran the length of the boat, but she was expected to walk from it to her cabin. Some cabins were better than others, and she did not get the best. She thought the attendant had been unfair, and spasms of rage shook her. The glass valves had closed, she could not go back. She saw, at the end of the vestibule, the lift in which she had ascended going quietly up and down, empty. Beneath those corridors of shining tiles were rooms, tier below tier, reaching far into the earth, and in each room there sat a human being, eating, or sleeping, or producing ideas. And buried deep in the hive was her own room. Vashti was afraid.

"O Machine! O Machine!" she murmured, and caressed her Book, and was comforted.

Then the sides of the vestibule seemed to melt together, as do the passages that we see in dreams, the lift vanished, the Book that had been dropped /31/ slid to the left and vanished, polished tiles rushed by like a stream of water, there was a slight jar, and the air-ship. issuing from its tunnel, soared above the waters of a tropical ocean.

It was night. For a moment she saw the coast of Sumatra edged by the phosphorescence of waves, and crowned by lighthouses, still sending forth their disregarded beams. These also vanished, and only the stars distracted her. They were not motionless, but swayed to and fro above her head, thronging out of one skylight into another, as if the universe and not the air-ship was careening. And, as often happens on clear nights, they seemed now to be in perspective, now on a plane; now piled tier beyond tier into the infinite heavens, now concealing infinity, a roof limiting for ever the visions of men. In either case they seemed intolerable. "Are we to travel in the dark?" called the passengers angrily, and the attendant, who had been careless, generated the light, and pulled down the blinds of pliable metal. When the air-ships had been built, the desire to look direct at /32/ things still lingered in the world. Hence the extraordinary number of skylights and windows, and the proportionate discomfort to those who were civilised and refined. Even in Vashti's cabin one star peeped through a flaw in the blind, and after a few hours' uneasy slumber, she was disturbed by an unfamiliar glow, which was the dawn.

Quick as the ship had sped westwards, the earth had rolled eastwards quicker still, and had dragged back Vashti and her companions towards the sun. Science could prolong the night, but only for a little, and those high hopes of neutralising the earth's diurnal revolution had passed, together with hopes that were possibly higher. To "keep pace with the sun," or even to outstrip it, had been the aim of the civilisation preceding this. Racing aeroplanes had been built for the purpose, capable of enormous speed, and steered by the greatest intellects of the epoch. Round the globe they went, round and round, westward, westward, round and round, amidst humanity's applause. In vain. The /33/ globe went eastward quicker still, horrible accidents occurred, and the Committee of the Machine, at the time rising into prominence, declared the pursuit illegal, unmechanical, and punishable by Homelessness.

Of Homelessness more will be said later.

Doubtless the Committee was right. Yet the attempt to "defeat the sun" aroused the last common interest that our race experienced about the heavenly bodies, or indeed about anything. It was the last time that men were compacted by thinking of a power outside the world. The sun had conquered, yet it was the end of his spiritual dominion. Dawn, midday, twilight, the zodiacal path, touched neither men's lives nor their hearts, and science retreated into the ground, to concentrate herself upon problems that she was certain of solving.

So when Vashti found her cabin invaded by a rosy finger of light, she was annoyed, and tried to adjust the blind. But the blind flew up altogether, and she saw through the skylight small /34/ pink clouds, swaying against a background of blue, and as the sun crept higher, its radiance entered direct, brimming down the wall, like a golden sea. It rose and fell with the air-ship's motion, just as waves rise and fall, but it advanced steadily, as a tide advances. Unless she was careful, it would strike her face. A spasm of horror shook her and she rang for the attendant. The attendant too was horrified, but she could do nothing; it was not her place to mend the blind. She could only suggest that the lady should change her cabin, which she accordingly prepared to do.

People were almost exactly alike all over the world, but the attendant of the air-ship, perhaps owing to her exceptional duties, had grown a little out of the common. She had often to address passengers with direct speech, and this had given her a certain roughness and originality of manner. When Vashti swerved away from the sunbeams with a cry, she behaved barbarically — she put out her hand to steady her. /35/

"How dare you!" exclaimed the passenger. "You forget yourself!"

The woman was confused, and apologised for not having let her fall. People never touched one another. The custom had become obsolete, owing to the Machine.

"Where are we now?" asked Vashti haughtily.

"We are over Asia," said the attendant, anxious to be polite.

"Asia?"

"You must excuse my common way of speaking. I have got into the habit of calling places over which I pass by their unmechanical names."

"Oh, I remember Asia. The Mongols came from it."

"Beneath us, in the open air, stood a city that was once called Simla."

"Have you ever heard of the Mongols and of the Brisbane school?"

"No."

"Brisbane also stood in the open air."

"Those mountains to the right—let me show /36/ you them." She pushed back a metal blind. The main chain of the Himalayas was revealed. "They were once called the Roof of the World, those mountains."

"What a foolish name!"

"You must remember that, before the dawn of civilisation, they seemed to be an impenetrable wall that touched the stars. It was supposed that no one but the gods could exist above their summits. How we have advanced, thanks to the Machine!"

"How we have advanced, thanks to the Machine!" said Vashti.

"How we have advanced, thanks to the Machine!" echoed the passenger who had dropped his Book the night before, and who was standing in the passage.

"And that white stuff in the cracks?—what is it?"

"I have forgotten its name."

"Cover the window, please. These mountains give me no ideas." /37/

The northern aspect of the Himalayas was in deep shadow: on the Indian slope the sun had just prevailed. The forests had been destroyed during the literature epoch for the purpose of making newspaper-pulp, but the snows were awakening to their morning glory, and clouds still hung on the breasts of Kinchinjunga. In the plain were seen the ruins of cities, with diminished rivers creeping by their walls, and by the sides of these were sometimes the signs of vomitories, marking the cities of today. Over the whole prospect air-ships rushed, crossing and intercrossing with incredible *aplomb,* and rising nonchalantly when they desired to escape the perturbations of the lower atmosphere and to traverse the Roof of the World.

"We have indeed advanced, thanks to the Machine," repeated the attendant, and hid the Himalayas behind a metal blind.

The day dragged wearily forward. The passengers sat each in his cabin, avoiding one another with an almost physical repulsion and longing to /38/ be once more under the surface of the earth. There were eight or ten of them, mostly young males, sent out from the public nurseries to inhabit the rooms of those who had died in various parts of the earth. The man who had dropped his Book was on the homeward journey. He had been sent to Sumatra for the purpose of propagating the race. Vashti alone was travelling by her private will.

At midday she took a second glance at the earth. The air-ship was crossing another range of mountains, but she could see little, owing to clouds. Masses of black rock hovered below her, and merged indistinctly into grey. Their shapes were fantastic; one of them resembled a prostrate man.

"No ideas here," murmured Vashti, and hid the Caucasus behind a metal blind.

In the evening she looked again. They were crossing a golden sea, in which lay many small islands and one peninsula.

She repeated, "No ideas here," and hid Greece behind a metal blind. /39/

PART II.   THE MENDING APPARATUS

By a vestibule, by a lift, by a tubular railway, by a platform, by a sliding door — by reversing all the steps of her departure did Vashti arrive at her son's room, which exactly resembled her own. She might well declare that the visit was superfluous. The buttons, the knobs, the reading-desk with the Book, the temperature, the atmosphere, the illumination — all were exactly the same. And if Kuno himself, flesh of her flesh, stood close beside her at last, what profit was there in that? She was too well-bred to shake him by the hand.

Averting her eyes, she spoke as follows:

"Here I am. I have had the most terrible journey and greatly retarded the development of my soul. It is not worth it, Kuno, it is not worth it. My time is too precious. The sunlight almost touched me, and I have met with the rudest peo- /40/ ple. I can only stop a few minutes. Say what you want to say, and then I must return."

"I have been threatened with Homelessness," said Kuno.

She looked at him now.

"I have been threatened with Homelessness, and I could not tell you such a thing through the Machine."

Homelessness means death. The victim is exposed to the air, which kills him.

"I have been outside since I spoke to you last. The tremendous thing has happened, and they have discovered me."

"But why shouldn't you go outside!" she exclaimed. "It is perfectly legal, perfectly mechanical, to visit the surface of the earth. I have lately been to a lecture on the sea; there is no objection to that; one simply summons a respira- tor and gets an Egression-permit. It is not the kind of thing that spiritually- minded people do, and I begged you not to do it, but there is no legal objection to it." /41/

"I did not get an Egression-permit."

"Then how did you get out?"

"I found out a way of my own."

The phrase conveyed no meaning to her, and he had to repeat it.

"A way of your own?" she whispered. "But that would be wrong."

"Why?"

The question shocked her beyond measure.

"You are beginning to worship the Machine," he said coldly. "You think it irreligious of me to have found out a way of my own. It was just what the Committee thought, when they threatened me with Homelessness."

At this she grew angry. "I worship nothing!" she cried. "I am most advanced. I don't think you irreligious, for there is no such thing as religion left. All the fear and the superstition that existed once have been destroyed by the Machine. I only meant that to find out a way of your own was — Besides, there is no new way out."

"So it is always supposed."

"Except through the vomitories, for which one /42/ must have an Egression- permit, it is impossible to get out. The Book says so."

"Well, the Book's wrong, for I have been out on my feet."

For Kuno was possessed of a certain physical strength.

By these days it was a demerit to be muscular. Each infant was examined at birth, and all who promised undue strength were destroyed. Humanitarians may protest, but it would have been no true kindness to let an athlete live; he would never have been happy in that state of life to which the Machine had called him; he would have yearned for trees to climb, rivers to bathe in, meadows and hills against which he might measure his body. Man must be adapted to his surroundings, must he not? In the dawn of the world our weakly must be exposed on Mount Taygetus, in its twilight our strong will suffer euthanasia, that the Machine may progress, that the Machine may progress, that the Machine may progress eternally.

"You know that we have lost the sense of /43/ space. We say 'space is annihilated,' but we have annihilated not space, but the sense thereof. We have lost a part of ourselves. I determined to recover it, and I began by walking up and down the platform of the railway outside my room. Up and down, until I was tired, and so did recapture the meaning of 'Near' and 'Far.' 'Near' is a place to which I can get quickly *on my feet,* not a place to which the train or the air-ship will take me quickly. 'Far' is a place to which I cannot get quickly on my feet; the vomitory is 'far,' though I could be there in thirty-eight seconds by summoning the train. Man is the measure. That was my first lesson. Man's feet are the measure for distance, his hands are the measure for ownership, his body is the measure for all that is lovable and desirable and strong. Then I went further: it was then that I called to you for the first time, and you would not come.

"This city, as you know, is built deep beneath the surface of the earth, with only the vomitories protruding. Having paced the platform outside /44/ my own room, I took the lift to the next platform and paced that also, and so with each in turn, until I came to the topmost, above which begins the earth. All the platforms were exactly alike, and all that I gained by visiting them was to develop my sense of space and my muscles. I think I should have been content with this—it is not a little thing—but as I walked and brooded, it occurred to me that our cities had been built in the days when men still breathed the outer air, and that there had been ventilation shafts for the workmen. I could think of nothing but these ventilation shafts. Had they been destroyed by all the food-tubes and medicine-tubes and music-tubes that the Machine has evolved lately? Or did traces of them remain? One thing was certain. If I came upon them anywhere, it would be in the railway-tunnels of the topmost story. Everywhere else, all space was accounted for.

"I am telling my story quickly, but don't think that I was not a coward or that your answers never depressed me. It is not the proper thing, it is not /45/ mechanical, it is not decent to walk along a railway-tunnel. I did not fear that I might tread upon a live rail and be killed. I feared something far more intangible—doing what was not contemplated by the Machine. Then I said to myself, 'Man is the measure,' and I went, and after many visits I found an opening.

"The tunnels, of course, were lighted. Everything is light, artificial light; darkness is the exception. So when I saw a black gap in the tiles, I knew that it was an exception, and rejoiced. I put in my arm—I could put in no more at first—and waved it round and round in ecstasy. I loosened another tile, and put in my head, and shouted into the darkness: 'I am coming, I shall do it yet,' and my voice reverberated down endless passages. I seemed to hear the spirits of those dead workmen who had returned each evening to the starlight and to their wives, and all the generations who had lived in the open air called back to me, 'You will do it yet, you are coming.'"

He paused, and, absurd as he was, his last words /46/ moved her. For Kuno had lately asked to be a father, and his request had been refused by the Committee. His was not a type that the Machine desired to hand on.

"Then a train passed. It brushed by me, but I thrust my head and arms into the hole. I had done enough for one day, so I crawled back to the platform, went down in the lift, and summoned my bed. Ah, what dreams! And again I called you, and again you refused."

She shook her head and said:

"Don't. Don't talk of these terrible things. You make me miserable. You are throwing civilisation away."

"But I had got back the sense of space and a man cannot rest then. I determined to get in at the hole and climb the shaft. And so I exercised my arms. Day after day I went through ridiculous movements, until my flesh ached, and I could hang by my hands and hold the pillow of my bed outstretched for many minutes. Then I summoned a respirator, and started. /47/

"It was easy at first. The mortar had somehow rotted, and I soon pushed some more tiles in, and clambered after them into the darkness, and the spirits of the dead comforted me. I don't know what I mean by that. I just say what I felt. I felt, for the first time, that a protest had been lodged against corruption, and that even as the dead were comforting me, so I was comforting the unborn. I felt that humanity existed, and that it existed without clothes. How can I possibly explain this? It was naked, humanity seemed naked, and all these tubes and buttons and machineries neither came into the world with us, nor will they follow us out, nor do they matter supremely while we are here. Had I been strong, I would have torn off every garment I had, and gone out into the outer air unswaddled. But this is not for me, nor perhaps for my generation. I climbed with my respirator and my hygienic clothes and my dietetic tabloids! Better thus than not at all.

"There was a ladder, made of some primæval metal. The light from the railway fell upon its /48/ lowest rungs, and I saw that it led straight upwards out of the rubble at the bottom of the shaft. Perhaps our ancestors ran up and down it a dozen times daily, in their building. As I climbed, the rough edges cut through my gloves so that my hands bled. The light helped me for a little, and then came darkness and, worse still, silence which pierced my ears like a sword. The Machine hums! Did you know that? Its hum penetrates our blood, and may even guide our thoughts. Who knows! I was getting beyond its power. Then I thought: 'This silence means that I am doing wrong.' But I heard voices in the silence, and again they strengthened me." He laughed. "I had need of them. The next moment I cracked my head against something."

She sighed.

"I had reached one of those pneumatic stoppers that defend us from the outer air. You may have noticed them on the air-ship. Pitch dark, my feet on the rungs of an invisible ladder, my hands cut; I cannot explain how I lived through this part, but /49/ the voices still comforted me, and I felt for fastenings. The stopper, I suppose, was about eight feet across. I passed my hand over it as far as I could reach. It was perfectly smooth. I felt it almost to the centre. Not quite to the centre, for my arm was too short. Then the voice said: 'Jump. It is worth it. There may be a handle in the centre, and you may catch hold of it and so come to us your own way. And if there is no handle, so that you may fall and are dashed to pieces — it is still worth it: you will still come to us your own way.' So I jumped. There was a handle, and — "

He paused. Tears gathered in his mother's eyes. She knew that he was fated. If he did not die today he would die tomorrow. There was not room for such a person in the world. And with her pity disgust mingled. She was ashamed at having borne such a son, she who had always been so respectable and so full of ideas. Was he really the little boy to whom she had taught the use of his stops and buttons, and to whom she had given his first lessons in the Book? The very hair that dis- /50/ figured his lip showed that he was reverting to some savage type. On atavism the Machine can have no mercy.

"There was a handle, and I did catch it. I hung tranced over the darkness and heard the hum of these workings as the last whisper in a dying dream. All the things I had cared about and all the people I had spoken to through tubes appeared infinitely little. Meanwhile the handle revolved. My weight had set something in motion and I span slowly, and then—

"I cannot describe it. I was lying with my face to the sunshine. Blood poured from my nose and ears and I heard a tremendous roaring. The stopper, with me clinging to it, had simply been blown out of the earth, and the air that we make down here was escaping through the vent into the air above. It burst up like a fountain. I crawled back to it—for the upper air hurts—and, as it were, I took great sips from the edge. My respirator had flown goodness knows where, my clothes were torn. I just lay with my lips close /51/ to the hole, and I sipped until the bleeding stopped. You can imagine nothing so curious. This hollow in the grass—I will speak of it in a minute,—the sun shining into it, not brilliantly but through marbled clouds,—the peace, the nonchalance, the sense of space, and, brushing my cheek, the roaring fountain of our artificial air! Soon I spied my respirator, bobbing up and down in the current high above my head, and higher still were many air-ships. But no one ever looks out of air-ships, and in my case they could not have picked me up. There I was, stranded. The sun shone a little way down the shaft, and revealed the topmost rung of the ladder, but it was hopeless trying to reach it. I should either have been tossed up again by the escape, or else have fallen in, and died. I could only lie on the grass, sipping and sipping, and from time to time glancing around me.

"I knew that I was in Wessex, for I had taken care to go to a lecture on the subject before starting. Wessex lies above the room in which we are /52/ talking now. It was once an important state. Its kings held all the southern coast from the Andredswald to Cornwall, while the Wansdyke protected them on the north, running over the high ground. The lecturer was only concerned with the rise of Wessex, so I do not know how long it remained an international power, nor would the knowledge have assisted me. To tell the truth I could do nothing but laugh, during this part. There was I, with a pneumatic stopper by my side and a respirator bobbing over my head, imprisoned, all three of us, in a grass-grown hollow that was edged with fern."

Then he grew grave again.

"Lucky for me that it was a hollow. For the air began to fall back into it and to fill it as water fills a bowl. I could crawl about. Presently I stood. I breathed a mixture, in which the air that hurts predominated whenever I tried to climb the sides. This was not so bad. I had not lost my tabloids and remained ridiculously cheerful, and as for the Machine, I forgot about it altogether. My one /53/ aim now was to get to the top, where the ferns were, and to view whatever objects lay beyond.

"I rushed the slope. The new air was still too bitter for me and I came rolling back, after a momentary vision of something grey. The sun grew very feeble, and I remembered that he was in Scorpio—I had been to a lecture on that too. If the sun is in Scorpio and you are in Wessex, it means that you must be as quick as you can, or it will get too dark. (This is the first bit of useful information I have ever got from a lecture, and I expect it will be the last.) It made me try frantically to breath the new air, and to advance as far as I dared out of my pond. The hollow filled so slowly. At times I thought that the fountain played with less vigour. My respirator seemed to dance nearer the earth; the roar was decreasing."

He broke off.

"I don't think this is interesting you. The rest will interest you even less. There are no ideas in it, and I wish that I had not troubled you to come. We are too different, mother." /54/

She told him to continue.

"It was evening before I climbed the bank. The sun had very nearly slipped out of the sky by this time, and I could not get a good view. You, who have just crossed the Roof of the World, will not want to hear an account of the little hills that I saw — low colourless hills. But to me they were living and the turf that covered them was a skin, under which their muscles rippled, and I felt that those hills had called with incalculable force to men in the past, and that men had loved them. Now they sleep — perhaps for ever. They commune with humanity in dreams. Happy the man, happy the woman, who awakes the hills of Wessex. For though they sleep, they will never die."

His voice rose passionately.

"Cannot you see, cannot all your lecturers see, that it is we who are dying, and that down here the only thing that really lives is the Machine? We created the Machine, to do our will, but we cannot make it do our will now. It has robbed us /55/ of the sense of space and of the sense of touch, it has blurred every human relation and narrowed down love to a carnal act, it has paralysed our bodies and our wills, and now it compels us to worship it. The Machine develops — but not on our lines. The Machine proceeds — but not to our goal. We only exist as the blood corpuscles that course through its arteries, and if it could work without us, it would let us die. Oh, I have no remedy — or, at least, only one — to tell men again and again that I have seen the hills of Wessex as Ælfrid saw them when he overthrew the Danes.

"So the sun set. I forgot to mention that a belt of mist lay between my hill and other hills, and that it was the colour of pearl."

He broke off for the second time.

"Go on," said his mother wearily.

He shook his head.

"Go on. Nothing that you say can distress me now. I am hardened." /56/

"I had meant to tell you the rest, but I cannot: I know that I cannot: good-bye."

Vashti stood irresolute. All her nerves were tingling with his blasphemies. But she was also inquisitive.

"This is unfair," she complained. "You have called me across the world to hear your story, and hear it I will. Tell me — as briefly as possible, for this is a disastrous waste of time — tell me how you returned to civilisation."

"Oh — that!" he said, starting. "You would like to hear about civilisation. Certainly. Had I got to where my respirator fell down?"

"No — but I understand everything now. You put on your respirator, and managed to walk along the surface of the earth to a vomitory, and there your conduct was reported to the Central Committee."

"By no means."

He passed his hand over his forehead, as if dispelling some strong impression. Then, resuming his narrative, he warmed to it again. /57/

"My respirator fell about sunset. I had mentioned that the fountain seemed feebler, had I not."

"Yes."

"About sunset, it let the respirator fall. As I said, I had entirely forgotten about the Machine, and I paid no great attention at the time, being occupied with other things. I had my pool of air, into which I could dip when the outer keenness became intolerable, and which would possibly remain for days, provided that no wind sprang up to disperse it. Not until it was too late, did I realize what the stoppage of the escape implied. You see — the gap in the tunnel had been mended; the Mending Apparatus; the Mending Apparatus, was after me.

"One other warning I had, but I neglected it. The sky at night was clearer than it had been in the day, and the moon, which was about half the sky behind the sun, shone into the dell at moments quite brightly. I was in my usual place — on the boundary between the two atmospheres — when I /58/ thought I saw something dark move across the bottom of the dell, and vanish into the shaft. In my folly, I ran down. I bent over and listened, and I thought I heard a faint scraping noise in the depths.

"At this — but it was too late — I took alarm. I determined to put on my respirator and to walk right out of the dell. But my respirator had gone. I knew exactly where it had fallen — between the stopper and the aperture — and I could even feel the mark that it had made in the turf. It had gone, and I realized that something evil was at work, and I had better escape to the other air, and, if I must die, die running towards the cloud that had been the colour of a pearl. I never started. Out of the shaft — it is too horrible. A worm, a long white worm, had crawled out of the shaft and was gliding over the moonlit grass.

"I screamed. I did everything that I should not have done, I stamped upon the creature instead of flying from it, and it at once curled round the ankle. Then we fought. The worm let me run all /59/ over the dell, but edged up my leg as I ran. 'Help!' I cried. (That part is too awful. It belongs to the part that you will never know.) 'Help!' I cried. (Why cannot we suffer in silence?) 'Help!' I cried. Then my feet were wound together, I fell, I was dragged away from the dear ferns and the living hills, and past the great metal stopper (I can tell you this part), and I thought it might save me again if I caught hold of the handle. It also was enwrapped, it also. Oh, the whole dell was full of the things. They were searching it in all directions, they were denuding it, and the white snouts of others peeped out of the hole, ready if needed. Everything that could be moved they brought — brushwood, bundles of fern, everything, and down we all went intertwined into hell. The last things that I saw, ere the stopper closed after us, were certain stars, and I felt that a man of my sort lived in the sky. For I did fight, I fought till the very end, and it was only my head hitting against the ladder that quieted me. I woke up in this room. The worms /60/ had vanished. I was surrounded by artificial air, artificial light, artificial peace, and my friends were calling to me down speaking-tubes to know whether I had come across any new ideas lately."

Here his story ended. Discussion of it was impossible, and Vashti turned to go.

"It will end in Homelessness," she said quietly.

"I wish it would," retorted Kuno.

"The Machine has been most merciful."

"I prefer the mercy of God."

"By that superstitious phrase, do you mean that you could live in the outer air?"

"Yes."

"Have you ever seen, round the vomitories, the bones of those who were extruded after the Great Rebellion?"

"Yes."

"They were left where they perished for our edification. A few crawled away, but they perished, too—who can doubt it? And so with the Homeless of our own day. The surface of the earth supports life no longer." /61/

"Indeed."

"Ferns and a little grass may survive, but all higher forms have perished. Has any air-ship detected them?"

"No."

"Has any lecturer dealt with them?"

"No."

"Then why this obstinacy?"

"Because I have seen them," he exploded.

"Seen *what?*"

"Because I have seen her in the twilight—because she came to my help when I called—because she, too, was entangled by the worms, and, luckier than I, was killed by one of them piercing her throat."

He was mad. Vashti departed, nor, in the troubles that followed, did she ever see his face again. /62/

PART III. THE HOMELESS

During the years that followed Kuno's escapade, two important developments took place in the Machine. On the surface they were revolutionary, but in either case men's minds had been prepared beforehand, and they did but express tendencies that were latent already.

The first of these was the abolition of respirators.

Advanced thinkers, like Vashti, had always held it foolish to visit the surface of the earth. Air-ships might be necessary, but what was the good of going out for mere curiosity and crawling along for a mile or two in a terrestrial motor? The habit was vulgar and perhaps faintly improper: it was unproductive of ideas, and had no connection with the habits that really mattered. So respirators were abolished, and with them, of course, the ter- /63/ restrial motors, and except for a few lecturers, who complained that they were debarred access to their subject-matter, the development was accepted quietly. Those who still wanted to know what the earth was like had after all only to listen to some gramophone, or to look into some cinematophote. And even the lecturers acquiesced when they found that a lecture on the sea was none the less stimulating when compiled out of other lectures that had already been delivered on the same subject. "Beware of first-hand ideas!" exclaimed one of the most advanced of them. "First-hand ideas do not really exist. They are but the physical impressions produced by love and fear, and on this gross foundation who could erect a philosophy? Let your ideas be second-hand, and if possible tenth-hand, for then they will be far removed from that disturbing element—direct observation. Do not learn anything about this subject of mine—the French Revolution. Learn instead what I think that Enicharmon thought Urizen thought Gutch thought Ho-Yung thought Chi-Bo-Sing /64/ thought Lafcadio

Hearn thought Carlyle thought Mirabeau said about the French Revolution. Through the medium of these eight great minds, the blood that was shed at Paris and the windows that were broken at Versailles will be clarified to an idea which you may employ most profitably in your daily lives. But be sure that the intermediates are many and varied, for in history one authority exists to counteract another. Urizen must counteract the scepticism of Ho-Yung and Enicharmon, I must myself counteract the impetuosity of Gutch. You who listen to me are in a better position to judge about the French Revolution than I am. Your descendants will be even in a better position than you, for they will learn what you think I think, and yet another intermediate will be added to the chain. And in time"—his voice rose—"there will come a generation that has got beyond facts, beyond impressions, a generation absolutely colourless, a generation

'seraphically free
From taint of personality,' /65/

which will see the French Revolution not as it happened, nor as they would like it to have happened, but as it would have happened, had it taken place in the days of the Machine."

Tremendous applause greeted this lecture, which did but voice a feeling already latent in the minds of men—a feeling that terrestrial facts must be ignored, and that the abolition of respirators was a positive gain. It was even suggested that air-ships should be abolished too. This was not done, because air-ships had somehow worked themselves into the Machine's system. But year by year they were used less, and mentioned less by thoughtful men.

The second great development was the re-establishment of religion.

This, too, had been voiced in the celebrated lecture. No one could mistake the reverent tone in which the peroration had concluded, and it awakened a responsive echo in the heart of each. Those who had long worshipped silently, now began to talk. They described the strange feeling /66/ of peace that came over them when they handled the Book of the Machine, the pleasure that it was to repeat certain numerals out of it, however little meaning those numerals conveyed to the outward ear, the ecstasy of touching a button, however unimportant, or of ringing an electric bell, however superfluously.

"The Machine," they exclaimed, "feeds us and clothes us and houses us; through it we speak to one another, through it we see one another, in it we have our being. The Machine is the friend of ideas and the enemy of superstition: the Machine is omnipotent, eternal; blessed is the Machine." And before long this allocution was printed on the first page of the Book, and in subsequent editions the ritual swelled into a complicated system of praise and prayer. The word "religion" was sedulously avoided, and in theory the Machine was still the creation and the implement of man. But in practice all, save a few retrogrades, worshipped it as divine. Nor was it worshipped in unity. One believer would be chiefly impressed by the blue /67/ optic plates, through which he saw other believers; another by the mending apparatus, which sinful Kuno had compared to worms; another by the lifts, another by the Book. And each would pray to this or to that, and ask it to intercede for him with the Machine as a whole. Persecution—that also was present. It did not break out, for reasons that will be set forward shortly. But it was latent, and all who did not accept the minimum known as "undenominational Mechanism" lived in danger of Homelessness, which means death, as we know.

To attribute these two great developments to the Central Committee, is to take a very narrow view of civilisation. The Central Committee announced the developments, it is true, but they were no more the cause of them than were the kings of the imperialistic period the cause of war. Rather did they yield to some invincible pressure, which came no one knew whither, and which, when gratified, was succeeded by some new pressure equally invincible. To such a state of affairs /68/ it is convenient to give the name of progress. No one confessed the Machine was out of hand. Year by year it was served with increased efficiency and decreased intelligence. The better a man knew his own duties upon it, the less he understood the duties of his neighbour, and in all the world there was not one who understood the monster as a whole. Those master brains had perished. They had left full directions, it is true, and their successors had each of them mastered a portion of those directions. But Humanity, in its desire for comfort, had over-reached itself. It had exploited the riches of nature too far. Quietly and complacently, it was sinking into decadence, and progress had come to mean the progress of the Machine.

As for Vashti, her life went peacefully forward until the final disaster. She made her room dark and slept; she awoke and made the room light. She lectured and attended lectures. She exchanged ideas with her innumerable friends and believed she was growing more spiritual. At times a friend /69/ was granted Euthanasia, and left his or her room for the homelessness that is beyond all human conception. Vashti did not much mind. After an unsuccessful lecture, she would sometimes ask for Euthanasia herself. But the death-rate was not permitted to exceed the birth-rate, and the Machine had hitherto refused it to her.

The troubles began quietly, long before she was conscious of them.

One day she was astonished at receiving a message from her son. They never communicated, having nothing in common, and she had only heard indirectly that he was still alive, and had been transferred from the northern hemisphere, where he had behaved so mischievously, to the southern — indeed, to a room not far from her own.

"Does he want me to visit him?" she thought. "Never again, never. And I have not the time."

No, it was madness of another kind.

He refused to visualize his face upon the blue /70/ plate, and speaking out of the darkness with solemnity said:

"The Machine stops."

"What do you say?"

"The Machine is stopping, I know it, I know the signs."

She burst into a peal of laughter. He heard her and was angry, and they spoke no more.

"Can you imagine anything more absurd?" she cried to a friend. "A man who was my son believes that the Machine is stopping. It would be impious if it was not mad."

"The Machine is stopping?" her friend replied. "What does that mean? The phrase conveys nothing to me."

"Nor to me."

"He does not refer, I suppose, to the trouble there has been lately with the music?"

"Oh no, of course not. Let us talk about music."

"Have you complained to the authorities?"

"Yes, and they say it wants mending, and referred me to the Committee of the Mending Ap- /71/ paratus. I complained of those curious gasping sighs that disfigure the symphonies of the Brisbane school. They sound like some one in pain. The Committee of the Mending Apparatus say that it shall be remedied shortly."

Obscurely worried, she resumed her life. For one thing, the defect in the music irritated her. For another thing, she could not forget Kuno's speech. If he had known that the music was out of repair—he could not know it, for he detested music—if he had known that it was wrong, "the Machine stops" was exactly the venomous sort of remark he would have made. Of course he had made it at a venture, but the coincidence annoyed her, and she spoke with some petulance to the Committee of the Mending Apparatus.

They replied, as before, that the defect would be set right shortly.

"Shortly! At once!" she retorted. "Why should I be worried by imperfect music? Things are always put right at once. If you do not mend it /72/ at once, I shall complain to the Central Committee."

"No personal complaints are received by the Central Committee," the Committee of the Mending Apparatus replied.

"Through whom am I to make my complaint, then?"

"Through us."

"I complain then."

"Your complaint shall be forwarded in its turn."

"Have others complained?"

This question was unmechanical, and the Committee of the Mending Apparatus refused to answer it.

"It is too bad!" she exclaimed to another of her friends. "There never was such an unfortunate woman as myself. I can never be sure of my music now. It gets worse and worse each time I summon it."

"I too have my troubles," the friend replied. /73/ "Sometimes my ideas are interrupted by a slight jarring noise."

"What is it?"

"I do not know whether it is inside my head, or inside the wall."

"Complain, in either case."

"I have complained, and my complaint will be forwarded in its turn to the Central Committee."

Time passed, and they resented the defects no longer. The defects had not been remedied, but the human tissues in that latter day had become so subservient, that they readily adapted themselves to every caprice of the Machine. The sigh at the crisis of the Brisbane symphony no longer irritated Vashti; she accepted it as part of the melody. The jarring noise, whether in the head or in the wall, was no longer resented by her friend. And so with the mouldy artificial fruit, so with the bath water that began to stink, so with the defective rhymes that the poetry machine had taken to emit. All were bitterly complained of at /74/ first, and then acquiesced in and forgotten. Things went from bad to worse unchallenged.

It was otherwise with the failure of the sleeping apparatus. That was a more serious stoppage. There came a day when over the whole world—in Sumatra, in Wessex, in the innumerable cities of Courland and Brazil—the beds, when summoned by their tired owners, failed to appear. It may seem a ludicrous matter, but from it we may date the collapse of humanity. The Committee responsible for the failure was assailed by complainants, whom it referred, as usual, to the Committee of the Mending Apparatus, who in its turn assured them that their complaints would be forwarded to the Central Committee.

But the discontent grew, for mankind was not yet sufficiently adaptable to do without sleeping.

"Some one is meddling with the Machine——" they began.

"Some one is trying to make himself king, to reintroduce the personal element." /75/

"Punish that man with Homelessness."

"To the rescue! Avenge the Machine! Avenge the Machine!"

"War! Kill the man!"

But the Committee of the Mending Apparatus now came forward, and allayed the panic with well-chosen words. It confessed that the Mending Apparatus was itself in need of repair.

The effect of this frank confession was admirable.

"Of course," said a famous lecturer—he of the French Revolution, who gilded each new decay with splendour—"of course we shall not press our complaints now. The Mending Apparatus has treated us so well in the past that we all sympathize with it, and will wait patiently for its recovery. In its own good time it will resume its duties. Meanwhile let us do without our beds, our tabloids, our other little wants. Such, I feel sure, would be the wish of the Machine."

Thousands of miles away his audience applauded. The Machine still linked them. Under /76/ the seas, beneath the roots of the mountains, ran the wires through which they saw and heard, the enormous eyes and ears that were their heritage, and the hum of many workings clothed their thoughts in one garment of subserviency. Only the old and the sick remained ungrateful, for it was rumoured that Euthanasia, too, was out of order, and that pain had reappeared among men.

It became difficult to read. A blight entered the atmosphere and dulled its luminosity. At times Vashti could scarcely see across her room. The air, too, was foul. Loud were the complaints, impotent the remedies, heroic the tone of the lecturer as he cried: "Courage, courage! What matter so long as the Machine goes on? To it the darkness and the light are one." And though things improved again after a time, the old brilliancy was never recaptured, and humanity never recovered from its entrance into twilight. There was an hysterical talk of "measures," of "provisional dictatorship," and the inhabitants of Sumatra were asked to familiarize themselves with the /77/ workings of the central power station, the said power station being situated in France. But for the most part panic reigned, and men spent their strength praying to their Books, tangible proofs of the Machine's omnipotence. There were gradations of terror—at times came rumours of hope—the Mending Apparatus was almost mended—the enemies of the Machine had been got under—new "nerve-centres" were evolving which would do the work even more magnificently than before. But there came a day when, without the slightest warning, without any previous hint of feebleness, the entire communication-system broke down, all over the world, and the world, as they understood it, ended.

Vashti was lecturing at the time and her earlier remarks had been punctuated with applause. As she proceeded the audience became silent, and at the conclusion there was no sound. Somewhat displeased, she called to a friend who was a specialist in sympathy. No sound: doubtless the friend was sleeping. And so with the next friend whom she /78/ tried to summon, and so with the next, until she remembered Kuno's cryptic remark, "The Machine stops."

The phrase still conveyed nothing. If Eternity was stopping it would of course be set going shortly.

For example, there was still a little light and air—the atmosphere had improved a few hours previously. There was still the Book, and while there was the Book there was security.

Then she broke down, for with the cessation of activity came an unexpected terror—silence.

She had never known silence, and the coming of it nearly killed her—it did kill many thousands of people outright. Ever since her birth she had been surrounded by the steady hum. It was to the ear what artificial air was to the lungs, and agonizing pains shot across her head. And scarcely knowing what she did, she stumbled forward and pressed the unfamiliar button, the one that opened the door of her cell.

Now the door of the cell worked on a simple /79/ hinge of its own. It was not connected with the central power station, dying far away in France. It opened, rousing immoderate hopes in Vashti, for she thought that the Machine had been mended. It opened, and she saw the dim tunnel that curved far away towards freedom. One look, and then she shrank back. For the tunnel was full of people—she was almost the last in that city to have taken alarm.

People at any time repelled her, and these were nightmares from her worst dreams. People were crawling about, people were screaming, whimpering, gasping for breath, touching each other, vanishing in the dark, and ever and anon being pushed off the platform on to the live rail. Some were fighting round the electric bells, trying to summon trains which could not be summoned. Others were yelling for Euthanasia or for respirators, or blaspheming the Machine. Others stood at the doors of their cells fearing, like herself, either to stop in them or to leave them. And behind all the uproar was silence—the silence which is the voice /80/ of the earth and of the generations who have gone.

No—it was worse than solitude. She closed the door again and sat down to wait for the end. The disintegration went on, accompanied by horrible cracks and rumbling. The valves that restrained the Medical Apparatus must have been weakened, for it ruptured and hung hideously from the ceiling. The floor heaved and fell and flung her from her chair. A tube oozed towards her serpent fashion. And at last the final horror approached—light began to ebb, and she knew that civilisation's long day was closing.

She whirled round, praying to be saved from this, at any rate, kissing the Book, pressing button after button. The uproar outside was increasing, and even penetrated the wall. Slowly the brilliancy of her cell was dimmed, the reflections faded from her metal switches. Now she could not see the reading-stand, now not the Book, though she held it in her hand. Light followed the flight of sound, air was following light, and the original void returned to the cavern from which it had been /81/ so long excluded. Vashti continued to whirl, like the devotees of an earlier religion, screaming, praying, striking at the buttons with bleeding hands.

It was thus that she opened her prison and escaped—escaped in the spirit: at least so it seems to me, ere my meditation closes. That she escapes in the body—I cannot perceive that. She struck, by chance, the switch that released the door, and the rush of foul air on her skin, the loud throbbing whispers in her ears, told her that she was facing the tunnel again, and that tremendous platform on which she had seen men fighting. They were not fighting now. Only the whispers remained, and the little whimpering groans. They were dying by hundreds out in the dark.

She burst into tears.

Tears answered her.

They wept for humanity, those two, not for themselves. They could not bear that this should be the end. Ere silence was completed their hearts were opened, and they knew what had been important on the earth. Man, the flower of all flesh, /82/ the noblest of all creatures visible, man who had once made god in his image, and had mirrored his strength on the constellations, beautiful naked man was dying, strangled in the garments that he had woven. Century after century had he toiled, and here was his reward. Truly the garment had seemed heavenly at first, shot with the colours of culture, sewn with the threads of self-denial. And heavenly it had been so long as it was a garment and no more, so long as man could shed it at will and live by the essence that is his soul, and the essence, equally divine, that is his body. The sin against the body — it was for that they wept in chief; the centuries of wrong against the muscles and the nerves, and those five portals by which we can alone apprehend — glozing it over with talk of evolution, until the body was white pap, the home of ideas as colourless, last sloshy stirrings of a spirit that had grasped the stars.

"Where are you?" she sobbed.

His voice in the darkness said, "Here."

"Is there any hope, Kuno?" /83/

"None for us."

"Where are you?"

She crawled towards him over the bodies of the dead. His blood spurted over her hands.

"Quicker," he gasped, "I am dying — but we touch, we talk, not through the Machine."

He kissed her.

"We have come back to our own. We die, but we have recaptured life, as it was in Wessex, when Ælfrid overthrew the Danes. We know what they know outside, they who dwelt in the cloud that is the colour of a pearl."

"But, Kuno, is it true? Are there still men on the surface of the earth? Is this — this tunnel, this poisoned darkness — really not the end?"

He replied:

"I have seen them, spoken to them, loved them. They are hiding in the mist and the ferns until our civilisation stops. Today they are the Homeless — tomorrow — "

"Oh, tomorrow — some fool will start the Machine again, tomorrow." /84/

"Never," said Kuno, "never. Humanity has learnt its lesson."

As he spoke, the whole city was broken like a honeycomb. An air-ship had sailed in through the vomitory into a ruined wharf. It crashed downwards, exploding as it went, rending gallery after gallery with its wings of steel. For a moment they saw the nations of the dead, and, before they joined them, scraps of the untainted sky. /85/

Problems
for
Investigation

QUESTIONS FOR DISCUSSION

C. P. Snow   *The Two Cultures*

1. Why does Snow assert that coming from a poor home helped him acquire the "credentials" for speaking on this subject? What are these credentials?
2. Snow declares (p. 4) that he intends to examine two of the most profound misinterpretations that prevent communication between scientists and literary men—"one on each side." What are these misinterpretations? Which side comes out the better in Snow's examination?
3. Snow remarks (p. 5) that some of his acquaintances regard the concept of "two cultures" as an oversimplification. Why do they think this? Do you yourself consider the two-part division to be too arbitrary? Why or why not?
4. How does Snow define a "culture"? What does he regard as the distinguishing features of the "scientific culture"?
5. Explain Snow's contention that literary intellectuals are "natural Luddites."
6. What does Snow mean when he asserts (p. 11) that in the face of the Industrial Revolution many intellectuals decided to "contract out"?
7. Discuss Snow's observation (p. 11) that "in any country where they have had the chance, the poor have walked off the land into the factories as fast as the factories could take them."

F. R. Leavis   *Two Cultures? The Significance of C. P. Snow*

1. Why do you suppose Leavis considers it necessary to discredit Snow as a novelist?
2. Explain what Leavis means when he declares (p. 14) that Snow "takes over . . . the characteristic and disastrous confusion of the civilization he is offering to instruct."
3. What values does Leavis find in the writings of D. H. Lawrence and John Ruskin that are fundamentally opposed to the values implicit in Snow's essay?
4. What does Snow mean by "jam"? What do you think of the mode of expression he employs? Do you feel that Leavis' objection to regarding the "standard of living" as an ultimate criterion is justified?
5. Explain what Leavis means when he remarks (p. 16) that Snow's "social hope" evokes "the vision of our imminent tomorrow in today's America." Do you feel that his assessment of America is accurate? Why or why not?
6. How does the sort of intelligence that Leavis describes in the concluding paragraph of this excerpt differ from the sort of intelligence with which Snow is preoccupied?
7. Some critics have objected to the tone Leavis adopts in this essay. Do you find the tone objectionable in the excerpt you have read? Discuss the question of "politeness" as an element in public controversy.

John Wain   *A Certain Judo Demonstration*

1. Wain adversely criticizes both Leavis and Snow. With which writer is he primarily in agreement?
2. Wain approaches the conflict between personalities with considerable zest. What passages contribute especially to the humorous tone of his article? How effective to Wain's argument do you consider this tone to be?
3. Do you feel that Wain's comments on Snow's experience with, and attitude toward, the Russians are relevant to the controversy between science and the humanities? If so, how?

Hilary Corke   *Snow vs. Leavis*

1. In Corke's opinion what are the main weaknesses in Leavis' essay? Does Corke's article display any of the same weaknesses? If so, in which passages?
2. Compare Corke's evaluation of Leavis, and of Snow, with Wain's.

Anthony West   *From the Top Drawer and the Bottom*

1. The first part of West's article introduces a new idea into the controversy. What is this? To what extent do you think this idea helps explain the nature of Leavis' attack on Snow? To justify it?
2. In the latter part of his article West passes moral judgment upon an affair not directly related to the main controversy. Do moral judgments of this character have any relevance to the larger issues of the debate? See Snow's observations on the moral qualities of science and scientists (p. 7).

Richard Wollheim   *Grounds for Approval*

1. Wollheim agrees with a good many of Snow's contentions. On what specific issue does he differ?
2. What is your reaction to Wollheim's argument that is summed up by the remark (p. 28): "The brutal fact is that certain things bore certain people"? How do you think Snow might respond to this?
3. Explain Wollheim's contention that a "philosophical deficiency" constitutes the main weakness of Snow's essay.

William F. Buckley, Jr.   *The Voice of Sir Charles*

1. What are the implications of Buckley's reference, at both the beginning and the end of his article, to Snow's voice as the voice of a machine?
2. In what ways does Buckley's treatment of Snow's attitude toward Russia differ from Wain's?

Martin Green   *A Literary Defense of "The Two Cultures"*

1. How does Green explain the popular interest aroused by Leavis' attack on Snow?
2. Green's attitude toward Wellsianism is a mixed one. Explain.
3. Which of Leavis' judgments about Snow's manner and public pose does Green specifically challenge? What specific values does he see in Snow's approach to his subject?
4. Green remarks that we must grant Leavis one important point. Explain this point. How is it qualified?
5. Green seems to suggest that Leavis errs in the direction of oversubtlety — that he misrepresents Snow's argument by deliberately refusing to take simple statements in the way they were meant. Indicate examples of this.
6. Why, in Green's opinion, has Snow failed to receive full support from either the literary world or the scientists?
7. Which of the criticisms directed against Leavis in the last two pages do you consider the most telling?

Lionel Trilling
Science, Literature & Culture: A Comment on the Leavis-Snow Controversy

1. What were the attitudes of Arnold and Huxley toward each other according to Trilling? How does this relate to the attitudes of the antagonists in the present controversy?
2. What does Trilling attribute as the motivation of Leavis' attack on *The Two Cultures?*
3. What are the chief points of Trilling's criticism of Leavis' assault on Snow?
4. What are the chief points of Trilling's criticism of Snow's *The Two Cultures?*
5. Towards the end of his essay Trilling introduces "the idea of the Mind." What does he mean by this concept? How does it relate to the controversy he is analyzing?

QUESTIONS FOR WRITING

1. On the basis of your experience discuss Snow's thesis that modern civilization may be divided into two mutually exclusive "cultures."
2. Snow suggests that both scientists and "literary intellectuals" must share the blame for the lack of communication and understanding between them. Analyze Snow's discussion — his specific statements, his illustrations, his choice of adjectives, etc., to show clearly the manner in which he weights the case heavily in favor of one side.
3. Write a paper enlarging on the implications of Snow's assertion that the scientists have "the future in their bones."
4. Would it be accurate to say that *many* of the participants in this controversy treat the issues in moral, rather than in purely intellectual, terms? Why or why not?

5. Evaluation of a writer's character and motives may, or may not, help clarify the issues of a controversy. Basing your discussion on the writings in this section, develop an essay on the subject of the use of personal attack in argument.

6. On the basis of your own experience and beliefs write a discussion of Wollheim's statement (p. 28): "A system of education in which people can't learn what they want to learn . . . would scarcely count for us as . . . education."

QUESTIONS FOR DISCUSSION

Francis Bacon   *The New Science*

1. What types of errors did Bacon believe had retarded the progress of science? Are any of these still prevalent?
2. Bacon anticipated opposition from the scholars and indifference from the public and the politicians of his time. Do any of the problems he raises still exist?
3. What evidence can you find for the assertion that Bacon's conception of the role of science was thoroughly utilitarian? What evidence can you find to *qualify* such an assertion?

William Wordsworth   *Preface to Lyrical Ballads*

1. What is the nature of the "truth" that Wordsworth believes poetry communicates? How does this differ from the "truths" communicated by the methods of science?
2. In what way does "pleasure" constitute an essential part in the activities of both the poet and the scientist?
3. What permanent and essential role does Wordsworth envisage for poetry? In the light of some of the previous readings in this collection, do you consider Wordsworth's conclusions unduly optimistic? Why or why not?

Thomas Love Peacock   *The Four Ages of Poetry*

1. What statements does Peacock make with which you are in general agreement? Does the picture he draws seem at any points to be deliberately exaggerated?
2. Peacock refers to Wordsworth as "a morbid dreamer." On the basis of the selection from Wordsworth, and any of his other works with which you may be familiar, discuss the validity of this description.

John Ruskin   *On Machine Labor*

1. Why does Ruskin believe that the worker in nineteenth-century England is less free than the workmen of the Middle Ages?
2. In what sense, according to Ruskin, does "the division of labour" refer not to the work but to the men? How accurately may this judgment be applied to the factory worker in our own society?

3. In what respects do Ruskin's views on machine-labor strike you as short-sighted?
4. Ruskin feels that the replacement of men by machines leads to consequences that are unfortunate both for the individual and for society. What are some of these consequences? Are any of the effects predicted by Ruskin visible in our own society?

Thomas Henry Huxley   *Science and Education*

1. What does Huxley find wrong with the proposition (p. 73): "literature contains the materials which suffice for the construction of [a criticism of life]"?
2. How does Huxley's summary of the history of Western culture serve his general argument?
3. What does Huxley mean when he accuses the Humanists of his day of possessing no solid basis for a true culture "not because they are too full of the spirit of the ancient Greek, but because they lack it" (p. 77)?
4. In the following selection Matthew Arnold refers to Huxley as "an excellent writer and the very prince of debaters" (p. 79). What characteristics of this essay would you point to as giving evidence that Arnold's description is just?
5. What evidence can you find in this essay to show that Huxley was well educated in the arts as well as in the sciences?

Matthew Arnold   *Literature and Science*

1. What does Arnold mean by "literature"? How does his meaning differ from Huxley's?
2. What does Arnold take up as the main point of difference between himself and Huxley in this essay?
3. What does Arnold mean by "instrument knowledge"?
4. Arnold claims (p. 84) that the knowledge men of science will give the world will be "to the majority of mankind, after a certain while, unsatisfying, wearying." What are his grounds for this claim?
5. How do Arnold and Huxley disagree on what is essential to human living?
6. Comment on the means Arnold proposes for developing an ideal national culture (p. 79): "to know the best which has been thought and said in the world." How is "the best" to be determined?

QUESTIONS FOR WRITING

1. Compare Bacon's conception of "two streams of knowledge" and "two tribes or kindreds of students" with Snow's idea of the "two cultures."
2. Compare Bacon's predictions in the *New Atlantis* with the developments in science and technology that have actually taken place.

3. Compare Wordsworth's views on the nature and function of poetry with those expressed by Peacock.
4. Shelley's famous essay "A Defense of Poetry" was conceived in part as a reply to Peacock's essay. Read Shelley's essay and discuss the difference in the two writers' conceptions of the nature and function of poetry.
5. With Ruskin's comments on machine labor compare Snow's assertion (p. 11) that "in any country where they have had the chance, the poor have walked off the land into the factories as fast as the factories could take them." Ruskin and Snow seem to employ different yardsticks in their value judgments. Write a paper on this topic.
6. Write a paper on the topic: the human and social effects of automation.
7. Would Huxley, if he were alive today, be satisfied with the state of scientific education in colleges and universities? What criticisms might he offer?

Part III   Contemporary Attitudes

QUESTIONS FOR DISCUSSION

Stuart Chase   *What Science Is*

1. Chase notes that the term "science" has been used to mean various things. List some of these meanings. How does Chase intend to use the term "science"?
2. Chase writes (p. 92) that "science is perhaps the most *moral* of all man's disciplines." What does he mean by this statement?
3. Explain the definition of science as "finding a pattern in a set of phenomena" (p. 92).

John Ciardi   *How Does a Poem Mean?*

1. Analyze Bitzer's definition of a horse in the light of Chase's comments on the meaning of science and the scientific method. In view of Chase's statement that "science is perhaps the most *moral* of all man's disciplines," would you consider Bitzer's definition to be superior morally to answers based on other disciplines?
2. What does Ciardi mean when he writes (p. 94) that the "horseman, gambler, and sculptor are involved in a living relation to a living animal"? Would the scientist be involved with a *living* relationship? With a *living* animal?

John R. Baker   *The Appreciation of Science as an End in Itself*

1. Baker tells us that apart from material benefits the discipline of science offers various pleasurable satisfactions. What satisfactions does he describe?
2. According to Baker, what determines the value of a scientific theory or discovery?
3. Baker writes (p. 95) that "there are reasons for thinking that science is potentially the greatest achievement of the human mind." What grounds does he advance for this assertion?

Maxwell Anderson   *Whatever Hope We Have*

1. What does Anderson mean by "the artist's faith"?
2. Referring to the boy turning over in his mind passages from *Doctor Faustus* as he ploughs corn, Anderson writes (p. 101): "It may be an impetus that will advance him or his sons an infinitesimal step along the interminable ascent." What is "the interminable ascent"? What evidence does he adduce to show the existence of such an ascent?

3. What, for Anderson, is the artist's role in relation to his nation and race?
4. In your own words, frame the theme of this essay.
5. Comment on Anderson's statement (p. 103): "the arts make the longest reach toward permanence, create the most enduring monuments, project the farthest, widest, deepest influence of which human prescience and effort are capable." Would this statement hold true if "science" were substituted for "the arts"?

Bertrand Russell *Science as an Element in Culture*

1. What is Russell's theme and where is it first stated?
2. Explain as fully as possible what Russell means by "the scientific attitude of mind."
3. At the beginning of the second part of his essay Russell writes (p. 107): "Two opposite and at first sight conflicting merits belong to science as against literature and art." What are the two merits? What does he mean by "as against literature and art"? Why does he refer to the second merit as depressing?
4. Toward the end of his essay Russell tells us (p. 110): "The desire for a larger life and wider interests, for an escape from private circumstances, and even from the whole recurring cycle of birth and death, is fulfilled by the impersonal outlook of science as by nothing else." What does he mean by "private circumstances"? Is the escape referred to desirable?

Archibald MacLeish *Why Do We Teach Poetry?*

1. Comment on MacLeish's statement (p. 112): "The exclusive proprietary right of science to know and to communicate knowledge is not only commonly recognized in our civilization: in a very real sense it is our civilization."
2. MacLeish tells us (p. 113) that poetry "does not abstract. Poetry presents." How can poetry "present"?
3. MacLeish writes (p. 112) that poetry "is capable of a kind of knowledge of which science is not capable." What kind of knowledge? Explain. Do you agree that such knowledge is more valid than the kind presented by science? Why or why not?
4. What do you think MacLeish means when he writes (p. 115): "Furthermore, abstractions have a limiting, a dehumanizing, a dehydrating effect on the relation to things of the man who must live with them"?

H. G. Wells *Is Life Becoming Happier?*

1. Wells envisages a number of obstacles in the path of the "march toward happiness." Identify as many of these as you can.
2. In which passages does Wells employ irony to make his point?
3. It has been remarked that Snow is in the direct line of descent from Wells. Do you find any evidence here for this opinion?

4. Look at Wells' prediction on p. 122 beginning: "The dictatorship of the proletariat may dictate what it likes. . . ." To what extent do you think that this prediction has been borne out by events?
5. Relate Wells' comments on the "once necessary drudge population" (p. 121) to the contemporary problem of automation.

D. H. Lawrence   *The Industrial Magnate*

1. What are the effects on the miners of Gerald's reorganization of the firm? What are the effects on Gerald? Explain as fully as possible.
2. Compare Ruskin's comments on machine labor in "The Nature of Gothic" with Lawrence's description of Gerald's reorganization.
3. Which controls the mine at the end — Gerald, or the efficient machine he has created? To what degree do you think machines dominate American life? Your life?

James T. Shotwell   *Mechanism and Culture*

1. On what subjects do you think that Shotwell and Snow would find themselves in agreement?
2. How damaging do you consider Shotwell's charge (p. 128) that "idealism failed to avert the desolation of Europe"? Might the same statement be made with equal validity about the beliefs and practices of those he refers to as "the practically-minded"?
3. What similarities does Shotwell see between the machine and the literary or architectural work of art? What differences?
4. Shotwell asserts (p. 132) that it is Dante's "larger vision, built of the universal hope and fear, that is the real *Divina Commedia*, not the epic locked in its stubborn Tuscan rhymes." In what sense is this true? What conception of poetry does Shotwell's statement imply?
5. What does Shotwell mean by "the immortality of use" (p. 131)?
6. At the conclusion of his essay Shotwell introduces a quotation from John Ruskin. Compare this with the ideas expressed in the selections from Ruskin's writings.

Erich Fromm   *The Sane Society*

1. Concerning the information presented in his tables, Fromm remarks (p. 142): "these data raise a question as to whether there is not something fundamentally wrong with our way of life and with the aims toward which we are striving." Explain this statement.
2. Do the data presented by Fromm give you any second thoughts about the predictions of Wells? About any of Snow's assumptions? Compare the implications of these data with those of Lawrence's "The Industrial Magnate."
3. Explain in your own words Fromm's concept of "alienation." Compare Fromm's description of the alienated worker in contemporary society with the picture drawn by Lawrence.

E. M. Forster   *The Machine Stops*

1. How does Forster communicate his belief in the supreme importance of "direct experience"? Compare his views on this subject with those expressed by MacLeish in his essay "Why Do We Teach Poetry?"
2. What are the implications of the manner in which the "religion of the Machine" developed?
3. Locate examples of Forster's use of irony in making his points.
4. Does Forster's story contain any element of hope for the future of humanity, or is it entirely pessimistic?
5. The rock formation in the Caucasus mountains that resembles "a prostrate man" is evidently intended to suggest Prometheus. What values does this symbol have in the context of the story?

QUESTIONS FOR WRITING

1. Chase writes (p. 93): "Science goes with the method, not with the subject matter." Explain. Could the scientific method, then, be applied to literature or art? For what ends?
2. Write an essay on the subject: the intrinsic values of science.
3. Develop an essay discussing the question of progress in the arts.
4. Discuss some work of literature you have read which you feel exemplifies the principles advanced by MacLeish.
5. Discuss MacLeish's statement (p. 114): "Colleges and universities do not exist to impose duties but to reveal choices."
6. Do you consider Wells' predictions unduly optimistic? Why or why not?
7. Wells implies that greater material prosperity leads inevitably to better and happier lives for the people who experience it. Discuss this idea, comparing Wells' views with those of Fromm.
8. Write a paper on the topic: Ruskin and Lawrence as "natural Luddites."
9. Write a paper on the topic: the uses of leisure.
10. Discuss evidences you have encountered of automation in education.
11. Lawrence says that "nothing matters but life," meaning by this that life resides in living individuals. Snow, on the other hand, seems to stress the social hope of a collective life envisaged for the future. Discuss the conflict between these two positions.
12. Shotwell implies that the increase in mechanical power and efficiency is to be valued simply for its own sake. Discuss this attitude, comparing it with the views expressed by Lawrence and Fromm.
13. Forster suggests that certain kinds of experience and certain ways of life are proper to human beings and that others are not. Discuss this idea.
14. Discuss trends in contemporary life that seem to be leading toward the situation that Forster envisages.

TEN POSSIBLE AREAS FOR RESEARCH

Bacon and the Origins of Modern Science
Scientific Utopias, or Anti-Utopias
Machine Labor in the Nineteenth Century
The Social Effects of the Industrial Revolution
A Defense of Automation
Anti-Mechanism in the Fiction of D. H. Lawrence
The Luddite Movement
Emphases in Russian and American Education
The Role of the Scientist in Politics
A Narrative Account of the Snow-Leavis Controversy